FROZEN SHIPS

The Arctic Diary of
Johann Miertsching
1850-1854

FROZEN SHIPS

The Arctic Diary of

Johann Miertsching

1850-1854

Translated and
with introduction and notes by

L. H. Neatby

1967 MACMILLAN OF CANADA TORONTO

Library of Congress Catalogue Card No. 67-21264

Parts of the introduction appeared
in an article contributed
by the translator to the December 1960
issue of *The Beaver*. The courtesy of Miss Malvina Bolus
editor of *The Beaver*, in granting permission for
their reproduction here is gratefully acknowledged.

Printed in Canada by John Deyell Limited
for the Macmillan Company of Canada Limited
70 Bond Street, Toronto

CONTENTS

73 - 7782

ILLUSTRATIONS

(between pages 94 and 95)

*(2, 3, and 4 are from photographs of colour sketches
by Lieut. S. Gurney Cresswell of the* Investigator.*)*

MAPS

INTRODUCTION

The theme of Miertsching's *narrative*, the 1850-4 voyage of H. M. S. *Investigator*, is the last episode but one (McClintock's voyage in the *Fox* was the last) in the grand epic of British discovery in the North American Arctic. Aiming at a short route to the East Indies by way of the North-west, Frobisher, Davis, Hudson, and Baffin had explored the two great basins of Hudson Bay and Baffin Bay, and had concluded that neither provided the western channel they sought. For the next two centuries little occurred except half-hearted and abortive attempts to disprove this theory by finding a waterway from Hudson Bay to the Pacific. In 1777 James Cook, attempting the Passage from the west, barely entered the Arctic before turning back from Icy Cape on the north-west shore of Alaska. In 1818 the north-eastern and northern shores of America remained utterly unknown from Repulse Bay (inside Hudson Bay) to Bering Strait, except for the mouths of the Coppermine and Mackenzie rivers where Samuel Hearne and Alexander Mackenzie, respectively, had just reached tidewater. Of the vast and complex archipelago that lay beyond, nothing at all was known except for some sections of the east shore of Baffin Island.

The 1818 cruise of John Ross in Baffin Bay did little but confirm the erroneous conclusion of William Baffin that this basin was a true bay and provided no passage to the west. In 1819 the British Admiralty, in a determined effort to find an ultimate solution of the problem, sent out two expeditions: Lieutenant John Franklin was dispatched overland to chart the arctic shore of America by canoe, while Lieutenant Edward Parry was given command of the ships *Hecla* and *Griper* with orders to renew the search for a western outlet from Baffin Bay. Parry's voyage was the most successful ever made in the Canadian Arctic by sail only. Ascending Baffin Bay to latitude 74° and turning into Lancaster Sound (dismissed by both Baffin and Ross as a closed bay), he sailed a distance of five hundred miles to the west, along channels which he named Barrow Strait and Viscount Melville Sound; and in the autumn he berthed his ships at Winter Harbour on Melville Island. In the spring of 1820 he made some explorations on foot on Melville Island, and to the south-west across the sound he took note of an unmistakeable "loom of land" which he entered on his chart as Banks Land. When the ice broke up he found himself unable to make headway west or south, and returned home. As no later sea-borne expedition came near to matching this achievement, Parry's observations were all that McClure had to guide him when, thirty years later, he passed through Bering Strait and approached the region of Banks Land from the west. (He named this land Baring Land, supposing it to be separate from Parry's Banks Land.)

The amphibious expeditions working by boat and canoe farther south along the continental shore met with better success. By 1840 the parties of Franklin and Richardson, Simpson and Dease, had charted the entire arctic seaboard of North America from Bering Strait to the Isthmus of Boothia, leaving unexplored only the peninsulas of Melville and Boothia and the intervening coast. As this region was not easy to approach by land or sea it was proposed to send in ships by way of Lancaster Sound with orders to grope their way south-west to some point on the continental shore west of Boothia, thus completing a salt-water

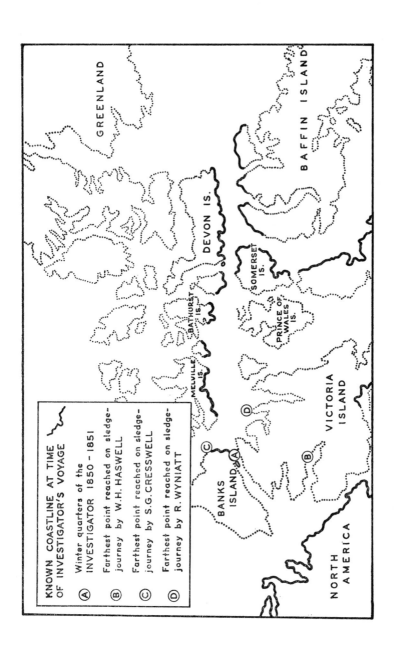

KNOWN COASTLINE AT TIME
OF INVESTIGATOR'S VOYAGE

Ⓐ Winter quarters of the
    INVESTIGATOR 1850 - 1851

Ⓑ Farthest point reached on sledge-
    journey by W.H. HASWELL

Ⓒ Farthest point reached on sledge-
    journey by S.G. CRESSWELL

Ⓓ Farthest point reached on sledge-
    journey by R. WYNIATT

GREENLAND

BAFFIN ISLAND

DEVON IS.

SOMERSET
IS.

BATHURST
IS.

PRINCE OF
WALES
IS.

MELVILLE
IS.

VICTORIA
ISLAND

BANKS
ISLAND

NORTH
AMERICA

Northwest Passage. In 1845 Sir John Franklin sailed with the ships *Erebus* and *Terror* to carry out this mission. In 1848, as the expedition was still unreported, Sir James Ross was dispatched with the ships *Enterprise* and *Investigator* to bring it aid. (Lieutenants McClure and McClintock were among Ross's officers.) Ross spent the winter of 1848-9 at Port Leopold on Somerset Island. The state of the ice prevented him from getting farther west in the ensuing summer, and he returned to England in the autumn without having found the least trace of the missing expedition.

It was now plain that a major catastrophe had overtaken Franklin's crews, and the British government and wealthy individuals in Great Britain and the United States equipped expeditions to bring them relief. Here the saga of the *Investigator* begins. It was resolved to send in a larger and better-equipped expedition by way of Lancaster Sound, and, as Franklin's ships might have penetrated far to the west before meeting disaster, Ross's two ships were hurriedly refitted to make the long voyage by way of Cape Horn, up the Pacific, and through Bering Strait, to search the Alaskan shore and the unknown seas of the Western Arctic. Captain Richard Collinson, a marine surveyor of distinction, took command of this expedition in the *Enterprise*. As his second-in-command the Admiralty chose a very unlikely aspirant to fame, an Irish lieutenant, Robert John Le Mesurier McClure. Then forty-two, McClure had previously served in a subordinate rank on two polar voyages, but was otherwise undistinguished. He was promoted to the rank of commander, and took command of the *Investigator*. Through the co-operation of the Moravian Society, Johann August Miertsching, a brother of that order and a missionary to the Labrador Eskimos, was enlisted as interpreter; he joined the expedition at the last moment.

A pious evangelist, Miertsching is one of the quaintest and by no means the least heroic of Canadian arctic travellers. Born in Saxony in 1817, and trained as a missionary of the Moravian Brotherhood, he spent the early years of his manhood at Ogkak on the Labrador coast where he learned the ways of his Eskimo flock and acquired great proficiency in their language. In 1849 he came home on furlough and was immediately enlisted by the British Admiralty to serve as interpreter on the expedition then setting out to make search for Sir John Franklin by way of Bering Strait. As there was no space on Captain Collinson's *Enterprise* he was given a temporary berth on the second vessel, the *Investigator*, and he remained one of her crew for the entire five years of that all but disastrous cruise. His personal record of the voyage is a most valuable document, furnishing as it does an outsider's view and supplying details that contemporary chroniclers either ignored or thought it prudent to suppress.

Though much applauded at the time, Captain McClure of the *Investigator* has not obtained the rank in arctic history to which the discovery of Prince of Wales Strait and the achievement of the Passage would seem to entitle him. The harshness of his discipline, doubts as to his discretion, censure (not wholly deserved) of his conduct in breaking away from Collinson to cruise off on his own, the subsequent revelation of Franklin's priority as discoverer of the Passage – all these have left him with a reputation that is somewhat ambiguous, and decidedly not of the first rank among the discoverers of his day.

Contemporary publications, of which there are two in English, do not provide the means for a full and just estimate of his worth. He produced no memoir of his own, but permitted Captain Sherard Osborn to use his journals; Osborn compiled a lively and interesting but quite uncritical panegyric. On the other hand, the ship's surgeon,

Alexander Armstrong, in a weighty and impressive volume, drew a most unfriendly portrait of his captain. Both records are biased and need to be checked against a less prejudiced source. It is this that Miertsching is able to provide.

Shortly after the voyage he published in German a memoir of the voyage in which he alluded to certain circumstances that Osborn had ignored and Armstrong (very bitter against his captain, but inhibited by his rank as naval officer) had passed over lightly. But Miertsching's account also was toned down to spare the feelings of former comrades, and his original journal rested in the family archives for over a century until through the kindness of Professor W. Jannasch of Göttingen, Germany, and of Mr. Niels Jannasch of Seabright, Nova Scotia, it was placed in the hands of the present editor.

The only part of this record that is a genuine diary is that relating to the tedious and protracted home-coming (from April 1853 to November 1854); Miertsching's original diary was lost when the ship was abandoned. As neither inclination nor training disposed him to organize his recollections into a regular history of the voyage, Miertsching drew upon his memory, aided by his own pencilled notes and the captain's personal journal, to reproduce as accurately as possible the missing portions of the diary (from January 20, 1850, to April 15, 1853). No reader will doubt that he did so with success. He was sensitive and, in an environment which he found strange and sometimes repulsive, he was susceptible to vivid impressions which an excellent memory enabled him to retain. A good deal of substance must have been lost, but the quaint, lively, and highly original flavour of the rest is unimpaired. The Captain's journal kept him informed as to dates, so permitting him to preserve the diary form, but the style and quality are all his own.

But to assert that our record is, as far as it goes, a faithful copy of its original is not to claim that it is accurate or well-proportioned. Miertsching is a romantic: he magnifies the horrors of the storm-tossed ice, just as the pompous Armstrong, with the reverse kind of affectation, seems to make light of them; his treatment of this theme is laboured and artificial compared with his charmingly natural portrayal of the Eskimos of the Mackenzie region and Prince Albert Land. Except for his constant association with McClure and his little devotional gatherings, he seems to have been something of a recluse: after almost four years in the same mess he admits to only a "tolerably" good acquaintance with Sainsbury; his journal is as poor in character studies as it is rich in incident and topographical description. He makes gratuitous errors in points of the compass, records exaggerated rumours which he subsequently fails to correct, and, despite the captain's journal, seems at times to be confused in his dates. But it is useless to censure him for neglecting the rules of historical composition by which he never professes to be bound; his journal is the record of his own experiences, observations, and emotions, and of these he presents a picture that is wholly natural and convincing.

If Miertsching does not tell us much of the dispositions of his brother-officers, he is very revealing about his own. Though a worthy member of the army of nineteenth-century missionary-pioneers, he is not quite representative of the type. He lacks the adventurous character of a Livingstone, is an explorer by compulsion only, and never ceases to pine for the quiet life of a missionary in Labrador. Nor is he a stoic: he often complains of uncongenial companions and of hardship. He seems to have been peculiarly susceptible to physical discomfort. It is the more to his credit that he "kept his head high" and exerted himself so strenuously for the spiritual and bodily good of his shipmates. His religious principles were surely founded: in five

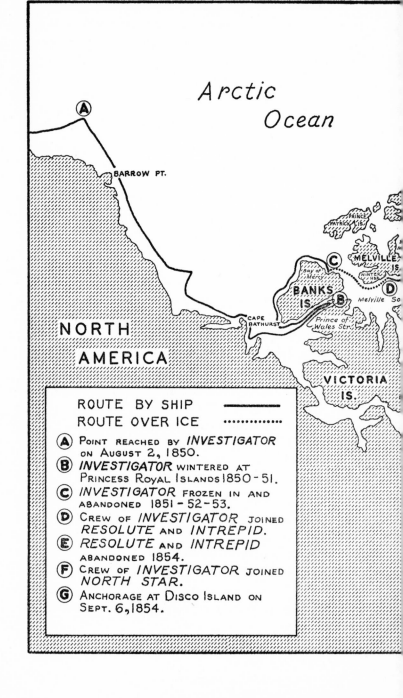

Arctic Ocean

BARROW PT.

PRINCE PATRICK IS.

Bay of Mercy

C MELVILLE IS.

WINTER HBR.

D

BANKS IS.

Melville So.

CAPE BATHURST

B

Prince of Wales Str.

NORTH AMERICA

VICTORIA IS.

ROUTE BY SHIP ⎯⎯⎯

ROUTE OVER ICE ············

(A) Point reached by *INVESTIGATOR* on August 2, 1850.

(B) *INVESTIGATOR* wintered at Princess Royal Islands 1850-51.

(C) *INVESTIGATOR* frozen in and abandoned 1851-52-53.

(D) Crew of *INVESTIGATOR* joined *RESOLUTE* and *INTREPID.*

(E) *RESOLUTE* and *INTREPID* abandoned 1854.

(F) Crew of *INVESTIGATOR* joined *NORTH STAR.*

(G) Anchorage at Disco Island on Sept. 6, 1854.

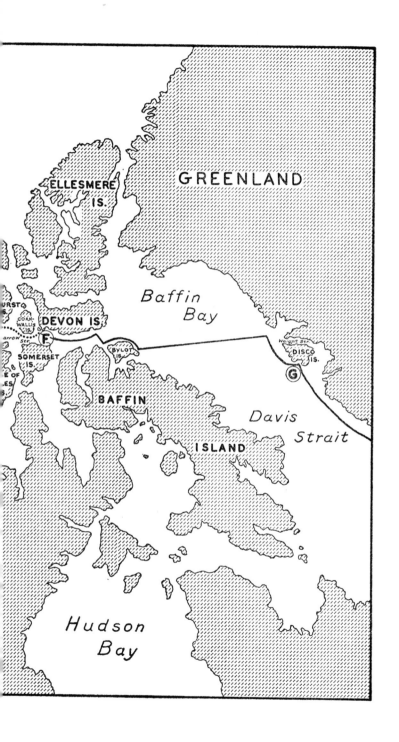

years of association with worldly companions whose example was the more seductive because they treated him
with personal kindness, he yielded not a jot of his austere
morality, and he is no more severe with the defective
Christianity of Captain McClure at the beginning of the
voyage than with that of Sir Edward Belcher at its close.
He must have been of a most amiable disposition: a high
degree of virtue, especially of that militant virtue which
feels bound to exhort and instruct, is seldom popular, and
yet he won a group of converts and the respect and affection of almost the entire company. Armstrong, who disliked
him, was a solitary exception; on the way home both the
genial Kellett and the morose Belcher went out of their way
to do him kindness, and sailors with "features hardened
by storm and foul weather were not ashamed to shed tears"
when they bade him a last farewell.

The simplicity and candour of Miertsching's style give
his narrative charm throughout and the occasional touch
of unconscious humour. His narrative has its defects as a
travelogue, but affords an excellent portrayal of a good
religious person who is both manly and lovable.

His later history is rather pathetic. When his furlough
expired the rulers of his Order, with the perversity that
executives sometimes display, sent him, not back to his
beloved Eskimos, but to South Africa, to practise among
the Hottentots the habits and dialect learned in Labrador.
After many years' service in this uncongenial field, he
retired to his native Saxony where he died, worn out, before
the age of sixty. But the family connection with Canada
was preserved; his daughter married a Labrador missionary; there a grandson was born, and today descendants of
the old pioneer are living in the country whose frontiers a
century ago he helped to extend.

THE OFFICERS OF THE *Investigator*
William H. Haswell, First Lieutenant: Commended by

Armstrong for the excellent care he took of his men on sledge-journeys. Miertsching implies that he was young and lacked self-confidence. This would partly explain the severity that McClure found necessary for the enforcement of discipline. Haswell subsequently attained the rank of rear-admiral.

Samuel G. Cresswell, Second Lieutenant: Hardly noticed in memoirs of the voyage. Cresswell was an artist and produced eight water-colours of the voyage, three of which are reproduced in this book.

Robert J. Wyniatt, Mate: According to Armstrong, energetic, especially as a hunter. From Miertsching we gather that he was inclined to be feckless and irresponsible.

Hubert H. Sainsbury, Mate: In poor health throughout the voyage.

Stephen Court, Second Master: The practice of appointing a sailing-master dated back to the wars of the sixteenth and seventeenth centuries, when the captain was commander of the fighting force and relied upon a professional seaman for the handling of the ship. The master was employed to care for the ship and his great merit was trustworthiness. Stephen Court amply met this requirement: he is never noticed in the memoirs except for the quiet, competent discharge of his duties. He later sailed to China with Sherard Osborn and ended his days as harbour-master at Shanghai.

Alexander Armstrong, M.D., Surgeon: Though only thirty-one when posted to the *Investigator*, Armstrong had already achieved distinction, having received the thanks of the trustees of the British Museum for work in the natural sciences, and of the commander-in-chief for improvements in naval sanitation. From his memoir of the voyage one gathers that he was shrewd, observant, much the best-informed man on board, and endowed with a gift for making those qualities unpalatable to his associates. One is not surprised to learn from Miertsching that he quarrelled openly with the captain and was made the victim of some rude horse-play by the wardroom officers. His success in the maintenance of health on board under the most adverse conditions was justly applauded. He seems to have been as intimate as his rank permitted with the men of the lower deck, and in view of the less than perfect efficiency on the quarter-deck we may assume that to him and to the sturdy Court the comparative good humour and discipline that prevailed throughout the cruise was largely due.

An old newspaper clipping preserved in the Stefansson Collection at Dartmouth College records a gathering at which the petty officers and men of the *Investigator* presented Armstrong with a chronometer in token of their gratitude for his exertions on the cruise. It is significant that neither McClure nor Haswell attended this ceremony, which was chaired by Lieutenant Bedford Pim.

H. Piers, Assistant Surgeon

John C. Paine, Clerk-in-Charge

William Newton, Ice-Mate: This officer was a civilian, recruited from the whaling trade as a specialist in ice navigation. Mr. Newton made his own contribution to a certain oddness evident among the ship's officers. We owe to Miertsching the account of his hallucinations, which Armstrong – apparently no psychiatrist – dismisses with a casual sneer.

TRAVEL NARRATIVE

OF A

NORTH POLE

EXPEDITION

IN SEARCH OF

SIR JOHN FRANKLIN

AND FOR THE

DISCOVERY OF THE

NORTHWEST PASSAGE

IN THE YEARS 1850-1854

BY

JOHANN AUGUST MIERTSCHING

As my daily journal was left behind on the ship in the frozen seas I have composed a second which naturally is incomplete and not so valuable as the first. To write this second journal I have been able to use the captain's personal diary and also numerous pencil-notes of my own which I was fortunate enough to preserve. Above all I have had my memory to draw upon and indeed that might be called my principal source. Scattered leaves thus put together form this most defective narrative.

JOHANN AUGUST MIERTSCHING

Daily temperatures are quoted according to the Fahrenheit scale, and when one figure only is given it is the mean for the twenty-four hours; latitude and longitude (west of Greenwich) are given as at 12 noon.

CHAPTER ONE

18 January 1850

After a pleasant journey of seven hours from London to Plymouth on the Great Western Railway, I reached Devonport with my companion, Brother Van Deurs, at 5.30, where we hired a boat and through pouring rain made our way to the ship *Enterprise*, which lay at anchor three miles away in Plymouth Sound near the ship *Investigator*. Arrived there, we found the crew busily taking on provisions, coal, etc.; a good many of them were drunk, and one was seated in irons near the wheel. Captain Collinson and his guest, Commander McClure of the *Investigator*, who had just finished their meal, welcomed me in the friendliest manner. Brother Van Deurs conversed for some time with the two captains, but I understood nothing of what they said. He then got into his boat and returned to Devonport. I was given temporary quarters in the captain's cabin where I enjoyed a good night's rest.

19 January

In the morning Captain Collinson took me with him to Devonport where he bought me an outfit of sailor's clothing and other articles. He also presented me to Admiral

Gedsch [Gage?]. I parted from Brothers Van Deurs and Schmith, and wandered about the town and dockyards until Captain Collinson, having finished his own business, brought me back at 6 p.m. to the *Enterprise*. On arriving there I was straightway transferred to the *Investigator*, because, as they explained to me, there was no cabin for me on the *Enterprise*: at Valparaiso, whither we were to sail in company, I would be brought back from the *Investigator* and quartered on my proper ship, the *Enterprise*. Commander McClure was busy writing letters, but he gave me a friendly reception, set before me wine, grapes, almonds, and olives, and said many things to me which I did not understand. On the ship was universal disorder; people were writing letters in frantic haste, etc.; provisions and a thousand other things were being taken aboard; casks, boxes, and chests lay in all directions, so that one could scarcely get out of his cabin. I wrote letters the entire evening. In the cabin assigned to me by the captain himself my new servant, Corporal Farquharson, had neatly disposed an excellent bed and a wash-stand.

20 *January, Sunday*

At 6 a.m. a good wind for sailing out of the harbour – the anchor hoisted – the sails spread – and out we go to sea. Shall we see England or Europe again? and when? These are the questions which force themselves against one's will on every man; but it is impossible to answer them. Quite indescribable are the emotions that overwhelm everyone when such a ship sails – as on an arctic cruise – to an unknown destination, perhaps for two years, perhaps forever. The future is wrapped in obscurity. To the Most High and Almighty Lord and Saviour, under Whose protection, unworthy as we are, we undertake this perilous voyage, is all this known; but from us it is hidden. Morning prayer alone in my cabin. Late in the morning I was presented by the captain to the officers; they accepted me most cordially as interpreter into the rank of officer. In one of the musters of the sailors held by the captain they were ordered to salute me and to treat me as an officer. The sailors were in very good humour, caused chiefly by the cocoa and grog enjoyed at breakfast. The midday meal, which I took for the first time in the company of English sea officers, was something very different from the harmony prevailing on our mission ships! It lasted from 3 to 8 p.m. After that there was tea and whisky punch.

Our ship, the *Investigator*, is a small frigate[1] of 423 tons with three masts (barque). The crew consists of sixty-six sailors: captain, Robert Le Mesurier McClure; two lieutenants, Haswell and S. G. Cresswell; two mates (sub-lieutenants), R. Wyniatt and H. Sainsbury; two ship's doctors, Dr. Armstrong and H. Piers; J. C. Paine, ship's clerk, in charge of supplies; S. Court, sailing-master.[2] These officers are called wardroom or gunroom officers. The men are divided into three classes; The first class are petty officers, to which four artisans, armourer, breadmaker, cook, sailmaker, etc., belong. The captain has a cook and two stewards, the officers the same. The sailors on the lower deck — where they sleep in hammocks — are divided into messes, eight men to a mess. Each officer sleeps in his own cabin, seven feet square, with bed, wash-stand, desk, and chair. Each officer has a servant who keeps his cabin in order, does his washing and mending, etc. As on our ship there are no boys; the eight marines, one corporal, and one sergeant are appointed as servants, and for that receive twelve shillings a month in addition to their regular pay. Of cannon we have only two pieces, but a large stock of muskets, pis-

---

[1] The *Investigator* was not technically a frigate, nor could she have been rated as such; a frigate was a post-captain's, not a commander's, appointment.

[2] Presumably Mr. Newton, the ice-master, also belonged to the wardroom.

tols, hand grenades, and Congreve rockets. Rations consist of salt beef and pork, fresh boiled beef and veal; vegetables are beans, dried cabbage, and meal. At breakfast, cocoa, at night, tea with biscuit. Vinegar, pickles, mustard, etc. are served twice weekly. Before our ship left England the officers pooled £450 sterling and purchased with it wine, beer, and a variety of foods. The day is divided into four-hour watches; each watch, consisting of an officer and fifteen to twenty men, is on duty for four hours; and this rotation is kept up day and night.

At 5 a.m. the reveille sounds; the interior of the ship is cleaned throughout and everything well polished; at 8 is breakfast; at 9 a general muster on the foredeck at which every man must appear; until 11.30 the sailors are usefully employed; at 12 the midday meal; until 1.30 the men are free, then work until 5; at 6 tea, and until 8 p.m. the men are expected to take part in sport (hands dance and *skitark* [skylark?]). At 8 o'clock to bed. The officers dine at 2 p.m., the captain at 4. The officers sleep when they please. Each day at noon rations are issued for the ensuing day to the various messes by the officer in charge of stores. The daily grog ration is one gill per man.

23 *January (lat. 48° 36'; long. 11° 10'; temp. 52°)*

The last three days we have enjoyed fine weather and a fair wind. I feel dreadfully lonely in a floating house and in the company of utter strangers. The captain and officers are most kind to me, but unhappily I do not understand what they say. My servant is a Scot, and we communicate more by signs than by words.

24 *January (lat. 48° 56'; long. 10° 7'; temp. 52°)*

Last night powerful headwinds, this morning a frightful gale; about 8 a.m. the upper masts snapped; in a moment down came main and fore topmast, main and fore gallant, along with the flying jib-boom. The waves beat incessantly on the labouring ship, and this catastrophe caused a regular turmoil[1] on board. *I began on this occasion to learn something of my captain's character.* I spent almost the entire day in a life so strange to me in my cabin, where the drenching sea water stood two inches deep. A fine beginning for me, a total stranger to the life and the language of the sea.

25 January (lat. 48° 56'; long. 10° 6'; temp. 52°)
Rain and a wind subsiding, but still foul. New masts rigged; five men engaged in this task fell overboard but were rescued. A bitter quarrel between the captain and the officers. The deeply laden ship creaks and groans in the heaving waves. I did not suffer from seasickness.

31 January (lat. 47° 48'; long. 20° 21'; temp. 55°)
The weather always most unpleasant; rain and rough seas do not cease; the ship rolls a great deal; all the cabins are drenched in sea water. Last Sunday the men rested, but there was no Divine Service. On the 29th I dined with the captain. Today the *Enterprise* (Captain Collinson) was seen and spoken to by signal. The ship was pumped out; four feet of water in her well.

1 February 1850 (lat. 48° 7'; long. 20° 52')
The whole day foul wind and rain; wave after wave breaking on the decks. The men, with nothing to do, are joyous, and the fiddle in full play.

4 February (lat. 42° 48'; long. 19° 17'; temp. 54°)
Fine weather and strong fair wind. The captain inspected

---

[1]So I translate "eine wahre Rebellion"; it seems incredible that veteran seamen should have shown a mutinous disposition in such a crisis. The phrase, however, may refer to recriminations between the captain and his officers.

the cabins, and arrangements were made for the living quarters to be dried. A small iron stove was heated, and red-hot cannon-balls were placed in corners and recesses. In the evening a fire broke out and was promptly extinguished by the deck watch. A number of new sails were burnt.

5 February (lat. 41° 17'; long. 19° '; temp. 57°)
Weather fine and wind fair; a wholesale washing of clothes by the sailors. In the evening frightful noise and dancing and singing. For me this is all so new that it is wholly incomprehensible and, alone in my cabin, I can hardly contain myself. I had expected something very different in our perilous cruise. O, Lord and Saviour! have patience and take not Thy mercy from us. Help, Lord! in whatever way and by whatever means it may be. My mother and my sister, Johane, today celebrate their birthdays; I would fly across seas for them. Ach! and I am and feel so wretched. I can scarcely control my feelings. And now the officers too are quarrelling; the captain prefers not to notice them.

7 February (lat. 38° 9'; long. 19° 45'; temp. 59°)
It is beginning to be delightfully warm. Wind and weather good. Today we are near the Azores. In the afternoon met two ships. I dined with the captain; after food there was whisky punch, but that liquor was too strong for me, for I am as yet no seaman: I do not enjoy it.[1]

8 February (lat. 36° 54'; long. 20° 4'; temp. 59°)
From today on every third day a keg containing notice of

[1]According to a tradition preserved by his descendants, Miertsching later developed — and retained to the end of his days — a taste for this particular beverage which other members of his order viewed with something less than approval.

our ship will be thrown overboard. From today also I am to go every day at 12 noon to the captain's cabin and drink a glass of wine with him (luncheon). My books and notes, which are all moist and damp, and also my guitar, I am henceforth to keep in the captain's cabin.

10 February (lat. 34° 52'; long. 21° 37'; temp. 62°)
Weather warm and fine. In the morning the captain held Divine Service on the upper deck, and read the Gospel and Epistle for the thirteenth Sunday before Trinity. We sighted three ships bound for the West Indies.

13 February (lat. 31° 27'; long. 23° 20'; temp. 66°)
The weather is becoming very hot. With the wind now steady and fair the ship is sailing eight to nine miles an hour; neither birds nor fish are seen. From today I have assigned myself the daily duty of devoting two hours to the study of English and two hours to the language of the Eskimo.

20 February (lat. 15° 36'; long. 26° 40'; temp. 73°)
Yesterday we came into the trade winds; a great many flying fish and black stormy petrels [*Sturmvogel*] seen. Today came the order to wear white socks, jackets, and straw hats.

21 February (lat. 14° 16'; long. 26° 36'; temp. 75°)
A glorious summer day; mild wind; the night I spent on deck; it was so agreeable that I cannot describe it. The moon gave no shade. In the evening music and dancing in which the officers took part.

22 February (lat. 12° 25'; long. 26° 12'; temp. 75°)
Oh, what a glorious evening it is! If only it were not for this

frightful noise and dancing. Yet I can often seek comfort in my guitar:

Ich darf Dich im Geiste kuessen
Und mit Freuden Dich geniessen;
Ja, wenn sich oft truebe Stunden
Manchmal bei mir eingefunden,
Dass mein Herz weint,
Weil kein Trost erscheint,
Gibt Er neue Gnadenblicke,
Dass Er mein Herz erquicke,
    O, wie treu ist Er!

24 *February* (*lat. 7° 48'; long. 25° 12'; temp. 79°*)
Each Sunday there is Divine Service; the captain stands and reads from the Prayer Book a psalm, two chapters from the Bible, the Ten Commandments, and the Gospel and Epistle prescribed for that Sunday. Oh, how grand it is on Sunday, when there is neither music, dancing, nor uproar. A sailor suddenly became ill and spat blood a great deal.

26 *February* (*lat. 4° 21'; long. 23° 26'; temp. 81°*)
For three days dull weather and dead calm; it is becoming unendurably hot. Today every man must bathe in the sea. Those who cannot swim are secured with lines around their waists; I was glad that as a boy I had learned to swim. The captain was the first to plunge into the sea.

1 *March 1850* (*lat. 3° 31'; long. 23° 26'; temp. 82°*)
Wind and weather both favourable. Many fish, sharks, and dolphins around the ship – everything most agreeable, if only I had a Christian friend or a Christian environment!!!

4 March (lat. 1° 6'; long. 26° 33'; temp. 81°)
All day rain and no wind. The heat is almost unendurable.
Two slave-ships sighted.

5 March (lat. 0° 6' south; long. 27° 16'; temp. 81°)
Today the captain granted permission to the crew to celebrate the famous festival of Neptune; the body of every
man who is crossing the equator for the first time is smeared
with tar, which is then scraped off with a razor fashioned
from the rusty hoop of an old keg. I do not hold it worth
while to give an exact description of this festival which I
would be very glad to forget entirely. It is truly more than
any Christian man can comprehend that such men as our
sailors should exist! One would suppose that men living in
perpetual danger of the sea would be incapable of the bru-
tality and insolence which one encounters frequently on
land; but alas! I have met insolent and godless men, yet
were they angels compared to these brazen sinners; I feel
as if my lot had been cast among half a hundred devils.
The harsh rules of naval discipline are barely enough to
keep them under control. A Brazilian ship hailed us and
received English newspapers.

6 March (lat. 1° 37'; long. 28° 24'; temp. 82°)
Winds very light, but glorious weather; now very very hot;
how gladly would I send a tenth part of this heat to Labrador, and in return obtain a little ice or a glass of water
from Bek's pond. The water which we drink is stale and
lukewarm. More ships seen, and one spoken to – from
Hamburg. Since we left England scarcely a day has passed
with no one under arrest; today three men are in confine-
ment.

10 March (lat. 9° 13' south; long. 31° 58'; temp. 81°)
Wind and weather good; yesterday a heavy shower of rain;

13

much water was caught. Today the captain again made a mistake in that this Sunday [the fourth Sunday in Lent] he made Trinity Sunday; I do not think that anyone noticed it. At luncheon, to which he invited me, I told him that now for the second time he had become confused in his Sundays, at which he laughed heartily and said: "We are seafarers, and have fifty-two Sundays – one just like another – and only one festival, Christmas, when Jack must have roast beef and plum pudding." We had a most interesting conversation. Only it is unfortunate that my English is so bad. Oh Lord, grant that I may soon learn this language; then I will use it to Thy glory.

12 *March (lat. 15° 44' south; long. 33° 15'; temp. 80°)*
Fine wind and weather; several ships seen; forty English miles from the Brazilian coast; flying-fish swarm around the ship. In the evening from 6 to 8 a grand spectacle, dramatics, and dancing. In the evening I sat alone as usual in the captain's cabin where I could, in the spirit of worship, play on my guitar and sing: "Wie wohl ist mir o Freund der Seelen . . ."

16 *March (lat. 20° south; long. 36° 9'; temp. 80°)*
The weather is heavenly fine. My talks with the captain go better every day. In the evening we go up to the quarterdeck, and there reclining gaze at the southern stars.

23 *March (lat. 27° 6' south; long. 44° 42'; temp. 75°)*
Oh, glorious weather! How pleasant it would be here if only we were all Christians. Ah, could I only share in the daily chorus: "O Bethanien du Friedenshuette . . ." Not far from here is the land of palm trees, but unhappily there are few there who would break off branches and welcome the King of Glory.

26 March (lat. 32° 37' south; long. 45° 34'; temp. 70°)
Today I had the opportunity of conversing with our comedian, the negro Anderson; for two years he had been cook on a vessel carrying German emigrants to America, and he had picked up a few words of German; unhappily he is the most godforsaken of men. He is universally popular because he provides so much amusement.

31 March (lat. 40° 9' south; long. 52° 44'; temp. 64°)
I spent a very happy Easter Day; I felt so soothed in the seclusion of my cabin. The weather is very fine. What an unhappy life those men lead who do not seek to know Christ, who seek pleasure where no pleasure is to be found. Today another bitter quarrel between the captain and his officers.

1 April 1850 (lat. 38° 40' south; long. 52° 25'; temp. 62°)
The southern stars are very fine, but I find the so-called Southern Cross of little significance; I have often sought it in the sky, and, had it not been pointed out to me, would never have found it. The two little nebulae of Magellan are interesting, especially when seen through the large telescope. Always we see many fish, especially sharks, and birds. The glow of the sea by night is wonderful. Until now we have had no sick; now two men are depressed and troubled with blood-spitting. Mr. Piers comes daily to me and we read English. This well-educated and, to me, very beloved man is attached to no religious denomination in England, and wishes to learn about the Brotherhood. His brother is a *Socianer*. At a depth of 170 fathoms the temperature of the sea water is 59°.

6 April (lat. 42° 17' south; long. 52° 25'; temp. 56°)
For several days most unpleasant weather; very stormy

and with much rain; a number of sea-fowl caught, also three albatross, which measure 10 feet, 5 inches, from wing-tip to wing-tip. Of the four men under arrest one today was given four dozen lashes on the bare back with the cat-and-nine-tails. A horrible punishment so to flay the back of a fellow creature, but with a rabble like our crew some such punishment there must be.[1]

7 April (lat. 43° 57' south; long. 52° 25'; temp. 54°)
On account of the stormy weather and rain Divine Service was held on the lower deck. With the captain at luncheon a very interesting conversation, only the English language is still very unfamiliar to me. Today in a depth of 180 fathoms 40° Fahrenheit.

9 April (lat. 47° 1' south; long. 63° 48'; temp. 53°)
Raw, damp, cold, and stormy weather. Three times bottom has been found at 60 fathoms, but no land is in sight. Yesterday evening the sailors were engaged in a brawl, in consequence of which five men were punished today. The three sick are most depressed and unhappily devoid of Christian faith.

14 April (lat. 57° 36' south; long. 68° 3'; temp. 47°)
For the last few days the weather has been foggy, but the wind fair. Many sea-fowl seen; two sea-eagles shot; colour, dark brown and white. The wings measure eleven feet. In the late afternoon land was sighted to the west. The ship tacked back and forth all night.

---

[1]Other arctic captains of the period were much less prone than McClure to make extreme use of their disciplinary powers. Collinson (Noel Wright, *Quest for Franklin*, p. 202), and Sir Edward Belcher (*Last Arctic Voyage*, introduction, p. 7) are instances. See also Parry, *Journal of a Voyage for the Discovery of the Northwest Passage*, entry for February 14, 1820.

15 April (lat. 52° 30' south; long. 68° 28'; temp. 47°)

In the morning land close aboard, Cape Virgin! Thousands of great white birds seen on the beach. Mr. Cresswell shot a white swan. 10 a.m. at the entrance of the Straits of Magellan. To the right the land of Patagonia, to the left Tierra del Fuego or Feuerland. On the green hills we saw grazing great herds of llamas [guanacos]. Here are no trees, only low bushes.

16 April (temp. 46°)

We passed the night at anchor not far from the land; the tide here runs five miles an hour; spring flood 40-50 feet. Great herds of llamas are grazing on the Patagonian side. The formation of the land is gently rising hills and great plains overgrown with bush. 10 a.m. we sighted the steam warship *Gorgon*, Commander Painter, in the distance ahead, lying at anchor. She had come from Valparaiso to give us a tow through the Straits of Magellan. At 11 a.m. we were overhauled by the American steamboat *New World*, which was sailing to California. On the shore near by had assembled upwards of three hundred Patagonians, most of them on horseback. At 1 p.m. the *Gorgon* approached us under steam and took us in tow; from her we learned that our consort—the *Enterprise*, which we had not seen since 26 January—had passed two days before. The further we sailed the more beautiful grew the land on the right shore and on the left; both sides were covered with beautiful woods. The Tierra del Fuegan islands rise to a great height. At Sandy Bay we met again many Patagonians, dressed in long cloaks of llama hair; these folk are very big and strong; the women six feet tall, and the men from 6 feet, 8 inches, to 7 feet, 3 inches; their faces are broad and well-proportioned, their long hair is black, their colour brown. Close to Sandy Bay lay a stranded ship which had

17

been caught in the forty-foot-high flood-tide and flung on to the land.

17 April (temp. 45°)

Sailed all night; at 8 a.m. at anchor at Fort Famine, a Chilian convict settlement. There we purchased bullocks and pigs. A number of other sailboats were anchored there. The country, covered with woods, is beautiful.

18 April (temp. 45°)

Late yesterday evening we anchored in Fortescue Bay (or Fort Gallant); near us lie at anchor the *Enterprise, Gorgon, New World,* and a number of other smaller craft. The day was stormy; fresh water was taken on board here; our three invalids were transferred to the *Gorgon,* and fit men received in their place. Throughout the day I was on land, collected flowers, etc.; was also on the American steamboat *New World,* where I met quite a number of Germans on their way to California, where they hope to make their fortunes without any trouble. The country, inhabited by Patagonians, is very beautiful; great forests. Fish very plentiful. On land I saw five large wigwams uninhabited, and boats which resembled the Eskimo *kayaks,* but made of bark instead of skin. In the afternoon to dinner with Captain Collinson on the *Enterprise,* where I learned that from here we were sailing not to Valparaiso, but direct to the Sandwich Islands. I was required (now, in the darkness and rain) to move with sack and pack to the *Enterprise* to occupy a new and comfortably fitted cabin. But this was not a positive order, and my captain, Mr. McClure, put in a good word for me, so I was permitted to remain on the *Investigator* until our arrival at the Sandwich Islands[1],

[1]Collinson paid dearly for this good-natured concession: three years later he was to pass within a few miles of the scene of Franklin's disaster, and had he had Miertsching with him to question the natives he might have ascertained that fact and achieved the success which later fell to the lot of McClintock.

where we were to remain for two weeks. I was much pleased at being allowed to remain on my ship, for the rain and high waves in the dark night would thoroughly have drenched me and my baggage in the passage from ship to ship. When the dinner was over I left Captain Collinson, Mr. McClure, and Painter to drink their whiskey alone, and spent the evening with the officers of the *Enterprise*.

19 April (temp. 48°)

The weather fine; the wind foul but not so strong. At 6 a.m. we got under way; the steamer *Gorgon* took both ships in tow, the *Enterprise* and the *Investigator*, and pulled us along at five to six miles an hour. In the afternoon, with a strong tide flowing against us, we went very slowly, and were approached by a number of Tierra del Fuegans (Pesheras) in little boats (canoes), resembling *kayaks*. Their appearance was wretched, and stirred our pity. Their stature is small, the women 4 feet, 2 inches, the men 5 feet, 1 inch, in head and body thick, arms and legs thin and curving inwards, hair black and long, while their colour, by reason of dirt, can no man distinguish, whether they are brown or a yellowish-grey; their dress consists of one small sealskin pulled over the shoulders and fastened at the breast. Their boats are canoes of ox-hide; one small boat, twelve feet by three, holds five full-grown men or two men and three women and children; in the middle of the boat a fire burns on a small flat stone; one woman tends the fire; two paddle; one man sits in the stern of the boat, the other in the bow. From time to time the women dive and bring up mussels and the like which are cooked on the fire and devoured by the men. To us their speech was unintelligible. One woman was crying "baki" and "bakunga". I tossed the poor naked being some tobacco and my pocket-handkerchief, which she bound on her head with her hair and swam to the nearest land. Should these poor heathen here be so degraded and never hear the Gospel? Ships bearing missionaries sail by them to distant lands, and these poor wretches occupying the lowest grade of humanity, our brothers according to the flesh, seem forgotten by man and Christ. The farther west we go, the loftier and more rugged becomes the coast on either side of the strait. The forests fade away completely; only small bushes and moss; great glaciers occur here as in the far north.

20 *April (temp. 48°)*
Today in the morning we emerged from the straits into the Pacific Ocean; but it was no more peaceful than it was small; north-westerly gales and heavy seas greeted us, so that the twelve-inch tow-rope parted, and the steamboat, being able to do us no further service, steamed off towards Valparaiso, and we were left to make our way in company with the *Enterprise* to the Sandwich Islands.

23 *April (lat. 54° 17′ south; long. 80° 33′; temp. 42°)*
The weather most cold and disagreeable; very tempestuous with heavy seas – the waves beat on the upper deck, and the bulwarks are beginning to shatter. We have not seen the *Enterprise* for two days.

30 *April (lat. 51° 2′ south; long. 81° 57′; temp. 42°)*
Wind and weather the same as last week; waves house-high dash one over another; now snow falls; now rain. The ship is tossed about like a nutshell; one can neither stand nor sit; and as for lying, one must brace himself with knee and elbow and all his limbs pain him; everything on the ship is wet.

1 *May 1850 (lat. 49° 6′ south; long. 79° 50′; temp. 43°)*
A very strong east wind is driving us to the west, and the

20

mighty ocean swell and the towering waves are coming from the north-west. The rolling of the ship is almost unbearable; a number of seamen, as well as Haswell, Wyniatt, and Sainsbury, have become sea-sick. Today there was again a sharp dispute between the captain and the officers.

8 *May*

For the last few days a devil of discord seems to have fixed his abode amongst us. It is as if each man were himself a devil. Towards me they are friendly and courteous, but it is most difficult to stand alone in the midst of such antagonists. Oh, loving Saviour, give me wisdom and guide me on the right path.

10 *May (lat. 38° 49′ south; long. 90° 30′; temp. 59°)*

Wind and weather very unfavourable: for the last fourteen days we have been able to carry only two small sails in the gale and the heavy seas. The bulwarks are smashed; there is much water in the ship, and the cabins and everything are drenched; fourteen seamen lie sick below. I caught a large bird, an albatross, fifteen pounds in weight, the wings 10 feet, 5 inches. The waves often deluge the upper deck and leave behind small fish and other creatures of the sea.

14 *May (lat. 30° 42′ south; long. 95° temp. 68°)*

Today three more men sick; there are now seventeen sick, suffering from colds, rheumatism, blood-spitting, and colic; calm weather, not a breath of wind stirring; yet the sea rages, and the ship is so rolled about that she dips the ends of her yards in the water. It is a miserable life, the life of a sailor; it is almost unendurable; one cannot stand, sit, or lie; in addition everything is wet through – clothes, bedding, everything – and in the ship there is a repulsive odour.

15 May (lat. 30° 30′ south; long. 94° 10′; temp. 69°)
Last night a terrific squall; everyone, even the captain, feared that the ship was lost. We sailed by some coral reefs, and saw a large fragment of a mast floating in the sea. 7 a.m. – another squall struck us with an overpowering blast, smashed the three topmasts, two yards, flying jib, and the main jib-boom; a sail was blown away. This happened while the first lieutenant, who was officer of the watch, had quitted the deck for a few minutes; the ship, now more than ever, was wallowing amid the waves – the fury of the captain was terrible, positively inhuman. The work which now began with the crippled ship was most difficult; for each man must hold on with one hand and work with the other, with the ship rolling and the waves breaking in cataracts over all.

16 May (lat. 30° 26′ south; long. 94° 37′; temp. 68°)
Praise and thanks be to God that this disastrous day is over: it has been the most unpleasant that I have yet experienced on board. I kept myself as much as possible to the dampness of my cabin, far from those exasperated folk; for yesterday the devil held high festival on our ship. Now the ship lies helpless, and only on the lower masts are a few sails spread; spare masts there are none; today stout yards are rigged in the place of masts. This morning there was held a solemn inquiry or trial of the seamen and officers; the outcome was that Lieutenant Haswell was placed under arrest; he is under the guard of two armed marines.[1] The wind is subsiding; the weather appears to be breaking.

18 May (lat. 27° 50′ south; long. 97° 48′; temp. 64°)
Today I also fell into the hands of the doctors: clothing,

[1]Perhaps this harshness was in part provoked by McClure's consciousness of his own shortcomings. He had no confidence in his officers; Haswell's efficiency was impaired by sickness, and the ship had almost capsized a few hours previously. It was a time for the captain to take immediate control.

linen, bedding, all are wet through; for fourteen days I have slept little, and that badly; in the evening before going to bed, I and my servant, also sick, have been compelled to wring out my bedding, which consists of woollen blankets, and then lie on damp sheets. I received medicine and orders to drink four glasses of sherry daily. The captain was very kind and ordered me to spend the day in his cabin. Our conversation was long and interesting; it seems to distress him that he had so forgotten himself on that day and had not handled the affair as a sincere Christian should have done.

19 May (lat. 27° 1' south; long. 98° 41'; temp. 68°)
Our doctor is sick also. Today fine weather; I dragged myself up on deck and warmed myself in the beaming kindness of the hot sun. Today is Whitsunday; Divine Service is held for the first time in six weeks. The captain told me that certain officers will be changed when we reach the Sandwich Islands. I also would be glad to bid the *Investigator* farewell.

23 May (lat. 26° 31' south; long. 101° 24'; temp. 71°)
Fine weather, with the occasional passing shower of rain. We have not sighted the *Enterprise* since 21 April. Our orders were to touch at Easter Island and there take on fresh water, but the captain will not do so: he is steering direct for the Sandwich Islands, and therefore from now on the daily ration of water is set at one pint per man. On clear nights we see the Southern Cross and the two nebulae. The clouds and star-pattern are quite different and more beautiful than in the northern hemisphere. We see very many birds, and during the last few days we have sighted not a few whales.

26 May (lat. 22° 54' south; long. 101° 2'; temp. 73°)
Wind and weather fair and fine. Our quarters are complete-

ly, and the interior of the ship moderately, dry. Of the nineteen sick there are yet twelve on the sick list. I feel almost completely recovered. Daily the men are busy hauling supplies up from the ship's hold to dry them out on the upper deck.

31 May (lat. 19° south; long. 105° 36'; temp. 73°)
Fine weather; north-east trade wind; the ship thoroughly cleansed, and repair work painted; many hundredweight of bacon ruined by sea water thrown into the sea. A seaman, Taylor, was today given two dozen lashes. With the weather again fine and the ship put in order, dancing and revelry is resumed. I was drying my books on the upper deck and took the opportunity of offering more very fine tracts to various seamen, who received them with thanks. I hope that they may not be read in vain. I dined with the captain, and when the meal was over had a pleasant talk on man's creation and his salvation through our Lord and Saviour. Ah! if only my English were better.

10 June 1850 (lat. 7° 15' south; long. 120° 24'; temp. 80°)
Every day fine weather and fair wind; in such agreeable weather it is grand to be a sailor. Lieutenant Haswell is still under arrest in his cabin with two men guarding his door; morning and afternoon he must pace the deck for two hours, but he may speak to no one. The sick are getting better, yet the captain will exchange a number of the invalids for fit men at the Sandwich Islands. My reading of English improves continuously, but there are still many words which I do not understand, and I must keep my dictionary by me.

15 June (lat. 0° 10' north; long. 131° 5'; temp. 81°)
This afternoon we crossed the Line for the second time; I am glad that there was no such ceremony as occurred when

we crossed it in the Atlantic Ocean. The continuous fair wind is sweeping us fast to the north. The heat is almost unbearable, and one's thirst is great, but no water is to be had. A sailor asked me for a tract, and I distributed among the crew all that I had. On learning of this the captain laughed heartily and gave it as his opinion that his people were not such simple folk as my Eskimos, etc.

29 *June (lat. 20° 6'; long. 154° 30'; temp. 76°)*
Until now always magnificent weather and fair wind. As we shall now soon be in the Sandwich Islands, drinking water is being issued without restriction. Most of the salt pork, cheese, smoked meat, etc., in the ship has been spoiled by dampness and heat. For the last little while the tone on the ship has been friendlier. Each evening I am with the captain on the quarter-deck until 11 p.m.; it is the pleasantest part of the day. The ship is repainted, and all the damage wrought by the waves repaired. Nine men are still sick. Frequently the captain grants the men an extra grog.

30 *June (lat. 21° 14'; long. 156° 33'; temp. 77°)*
Yesterday land was sighted which is the island Owahi, and belongs to the Sandwich group. Two lofty mountains, Mauna Roa and Mauna Koa, rise 13,000 and 15,000 feet above sea-level; one of these mountains is volcanic. During the night we passed the first and largest of the Hawaiian or Sandwich Islands. This morning the second island, Maui. In the clear weather we saw on the top of the mountains the everlasting snow; before midday the third island, Molokai, was passed; we sailed close to the land; saw a number of missionary establishments, heard the sound of church bells, saw the brown natives, clad in white, hurrying to church to worship God. Frankly, my present lot — which is not likely to change for a year or two — does not please me. But all must be good and right; it is God's will

that I should be where I am. At midday we drew near a large ship which was unknown to us; we hoisted our ensign and pennant, but the stranger showed no flag; the captain ordered a gun to be loaded and fired; the shot struck the water near the ship, and this had the desired effect, for a flag was straightway hoisted – the ship was a Yankee. At 6 p.m., just as we came up on deck after dinner, we sighted the island Owahu, where stands the city of Honolulu with its spacious harbour and royal residence, and where we are to remain for fourteen days. In the evening we rounded the dangerous Cape Kawaikao, and were only twenty English miles from the harbour; but as our sailing-master, Mr. Court, was unfamiliar with these waters, and had no chart to inform him, we took in our sails and hove to for the night, intending to run in next morning by daylight. Numerous ships were passing us, sailing to and from the port.

CHAPTER TWO

1 July 1850 (temp. 86°)

Weather superb. At 6 a.m. I had coffee with the officers on
the upper deck. The ship is drawing near to land; here also
are many swarms of flying-fish. The land is covered with
tropical fruits and trees; on the lowlands the coconut, on
the higher ground forests of sandalwood. No house or
human being in sight. At 8 o'clock guns were fired and a
flag hoisted to summon the pilot; he arrived at 9, and his
first article of news was that the *Enterprise*, after lying
here for four days, had set sail only yesterday morning for
Bering Strait. This caused our captain no small alarm.
Canoes of wood approached us bringing bread, butter,
eggs, etc., for sale; the brown canoemen spoke broken English. Other boats also came and took our soiled clothing to
land to wash it; for a dozen pieces we paid two dollars. We
anchored about 10 a.m. I was granted permission to go
ashore. Mr. Piers accompanied me and we visited the city
which has a population of over 30,000; many English,
Americans, Chinese, Jews, and Germans, mostly merchants
and business men, are met here. A German merchant,
Altin, from Hamburg, welcomed me kindly and invited me
to break bread at his home; but I was eager to meet the
missionaries, though to be sure they are hated by many

here in the city, and especially by our officers and men. However I was given a brotherly reception by the Reverend Mr. Clarke, and invited to tea and a religious meeting on the following day. My companion, Mr. Piers, caught some rare butterflies in the garden of the mission house; and so we went back to our ship, which lay between an English and a French man-of-war.

2 *July (temp. 86°)*

Yesterday evening a little English warship arrived from Panama bringing us letters, newspapers, etc., from England, and, for me, also from Germany. Oh, how I rejoiced over the beloved letters and an English *Losung*[1] and missionary leaflets from Brothers Mallalieu and Latrowe [Latrobe?]. Also the letter from Brother U. A. L. cheered me greatly. Thanks to Thy love, my joy was indescribable. Yesterday morning the captain sent for me and told me that we were to remain here for fourteen days, and advised me for the good of my health to rent a lodging, for which he offered me a sum of money; but I still had sterling, and so needed none. The captain further told me that I was to remain on his ship until we reached Bering Strait, where we would meet the *Enterprise*. I was also introduced to the English consul, Mueller. I went to the mission house, and the Reverend Mr. Clarke, who is also chaplain to the Court, took me to all the families connected with the mission, and by all I was received with friendship and affection. They offered me a room at the mission house, which I accepted with thanks. Here I feel absolutely at home. By my servant I was introduced to the Reverend Mr. Damon, a preacher well known to seafarers: he is a true brother in Christ; his fine newly-built church is open to seamen of all nations; it has a library and writing-room attached. The

[1]The Moravian *Manual of Devotion.*

merchant, Altin, and his wife are very fine people; their son, nine months old, is not yet baptized, because no priest is here except the missionaries, and these worthy folk refuse to baptize the child, because the father, a very upright and respectable person, drinks a glass of wine daily at his midday luncheon. The missionaries put a ban on every kind of spirituous liquor,[1] and if a member of their church takes a glass he is promptly excluded from the religious community. The equipment of the mission here is impressive. This is the main station; from here all other stations are furnished with what they require. Central management is in Boston. Close to the city of Honolulu is a large school which many scholars, brown and white, boys and girls, attend; there the children of the missionaries are trained to become teachers; and then, after two years of study at Boston, they are ordained as preachers or missionaries. The missionaries own considerable tracts of land, but for the most part they are uncultivated. The schools are run by brown teachers. In the evening I attended a meeting. Oh! how grand it is to find one's self again among brethren who preach Jesus, the crucified One, without shame. There is a morning and evening meeting daily. In the evening I wrote letters.

3 July (temp. 86°)

In fine but very hot weather, morning and afternoon, I visited the country around Honolulu with horse and carriage in the company of the Reverend Mr. Damon. A country of marvellous beauty: in the lowlands tropical, and in the hills European plants. Lunch at the home of the school director, Dr. Armstrong, a truly Christian family. In the evening with the seminary inspector, the Reverend

---

[1]No doubt this rigour was for the protection of their native flock, but it was naïve to hope that this wholesome restriction would have any effect in an international seaport.

Mr. Price. Today they held a sort of court-martial or rather court of inquiry on our ship. After a five-hour session and much debate, the officers promised the captain exact obedience, etc.[1]

4 July (temp. 86°)

In the morning visited the royal garden and the great verandah and the fortress. The fortress was recently utterly destroyed by a French frigate, and is a sad spectacle of ruin. The king, Kamakea III, like his queen, seems a dull sort of person. Clothing of European fashion, all silk; red, green, and black seem to be the colours favoured. 130 foot-soldiers, equipped as Europeans with musket and bayonet – all barefoot. How far civilization, and especially Christianity, has actually progressed with the natives of Hawaii I could not in my short stay determine; yet my scanty observations revealed many baptized persons who were not true Christians. The missionaries have much to lament. The king, much fonder of the wine-flask than he is of Christianity, is not yet baptized; on the other hand, the Princess L. Elis. Kaluaikakuli seems to be a very Christian person; she lives the whole time with the missionary family of the Clarkes. English is the language of the Court. The dusky inhabitants of the city use both languages, Hawaiian and English; the country folk do not speak English. The city of Honolulu, with its fine harbour, grows daily; pre-fabricated houses of iron and wood are brought from England and America, and are quickly set up and readied for occupation. The English ship *Swift* has been here for three weeks, and in that time fourteen new houses have sprung up. There is anchorage for two hundred ships

[1]There can hardly have been at Honolulu any officer competent to convene a naval court. We may suppose that the officers of the *Swift* at an informal meeting persuaded McClure (with difficulty, it appears) to reinstate Haswell, and that in return the captain required some sort of an apology for past disorders.

in the harbour. Here dwell many Americans, so today the American Independence Day is being celebrated. Also the missionaries have prepared a banquet at the Seminary about an hour's journey from the city, to which I was invited. About 12 noon I received a letter from the captain in which I was ordered to rejoin the ship by 4 p.m.; circumstances compelled him to get under sail today. I was somewhat perturbed by this, to me, very unwelcome command; I was compelled – for I had completed only a few unimportant letters – now to write one letter only, and that in great haste, to the brothers in London and U. A. L. The invitation to have lunch with a gathering of the missionaries of Owahu and their families I neither could nor would decline, for I enjoyed sweet hours of refreshment with these dear people, and, besides, I would have another opportunity of sending letters to Europe when we arrived at Bering Strait. At 1 o'clock I found myself in this great family circle of missionaries, which consisted of about thirty-five persons. Spirituous liquors were here strictly forbidden: only a variety of lemonades were enjoyed. After the banquet there was a parting love-feast with hymns and prayers; in particular, the Reverend Mr. Rice delivered an especially loving prayer in which not only I but our entire company were with all love and reverence committed to the gracious care and protection of our Saviour. Oh, how comforting and cheering are such hours!! Oh, how cheered I was! Children brought me flowers and books as remembrances. I had sent the princess an English hymn-book, and before I departed we sang the verses of "Die wir und allhier zusammen finden" with tears running down our cheeks. The parting was truly painful for me, especially with the immediate future and the sort of men with whom I was to spend perhaps several years before my eyes. Accompanied with heart-felt blessings I took my leave of brothers and sisters who had grown so dear to me. Messrs.

Damon and Clarke went with me to the beach where a boat awaited me, and gave me some watermelons for the journey.

When Jesus calls, we ready stand;
Our future life is in His hand;
Though separated for a time,
We yet continue one in Him;
And therefore, while we part need not complain,
As if we were never to meet again —

were the last words which these loving brothers called to me as I was getting into the boat. Before I reached the ship I sighed:

Lord, let Thy Presence with us go,
Throughout our journey us direct;
Thy angels guard us and protect,
Yea, prosper Thou whate'er we do.
— Hear my prayers;
— See my tears.

I am incapable of expressing my emotions on paper; forget them I never will. As soon as I was on board I went and reported to the captain; he invited me to a glass of wine and showed a composure which was forced. The crew were all busily engaged in making the ship ready for sea, and, as generally happens when a ship is getting under sail, so was it also here: the men were half out of their wits; noise, singing, whistling, and profanity gave me an unpleasant reminder of what lay before me. Everyone was now aboard, including a number of men whom the sergeant and his marines had escorted from the city jail, and whose release the captain had procured by paying their fines. At muster and roll-call it was discovered that three sailors had got away with their belongings. Five invalids had been trans-ferred to the *Swift*, and nine new sailors added to our company. The few letters which I had written for Europe I now sealed and consigned to the English consul. At 5 p.m. we were clear of the harbour and in the open sea, and, as we had a very good wind and sailed fast, the city of Honolulu soon sank from sight. The captain's presence was required on deck, so I went to his cabin and sang to my guitar:

> Give me Thy strength, oh God of power,
> Then let winds blow or thunders roar;
> I need not fear by sea or land,
> For Thou, my God, wilt by me stand.

5 *July (lat. 22° 8'; long. 158° 46'; temp. 77°)*

Fine weather and fair wind. The island of Atoi passed. Today the captain explained to me all the very disagreeable circumstances which had compelled him to put to sea after only four days' stay in the port of Honolulu.[1] He told me also that he was not following the *Enterprise* from here to Petretanlovsky [Petropavlovsk?] in Kamchatka, but on the advice of certain merchant seamen was sailing direct for Bering Strait. Our ship has been equipped with new *zweifachen* [upper and lower?] masts and other rigging; also supplied with thirty tons (at twenty-one hundredweight) of coal, and food supplies (only a part of what we would have liked to obtain), a dozen live sheep and one bullock, and a hundred melons. The antagonism between the captain and his officers has been changed in a few days into a very agreeable and friendly relationship. Ah, could it only remain thus! The captain joined us at the table; it was very pleasant. The Reverend Mr. Damon has

[1]His fear that if he did not reach Bering Strait as soon as Collinson the latter would take the *Plover* with him into the ice and leave to the *Investigator* the relatively inglorious post of a lookout ship in Kotzebue Sound (Noel Wright, *Quest for Franklin*, p. 189). Hence his decision to attempt a passage through the uncharted and fog-bound Aleutians.

supplied our sailors generously with books and tracts through my servant, Corporal Farquharson. Ah! may these be a great blessing to us.

12 July (lat. 35° 4'; long. 164° 4'; temp. 74°)
Every day favourable wind; the weather very fine; we are steering as directly as possible for Bering Strait. The crew are in good humour; a number of them are on the sick list, because they could not refrain from frightful excesses in Honolulu. Daily we note that we are approaching the cold North; for the tropical heat is leaving us. It does not seem right to the captain that the men should read tracts, so he ordered the ship's fiddler to play a tune and the men to dance. A seaman, Boyle, a gifted singer and dancer, received from the captain a large glass of wine as a reward for his skill.

19 July
For several days raw, cold weather and fog; wind favourable; five sailors still under the doctor's care and regretting the frightful diseases which they contracted in Honolulu. I often have interesting discussions with the captain about the missionaries to the heathen and civilization itself: we hold very different views on these matters. Today we had a long discussion on the words, "it is easier for a camel to pass through the eye of a needle, etc." I still lack faith in my English, so I advised the captain to refer his mistaken views to his own writings and books; for he has a fine library, and in it some rare and precious works on Christianity. With the officers I associate much more agreeably than formerly. In the last few days we have seen countless varieties of sea-fowl.

20 July (lat. 51° 26'; long. 172° 30'; temp. 46°)
Close to the Aleutians. Wind and weather good. In the

afternoon Amlio, Sequam, and Tschunan passed; Amlio and Tschunan are inhabited. In the evening strong breeze from the west. We dined with the captain, and it went off pleasantly.

21 July (lat. 53° 44'; long. 172° 29'; temp. 46°)
Weather very foggy; strong south-west wind. In the afternoon in 137 fathoms depth. Countless sea-fowl around the ship; every one known to me from Labrador. In the evening steering for Unalaska where the captain wishes to buy fresh meat from the Russian traders.[1]

24 July (lat. 58° 42'; long. 173° 12'; temp. 45°)
For two days we have been experiencing very changeable weather; at times the wind very strong; the weather so foggy that one can scarcely see a ship's length ahead. Gore's Island passed in soundings of 25 fathoms. Violent tides in this still very poorly known archipelago, full of shoals and reefs, cause the captain and officers much uneasiness.

26 July (lat. 63° 11'; long. 168° 3'; temp. 45°)
Wind most favourable, but the weather is and remains very foggy and dim; nipping, damp cold. We passed St. Lawrence Island, small, but lofty, and overgrown with grass. The seamen are in excellent humour, but the captain is far from happy in these wholly uncharted seas; for a week neither sun, moon, nor stars visible, and the ship has been driven now backwards, now sideways by the current, so that one does not know where we actually are. The land is hidden in fog, and the charts of these seas are most untrustworthy.

[1]He must have altered his purpose, owing to the dangers of navigation.

***27 July** (lat. 65° 30'; long. 168° 30'; temp. 43°)*

An island, presumably King's, passed; fog thick; swell very strong and high; the captain, the officers, and a double watch remained on deck all night through; during the night passed Prince of Wales Cape without knowing it. 8 a.m. the islands of Baranof (Nunawuk) and Krusenstern (Ignaluk) passed to the east; these islands proved that we were almost through Bering Strait. For three days, day and night, every fifteen minutes the lead has been heaved; the depth varied from 7 to 12 fathoms. In the afternoon a depth of 16 fathoms; no land in sight.

***29 July** (lat. 68° 13'; long. 167° 10'; temp. 40°)*

Yesterday very disagreeable weather, but fair wind; today, after many days, again bright but cold weather. In the neighbourhood of Escholtz Bay in Kotzebue Sound guns were fired as a signal to the *Enterprise*, should she be anchored there. A dead whale seen. About midday two whaling-ships spoken to. 3 p.m., H.M.S. *Plover*, Captain Moore, met and spoken to. They know nothing of the *Enterprise*. Captain Moore has employed a young Eskimo woman to act as interpreter among the natives; she dwells in his cabin.

***30 July** (lat. 68° 57'; long. 168° 37'; temp. 44°)*

Weather fine and wind very light. We were very busy writing letters. The ship *Plover* is lying near us. This ship, a twelve-gun brig, was sent from England in 1848 to Kotzebue Sound with orders to lie at anchor here as a depot for the crews of Sir John Franklin, should they make their way from east to west through the frozen seas into Bering Strait. To this ship supplies are sent annually from the Sandwich Islands, and she lies here anchored in the ice for eleven months, and for one month cruises to the northwards from Bering Strait. A great number of friendly

Eskimos have gathered on the shore opposite the ship; unfortunately there is no one on the ship to use this grand opportunity of teaching them something of their creation and salvation; rather the men – and this includes high-ranking officers – behave themselves so shamelessly that here one will soon have an Anglo-Eskimo colony.

31 July (lat. 69° 9'; long. 166° 37'; temp. 45°)

The English warship *Herald*, Captain Kellett, which has been cruising for three years in the South Seas,[1] and is seeking here the ship *Plover*, met us today. We delivered to her our letters for Europe. They know nothing of the *Enterprise* and cannot believe that she has already arrived in these waters. Our captain was requested to wait here a few days for the *Enterprise*, but he excused himself on the grounds that Admiralty orders required him to be in the ice by the 1st of August.[2] The ship *Herald* drew close alongside, and her 230 men mounted the masts and yards and gave us three loud hurrahs.

1 August 1850 (lat. 70° 19'; long. 166° 55'; temp. 42°)

Weather fine and wind fair for a northern course. Yesterday evening as we parted from the *Herald* and set sail, Captain Kellett signalled again that we should wait at least twenty-four hours, but our captain, believing that he had grounds for asserting that the *Enterprise,* a faster-sailing ship than ours, had already passed this way unob-

[1]To chart the Lower California coast. When the Franklin search began he was ordered north every summer to supply the *Plover* and to cruise beyond Bering Strait. The previous summer in discharge of this duty he discovered Herald Island in the Arctic.

[2]In his *Personal Narrative of the Discovery of the Northwest Passage*, Dr. Armstrong, the *Investigator's* surgeon, insinuates that McClure practised deliberate deception on this occasion.

served, answered through signals or flags: "Cannot wait."[1] In the fine weather a watch was kept from the crow's-nest all day, but no ship was descried. We were an entire day in the vicinity of Cape Lisburne and Jie [Icy?] Cape, and from there set a course N.N.W. We counted forty-five whales, many walrus and seals on today's cruise. Here, where one sees no land, the depth is only 25 fathoms. The sun shines day and night through the entire twenty-four hours.

2 *August (lat. 72° 1'; long. 166° 12'; temp. 40°)*

Wind strong and fair; weather bright and cold. At 9 a.m. resounded the cry from the crow's-nest, "Ice", and in two hours we were ringed around with huge masses of ice, but sailed ever deeper therein, and the ship suffered many severe shocks. At 2 p.m. we were fixed and motionless. As far as sight extends from the crow's-nest the ice appears a solid, unbroken mass; with much toil and labour the ship was got about, and by night made her way into open water; we began now, instead of north, to steer east along the mainland shore. We saw several hundred – some, including the captain, asserted a thousand – walrus, young and old, lying on the ice; if the ship came near them at a

---

[1]Not expecting the *Investigator* to arrive first at Cape Lisburne, Collinson had not instructed her what to do in that event; and McClure's action was not without excuse. (See L. H. Neatby, *In Quest of the North-west Passage*, pp. 145-7). Yet the manner of his getaway is somewhat damaging to his "image". If he gave his superior officer, Captain Kellett, the assurance which Armstrong, and apparently Miertsching, believe that he did, he was not sincere, for it was doubly improbable that Collinson was already in the Arctic, since had he altered his purpose and come straight through the Aleutians he would hardly have failed to leave dispatches with the *Plover*. Still it was possible that he had done so, and Kellett preferred not to use his rank where he had no express commission to give an order.

A commander does not address a post-captain officially in the terms stated by Miertsching. McClure's signal read: "Important duty. Cannot upon my own responsibility."

given signal all dived and made a great commotion in the water; but they soon returned to the ice again.

3 *August (lat. 71° 55'; long. 166° 5'; temp. 39°)*

Wind and weather good. Sailed by ice all day. It consists of level floes six to eight feet above the water, and if, as informed persons declare, seven parts are in the water and one part above it, it follows that the ice hereabouts is fifty to sixty feet thick. Icebergs, such as one sees in Davis Strait and Baffin Bay, do not occur here. We tried to sail into the ice, but were soon again forced to turn back. There are no whales to be seen, but an abundance of walrus and seal. Today we put away our summer clothing, and put on something better suited to this climate. Time and again the question intrudes: How long will we have to cope with these frightful ice-masses in order to make our way through to Greenland? The novices, who have never before seen polar ice, had not imagined that the ice would resemble what, to their great astonishment, they find it to be. One hears them saying: "Had I known that the ice was so hard and strong, I would have been only too glad to stay at home."

> Lord, speed our vessel in its course:
> Let wind and waves propitious be;
> Let Thy divine protection shield
> All whom we now commend to Thee.

4 *August (lat. 71° 21'; long. 164° 53'; temp. 38°)*

No favourable wind; the ice forced us to sail back towards Cape Lisburne; from there along the coast in an easterly direction; Wainwright Inlet passed. Many familiar types of sea-fowl seen, especially many eiders. The coast is sandy, hilly, and green. In the evening close to heavy ice.

5 August (lat. 70° 28'; long. 160° 10'; temp. 41°)

During the bright, sunlit night sailed on through drift-ice, and took some hard knocks; in the morning fog and rain, but a very favourable land wind, which holds the ice off shore, so that the ship can make progress near to the land. 9 a.m. a ship was seen, which signalled its name: it was the *Plover*; we signalled our name and continued along shore without altering course. Towards evening we came upon very heavy drift-ice. Soundings 5-13 fathoms.

6 August (lat. 71° 35'; long. 155° 12'; temp. 41°)

The weather very dull and foggy; strong tide from west to east. The ship is beset in the ice and can move neither forwards nor backwards; no land is in sight; where we actually are is unknown even to the captain and the officers. Depth 5-7 fathoms. Spirits were not of the best; yet through the grace of God could I sing:

> My All in all, my faithful Friend,
> Upon Whose mercy I depend;
> Than aught in earth or heaven more dear;
> My Paschal Lamb from year to year;
> My Shield, my Rock, my Polar Star, my Guide,
> Thou art my God, and ever shalt abide.

7 August (lat. 71° 5'; long. 154° 43'; temp. 37°)

In the morning it was bright and clear; all the fog had vanished; we found ourselves close to land, and had, without anyone knowing it, rounded Point Barrow, and find ourselves now to the east of that cape to which no ship before us has forced its way. Frightful ice is all around us. Five boats, and in each eight men, have towed the ship through the ice all day; very exhausting work; hence this evening the fiddle is given a rest.

8 August (lat. 70° 54'; long. 154° 43'; temp. 37°)

Yesterday I had another long talk on Christianity with the captain: he asserted that on a ship at sea no one could hold that form of Christianity which is observed on land: at sea a man must have spirit and not hang his head; I told him that I would gladly call myself and really *be* a Christian, and yet I held my head every whit as high as he, and among other things quoted St. Paul: "Freut euch", etc., along with other texts. He could only reply that "I was not yet a true seaman, or I would have other views; Mr. Marx, who had formerly been a lieutenant on a number of warships, had adopted my sort of land-Christianity, and had learned by experience that it did not serve on board ship; so he gave up the sea, and became a parson and writes tracts for old wives; I should have given the leaflets which I had distributed among the seamen to lost women, who would have given me more thanks than his sailors." The captain broke off the discussion and asked me to sing something; he himself handed me my guitar – I opened my hymn-book and sang the hymn, "How great a bliss to be a sheep of Jesus, and to be guided by His shepherd staff", etc.; he listened with pleasure to three verses, and then thanked me and wished me good night.

At 3 o'clock this morning I was awakened to go ashore, because from the crow's-nest people could be seen on land. Six seamen, Mr. Court, and I came to the beach where three Eskimo men stood and waited unarmed until we came to them; I believed myself transported to Labrador when I saw these people: the same stature, features, hair; even the same clothes, and boots of sealskin, and of the same style; their speech was also the same, but of a slightly different dialect, so that I could understand them well, as they did me. They led us to a small hillock from where we could see their tents, a half-hour's walk away, and urged us to go with them and see their families, which we did not deem at all necessary. When they saw that we would not go to their tents they ran off at full speed without listening to us or accepting any gifts. We set up a small cairn, and ten feet east from it buried a small bottle containing notice of our search; and then returned to the boat. The land, a vast plain as far as the eye could reach, was covered with grass and little flowers, but all hard-frozen. We had scarcely got back to the ship when there came a boat made of hides (women's boat, *umiak*, *baidar*), with fifteen men and women, to the ship from the other side of the bay. They clambered on board and seemed to be quite at home on the ship, and soon began to sing and to dance. I could understand these people also very well. It appeared that they called themselves *koegarmints*, traded with "foreigners" (Russian traders) in the country by the "great river" (Yukatan, also called Yukon); already two ships had come to them from the west; presumably the *Plover*. No ship had ever been where our ship now was. These Eskimos, living at Point Drew, are a poverty-stricken folk, filthy and ragged to the skin. The women tattoo their faces as do the heathen in Labrador; their dress is also the same. The men wear two large glass beads or round stones on the lower lip towards the side of the mouth. Their dress is the same as in Labrador, but they wear their hair cut short or singed on the crown of the head. They know what fire-arms are, though they themselves have none; their weapons are big iron knives, spears, bows, and arrows. These people told us that the land (coast) was inhabited by men (Eskimos) from Nutka to the river (Kouamut) Yukatan or Colville. The captain distributed a few gifts among them, whereupon they took their leave. In the afternoon came four boats, full of Eskimos, to the ship, bringing for sale fish which were paid for with tobacco: for one fish one plug of tobacco; but, as only small fish were offered, I divided a plug of tobacco and gave out small pieces; promptly the

Eskimos did the same, and carved a tiny fish into four parts. Our sailors bought bows and arrows; even the natives' clothes were up for sale. These Eskimos do not understand the use of money. Gifts were distributed to these people also, and they were instructed that if white men came from the ice to their land they should receive them with kindness and give them food, which the Eskimos, for their part, promised to do. Now they began to steal various small articles; this could only be stopped by a measure of force; and very soon they were conducted to their boats, and none permitted to return to the ship. The coast is very flat and covered with green turf: there is no rock or stone. The depth of the sea is from 4 to 7 fathoms two English miles from the shore; near the beach the water is barely deep enough for a ship's boat. The sea-bottom is white sand. The tide rises eighteen inches. In the evening the ship grounded on a sand-bank, and cost much toil and labour before she could be refloated.

9 *August (lat. 70° 55'; long. 152° 2'; temp. 36°)*
Strong headwinds and frequent showers of rain. Depth 3-6 fathoms seven miles from land at the mouth of the Colville River. The ship beats to windward all day: every fourth hour she tacks; on the left is heavy ice; and on the right shoal water. Today in the bitter wind no Eskimos came to the ship. We saw many of their tents on this coast. To-day the captain entertained the officers at lunch [*Weinfruehstueck*]. The painful misunderstanding which earlier had embittered the lives of everyone of them is no more; since we left the Sandwich Islands relations have been better; wholly good they can never be; for the captain has no confidence in his young officers. Lieutenant Haswell, who had been under arrest for some weeks, does his best to carry out exactly his captain's wishes. Towards me both the captain and my mess-mates, the officers, have been

43

most friendly and obliging from the beginning of the voyage until now; yet it has often been most disagreeable for me to stand between factions so harshly divided; now conditions are a good deal better; yet one can see the red-hot embers still glowing under the ashes. I keep very much to myself; the management of the ship is no concern of mine; so I often spend a sacred hour alone in my little cabin. I must acknowledge it as a dispensation of my gracious Saviour that Corporal Farquharson has been assigned to me as my servant; he is one of those who loves what is good, is faithful and painstaking in his duty, and seeks to influence his mess-mates with Christian behaviour, speech, and leaflets, and for so doing endures much mockery and antagonism. I have already spent many happy evening hours with him in my cabin.

11 *August (lat. 70° 36'; long. 150° 16'; temp. 35°)*

Today at 3 a.m. I was aroused to go ashore in a boat; the thick fog of yesterday had disappeared and the weather was clear; the headwind weak; the land was a low island of gravel, devoid of vegetation, but covered with driftwood, containing trees fifty-six feet long, and two and a half feet in diameter towards the root. Of men or of their dwellings no trace could be seen. Our task was to bury a bottle containing notice of our search, and to set up a cairn; we shot a good breakfast and lunch for ourselves and went back to the ship. 9 a.m. came two *umiaks* full of Eskimos bringing small fish and sea-fowl to barter with; for these they were paid well and received an assortment of gifts. In the time of Divine Service, which began at 10 a.m., an ample watch was posted on deck, but nonetheless the Eskimos contrived to convey some articles from the deck to their boats, and before either the thieves or the missing things could be identified, they and their *kayaks* had disappeared among the masses of floating ice. In the afternoon splendid weather; we sailed close to land, an island (John's Island), to the east of the mouth of Colville River. In the distance we saw many Eskimos, who had hoisted a flag on a pole. At 4 p.m. I accompanied the captain in a boat; a second (the cutter) bore the second lieutenant and the doctor, all armed, and with the English flag flying we landed on the island. Although the Eskimos, with knives drawn, spears and bows made ready, wished to hinder us, and although a few arrows flew past our heads, yet these people, who had never before seen white men (*kablunaks*), soon became so friendly and childishly delighted that the friendly gesture of rubbing noses was offered to each of us, often two or three times. These Eskimos had a very pleasing appearance; they were well clad and clean. Their headman (chief), a very fine and sympathetic old man named Attua, had three wives and thirteen children. These people knew nothing of Franklin's ships. To these simple folk our ship seemed some sort of great monster; they called it a swimming island, etc. At every movement of the ship, although it was half an hour's pull distant, they showed fresh alarm and an electric shock, as it were, went through them all. Their fine clean tents with their families stood on a sandy knoll at a little distance from the beach. During the winter, they told us, they live three days' journey inland; for three months only in the summer do they bring their families to live in tents on the seashore. Some of these families travel each summer to Nuniwokingak along the coast, where they meet and do business with the Eskimos who dwell farther to the east. Attua told me that not far from here dwell the Nunatarmints; but he knows them only by name. I conversed with these people a long time, and wished to tell them of God, the Creator of all things, including ourselves; and that it is His will that we should be good and not bad, etc., but to explain even one fact to these simple children of nature, and to make them grasp it, requires a longer period of time than our very brief visit afforded. They have no conception of a high and Divine Being, yet they have a notion of two contrasted beings, one good and one bad, living in different regions where they themselves go after death, many to one, others to the second place, depending on their conduct in this life. Whilst I was so employed the captain, officers, and doctor, who had been examining the features of the country, came and asked me to distribute the gifts which we had brought with us: these naturally caused much pleasure. The captain gave his friend Attua a boat's flag, and asked him to forward a letter to the Russian traders on the Colville River; which he promised to do. Unhappily among the Eskimos – as far as I know them – a promise is held very casually. At 7 p.m. we reached the ship where a good supper awaited us in the captain's cabin.

12 August (lat. 70° 37'; long. 149° 17'; temp. 37°)
Throughout the night we had a fresh sea wind and bright weather. At 8 a.m. four *umiaks*, full of Eskimos, approached us; but we had much difficulty in enticing them to the ship; they offered ducks, eiders, and white swans for trade. Also a few fine fox, wolverine, ermine, and other skins. These natives were very well dressed; now saw a ship for the first time; one of them had an English gun (musket) with the name Barnett on the lock, but he had neither lead nor powder, nor did he obtain any from us. Also these Eskimos seemed to be highly accomplished thieves; they stole wherever they could; even from our pockets knives, handkerchiefs, and telescopes were stolen. Mr. Ford, our carpenter, detected in the skin-boat a small ice-anchor and the iron crank belonging to the windlass; on the latter sat a woman in order to hide it. I scolded her and called her "thief"; she retorted that *she* was no thief – her husband, not she, had taken it into the boat. These

people were required to leave the ship at once without receiving any gifts.

In the morning the weather was fine; in the afternoon thick fog and a headwind. The tide brought the ice into three fathoms of water where it took the ground. In the evening fast beset with ice.

3 August (lat. 70° 29'; long. 149° 20'; temp. 34°)
Weather very foggy, wind contrary, and encircled with very heavy ice, against which the ship is constantly being dashed. At 10 a.m. we could go no farther, neither forwards nor backwards; we cast two anchors and lay still. Fresh water was discovered on the surface and the ship's casks were filled. We did some target shooting. The captain gave me a double-barrelled gun which I shall keep and use industriously until we arrive at Davis Strait. In the evening I locked myself in my cabin; I was homesick, and joined the Brotherhood in spirit.

4 August (temp. 34°)
Today the weather somewhat better, but the wind foul. At 7 a.m. we quitted our icy anchorage. Navigation among these weighty ice-masses is extremely difficult: we thought that the ship would be broken to pieces by the thunderous blows of the ice. At 3 p.m. we reached free-sailing water, 3-5 fathoms (at six feet) in depth. At 5 p.m. we discovered a hitherto unknown island; because of sandbars we had to go around it; a boat was sent to find a channel by sounding; the ship followed her – unhappily too closely – and at 6 p.m. she took the ground in two fathoms of water. An ice-anchor was laid out in order to draw the ship off with the capstan; but this, and all means, proved fruitless. The tide drove ice against the ship until she lay over on her broadside and so remained. Boats were laden with the weightiest pieces of cargo in order to lighten the ship;

unfortunately one boat with eleven barrels of salt beef was capsized by the ice and the meat lost.[1] At 11 p.m. the ship was again afloat.

15 August (lat. 70° 31'; long. 148° 4'; temp. 37°)
Calm and pleasant sunshine. At 8 a.m. anchored the ship in the ice near a sandy islet. Wherever one looks from the crow's-nest there is nothing but heavy ice; no open water. In the evening heavy rain. Cresswell, Court, Paine, Sainsbury, and Newton went to the island to set up a cairn, and came back to the ship at 7 p.m.

16 August (temp. 37°)
Today calm and rain. Two Sandwich Island invalids, on the sick list until today, are declared well. At 8 a.m. the ship was freed from the ice; five boats took her in tow through the masses of ice until 12 noon, when we came to fast (pack) ice where no further progress was possible. The ship was anchored near a little islet. Today we discovered a small archipelago of sandy islets barely fifteen feet high. Sailors went out to fish with a great net, but after ten hours came back without a single fish. I landed with the officers; we shot numerous eiders and sandpipers. Innumerable nests of eiders are here; and we gathered a great heap of eiderdown. Two huge whale bones lay in the middle of the island; traces also of the polar bear were found imprinted in the sand. Many pieces of driftwood were found and taken to the ship. Vegetation is scanty or non-existent on these islands; some moss occurs. No traces of human beings were discovered. In the evening at 10 o'clock again to the ship.

[1]According to Dr. Armstrong, a prejudiced but by no means contemptible witness, this loss — a most damaging one as it proved — was due to McClure's stubborn refusal to heed the advice of his officers.

17 August (lat. 70° 9'; long. 148° 3'; temp. 35°)

In the morning foggy and still. The rudder was hoisted up and repaired. At 12 noon came the north wind; we made sail and had an appalling time in the drifting ice-masses. At 6 p.m. we came into open water and sailed east.

18 August (lat. 70° 30'; long. 148° 5'; temp. 35°)

Snow was falling the whole day. On account of the difficult navigation in the ice and the violent shocks sustained, there was no open Divine Service. At 11 a.m. we passed an island, Flaxman, and saw plainly the low-lying shore of the mainland. Here it occurred to the captain to go into the ice and, as he said, sail straight to the Pole. The wind was strong and fair; the lanes between the ice-masses were so narrow that on both sides of the ship not only the copper plating in which she was sheathed, but also splinters of wood were torn from her sides and remained hanging from the ice-blocks. The wind drove us at seven to eight English miles an hour. The shocks sustained were frightful; many articles were smashed and heavy weights were thrown about by the shuddering blows.

19 August (lat. 71° 32'; long. 144° 50'; temp. 33°)

Last night was sleepless and full of anxiety; I was twice thrown from my bed by the thunderous shocks of the ice. Today snow, rain, and fog, so that one can barely see for two hundred paces. Strong west wind and appalling ice. The ice grows ever heavier and the water-lanes narrower. At 11 a.m. the ship was beset and jammed amidst immovable masses of ice. The ice-masses, floating closely packed one against another, rose twelve to fifteen feet above the surface of the sea; and many are so broad that one could plant a city thereon. After three hours' hard work the ship could again be sailed back by the way we had come, but in the next half-hour of sailing we were again fast beset; again two hours' hard work; and now there was no more hope of going to the north through the ice, for all perceived the impossibility; so the captain gave up the plan; the ship was put about, yet we could not go back, but lay there quite helpless. The temper of the crew was far from pleasant: to the captain no man dared to speak.

20 *August (lat. 69° 41'; long. 136° 15'; temp. 35°)*
Thick snowy weather and calm. From 3 to 8 a.m. the ship was freed from the thick-packed ice-blocks and towed back by five boats through the ice – the work of galley-slaves. At 4 a.m. we came finally into more open water, and as early this morning and even yesterday the sailors had worked very hard, and now had spent eight hours at the oars, they could do no more, so the ship was anchored. A number of things broken by the ice were now repaired, then the ship was cleaned and put in order, as is done daily, and the men were given a chance to rest. Certainly they did not dance: that evening a tranquil silence reigned on the ship.

21 *August (lat. 69° 37'; long. 136° 34'; temp. 34°)*
Strong north wind; passed Flaxman Island, and saw men and tents there.[1] In the evening we neared Pelly Island, which lies at the mouth of the Mackenzie River. We moored the ship to an ice-floe, which we measured; it was twelve English miles long by seven broad. My birthday today I could celebrate with fitting quietness. In the evening two most pleasant hours in my cabin with Mr. Piers and Farquharson.

22 *August (lat. 69° 34'; long. 136° 9'; temp. 39°)*
Cloud, rain, and snow all day; also headwinds; but little

[1]In the entry for August 18, Flaxman Island is placed twelve degrees to the west – where it properly belongs.

ice. We came here upon a small archipelago consisting of five islands: Pelly, Garry, Kendal, Richard, and Guerney. The captain wished to send letters and dispatches from here to Fort Good Hope, the Hudson's Bay post on the Mackenzie. He wished therefore to land on this island and seek Eskimos, but owing to the strong wind and shoaling water this was impossible. Here more casks were thrown overboard containing the report of our cruise up to this point; perhaps one of them may be driven by the strong nor'wester into the river, and news of us may reach the Europeans who dwell there. The water here is of a muddy colour, and not very salty – brackish. Neither seal nor wild-fowl were to be seen.

23 *August (lat. 69° 54'; long. 133° 23'; temp. 40°)*
Weather bright and not cold. Wind contrary and very strong. So far what we were told by the Eskimos of Point Barrow has been found to be true: namely that each summer open water occurs between land and the compact ice-fields; therefore the captain ventured to sail east, and we have found the statement true until now; here the channel is growing wider, and today, in the teeth of a strong head-wind, the ship is beating to windward in a channel seven English miles broad. The continental shore is very low and flat; so also is the ocean-shelf; two English miles from the land the sea is only 3 fathoms deep (18 feet). Every time we tacked towards the land we saw also Eskimos and tents; from which I concluded that the coast was thickly or at least well populated. What a wonderful field for a missionary!

24 *August (lat. 69° 43'; long. 131° 57'; temp. 37°)*
By continuous beating to windward we make a little head-way; in the last two days only fifty English miles. Today at 10 a.m. as we slanted in towards the shore we saw Eski-

mos as usual; but some of the sailors – who, one may note, have keen eyes – insisted that they could make out a man in European dress. Thereupon the captain determined to land in person. He wrote a letter in the hope that through these people (who were sure to be in communication with the inhabitants of the Mackenzie valley) it might be forwarded to the Europeans who dwell there. The colours were hoisted on our ship. At 12 noon we quitted the ship – the captain, Dr. Armstrong, and I, with six seamen in a boat – and pulled for the land; we saw only a few Eskimos, and these received us in no friendly manner as we disembarked; they faced us with spears, long knives, and drawn bows. Every attempt to approach the savages in friendly fashion was unsuccessful; but the captain was determined not to go back without questioning them; finally after several unavailing endeavours I managed to get within ten paces of these hostile folk, and spoke to them in a friendly tone; and finally they began to listen and ceased their horrible shrieking and howling. They bade us go away and pointed to the ship which was just then in motion. I picked up a few arrows, bore them in my hand (I was without weapons) and, approaching, gave them back; again they grew very excited, so that I thought it best to draw from my pocket a pistol loaded with blank shot and fire it in the air; this device helped; they grew somewhat quieter and began to listen to me, trembling the while all over and with a white foam on their lips; and finally they were persuaded to lay down their weapons; and the captain and the rest came forward, also without weapons, and at last we were good friends. They invited us to their fine new-built wooden homes, and gave us fowl, fish, and reindeer skins in exchange for knives, saws, etc. Their friendship was even warmer than that, already recorded, of Attua. Old Kairoluak (chief in this region) especially enjoyed himself. This man had a fine house and two tents;

everywhere was order and cleanliness, such as I had never seen among Eskimos; great heaps of reindeer, bear, fox, and wolverine skins, were ready for bargaining purposes. These people have never seen Europeans before and have no traffic with the Hudson's Bay traders on the Mackenzie River, but dispose of their wares westwards where they do business with Attua. Old Kairoluak's son had recently had the misfortune to break the bone of his leg a little above the ankle, and now lay helpless and in great pain. The doctor examined him, but our stay was too short for anything to be done; and probably in a few weeks this fine young Eskimo would no longer be alive. If the Eskimos see no prospect of the speedy cure or improvement of an invalid they quickly give up hope altogether, and when the family moves to another region they leave the sick one in a lonely place where no Eskimo dogs come, set a little food by him, and thenceforth think of him no more. On a little sandhill we saw a peculiar wooden monument, and asked what it was. The people told us that strangers (*tujormints* or *kai-maraijets*) had come to this place without a boat, and had built a house of driftwood on the cape, and lived there; in time all fowl, seal, and reindeer had disappeared, and they must have been starving; then all but one of these strangers disappeared and the last – when the Eskimos came seeking the game which had vanished – was found dead on the ground, and Kairoluak had buried him there. I could not ascertain the date of this occurrence. Probably it is an old legend derived from some fight with the Indians.[1] I would gladly have talked longer with the Eskimos about this story and about more important matters, and to tell them something of a God, their Creator and Preserver, but suddenly the captain shouted, "The ship is aground!" and bade

[1] This meeting took place at the Tuktoyaktuk where Vilhjalmur Stefansson spent part of the winter of 1906-7.

us hurry to the boat. We had scarcely reached the ship — which was *not* aground — when a fog descended so thick that one could not see twenty paces. Deeming it his duty, the captain determined to visit the cape pointed out by the Eskimos, where the *tujormints* had built a house, in order perhaps through relics to learn more of the tragic story, but the thick fog prevented him from doing this today. It always grieves me and especially on this occasion to leave these poor people to lead their lives in heathenish ignorance without being able to impart to them something of an abiding faith. The Eskimos put to shame so many Christians in this that they go on long journeys to dispose of their wares, in order not to receive worthless stuff in exchange, but articles that are good and useful to them.

25 *August (lat. 69° 56'; long. 131° 48'; temp. 34°)*

This morning we found ourselves off Point Warren, and at 3 a.m. the captain, Dr. Armstrong, and I landed on the point indicated by the Eskimos where the strangers supposedly had dwelt. This is distant from the Eskimo village about ten English miles. We found the ruins of two Eskimo winter-houses built of driftwood, the fragments of old stone blubber-lamps, and other small articles, but all very old and moss-grown. We found not the least evidence to suggest that Europeans had lived here. Also the houses had been built in Eskimo style. Near by lay the wreck of a *kayak*, and everything suggested Eskimo techniques. We shot a number of eiders, and I reaped a harvest of plants and flowers, especially a fine blooming lupine; at 8 o'clock we got back to the ship. The regular Divine Service was held at 10. The weather was dull, damp, and cold. We sailed along the coast eastwards. I thought much of the Eskimos everywhere hereabouts dwelling so near me, and felt very homesick.

28 August (lat. 70° 27'; long. 128° 49'; temp. 34°)
For the last three days dull weather with snow, rain, and light contrary winds. The captain is often very impatient. The channel here is again very narrow: on the one side great impenetrable ice-masses, on the other very shallow water, although the shore is two English miles distant. It is a time when life at sea again becomes very disagreeable and repulsive. Everywhere I see Eskimo huts on shore, but cannot visit them.

29 August (lat. 70° 17'; long. 129° 46'; temp. 32°)
Bright weather and very favourable wind: we sailed rapidly forward; in the afternoon drew close to shore, saw traces of Eskimos, but no tents or houses; the ship took the ground solidly, and I was granted permission to go ashore. Messrs. Piers and Paine accompanied me; we rowed ourselves and remained on shore several hours until recalled by signal to the ship. By myself I enjoyed an undisturbed *Bruderfest*, sought plants and blooms, sang hymns, and was in spirit sharing in a love-feast of the Brotherhood. We found here many recently abandoned tenting-grounds and a number of caches with much winter provision, but Eskimos we saw none. The land, an interminable flat expanse, was covered with green sod and moss. We saw no rock anywhere. The caches are earthen pits, square and lined with driftwood; the provisions, consisting of reindeer, seal, and bear's flesh and blubber, were packed in wood covered with moss and then buried in a heap of sand; others, in which only feathered creatures, such as sea-fowl, are preserved, are similar, but somewhat smaller. We shot a number of birds, fine specimens for stuffing, and made a great fire on the beach where we roasted sandpipers, which tasted very good. Driftwood was in abundance here. We had a most pleasant afternoon and then made tea for ourselves and had a pleasant evening.

30 August (Cape Bathurst, temp. 29°)

We were under sail all night; the wind, though weak, was fair. In the morning a dead calm, and as the water was very shallow, only two feet under our keel, we cast anchor. The weather was bright and clear, and we saw two men on shore with a few dogs. This was an opportunity for the captain to send a letter to a Hudson's Bay station and thus forward news of us to England. We manned two boats and, taking an assortment of gifts for the Eskimos, set out for the land. There we met only two Eskimo women, Kunatsiak and Renalik, who told us that all the men were at Nuvoksua hunting whales. They said that they were not far off, and offered to guide us, an offer which the captain accepted. He ordered the boat to follow us along the shore, and we went with the two women by land along the beach. On the way they told us that recently Europeans had been there with three boats and remained in their land for two days;[1] they showed us various trifles which they had received as gifts; they placed a special value on finger-rings and glass beads as mementoes. After an hour we arrived at two Eskimo houses, the homes of these two women, and in answer to the question as to how far we must yet go to meet their men who were whale-fishing they said, "twice as far as we had already gone". As it was already late in the afternoon the captain decided to return to the ship and visit the Eskimos in the following morning. The women were given useful gifts, and gave us fish in exchange for a copper kettle. The captain bought a bear skin also. In the water were two nets made of *pergak* [woven reindeer sinew]. We went to the ship.

31 August (Cape Bathurst, temp. 29°)

All night we lay at anchor, and today, although the

[1] Richardson and Rae on the first amphibian Franklin searching expedition.

56

weather is fine and the wind fair, the ship remained at anchor, because the captain wished to visit the Eskimos.[1] After breakfast the captain, Armstrong, and I, with eight seamen, a day's rations for ourselves, and gifts for the Eskimos, took boat for the place where yesterday we had left the two women at their homes, in order to sail on from there to the camp of the Eskimos. The land, yesterday without snow and covered with plants and flowers, had become white overnight; the new-fallen snow lay seven inches thick. We pulled along a shore devoid of rock and stone, a mixture of clay, sand, and ice, making directly for a headland which the women had pointed out to us as the resting-place of their men. We touched bottom several times, for though we were a half-hour's pull from the land yet the water was only eighteen inches deep. We had put ten English miles behind us before we reached the cape, and yet no trace of Eskimos was to be seen. Five miles farther on we came to another cape or headland, and still no sign of Eskimos. The captain grew impatient, but let himself be persuaded to sail a little farther around an angle of the shore. We found ourselves in a deep inlet, with land on both sides of us; depth of water 12 to 30 inches, which was proof positive that neither whale nor seal would come here, and consequently no Eskimo either. I sought everywhere with my telescope in the hope of making out some hut, tent, or Eskimo, but found my efforts wasted. The water was so shallow that the sailors were compelled to get out of the boat and drag her around in order to launch her on her homeward course. Through my glass I noticed on the flat cape near by a few humps, veiled in a light mist, which, as neither stone nor rock was in sight, I took for a herd of reindeer. The captain and doctor called them ant-hills, because they did not move. In the twinkling of an eye the

[1]McClure's conduct here seems to disprove the criticism that he cared nothing for Franklin, but thought only of discovering the Passage.

mist disappeared, and to our joy we counted thirty tents and nine winter huts; thereupon we quickly perceived farther down the beach thirteen *umiaks* or skin-boats and a multitude of *kayaks*. Across a low, narrow sandspit – isthmus – we could see the sea and were now assured that we had arrived at Cape Bathurst. We had barely got out of the boat when a swarm of Eskimos came pouring down towards us with long spears, knives, harpoons, and bows ready drawn; they let fly several arrows and set up a hideous outcry. The women were following behind them with more weapons. In his desire to avoid unpleasantness the captain kept on asking, "What is to be done? What is to be done?" I handed the captain my gun, securely fastened my Eskimo frock, and ran as fast as I could towards them; which caused in their ranks a – to me – most disagreeable disturbance. I drew my pistol from my pocket, discharged it in the air before their eyes, and shouted to them to throw down their weapons. But they only shouted all the louder: "Shuitok, shuitok, Kalauroktuta." I took my stand before them with my pistol in my hand, unloaded – but the Eskimos did not know that, being unaware that one must load a fire-arm before discharging it – and told them that we were friends, brought gifts, and intended to do them no harm whatever; whereupon they became more quiet and peaceful; the captain came forward to join me, and finally, after much debate and giving of pledges, they laid down their weapons, but left their knives within easy reach on the ground. I marked a line on the snow between them and us which no one was to cross, and this also impressed them. They became more friendly, and finally all fear vanished, and they brought wives, children, and sucklings, and laid their little ones in our arms that we might observe them more closely. These Eskimos exchange wares with the Locheaux or Hare Indians, who dwell inland, also in a state of heathendom; whose speech the Eskimos understand, and

58

who carry their goods to Fort Good Hope on the Mackenzie River. After the captain had ended his business – which consisted of asking the Eskimos questions – and was convinced that these people knew nothing of Sir John Franklin and his unlucky crews, he handed to the Eskimo Kenalualik the letter directed to the Hudson's Bay station, along with many gifts for himself; the man promised to do his best to attend to it. While the captain was studying the features of the country I took advantage of my freedom and entertained myself with these poor, wild, simple folk; they listened gladly to me, and asked many questions, helping me with signs when their words and expressions were unknown to me. These people also know nothing of a Divine Being on high, and have apparently never thought that the sun, moon, rocks, and water were created by anyone, and were much astonished when I told them of a great, good Spirit, Who can do whatsoever He wills, and to Whom nothing is impossible – that He dwells above the sun, moon, and stars and watches all that we do, that this Spirit has created everything, including the first men, etc., at which they stared at me in amazement, and frequently cried out in wonder. They accepted all that I told them, but in connection with the stars old Kenalualik thus informed me: Above us is a great blue chest, the Sun's house; in daytime and through the long arctic summer the sun is not in his house, but when he goes there it becomes dark, but there are clean-cut little holes through which he can view the water and the land, and these are the stars. These Eskimos also have their own peculiar conception of the life after death. It is that there are two lands, one good, and one not good. In the good land dwells a good spirit who looks after the wild animals, that they do not disappear from the land. In the bad land dwells also a spirit who is bad and always does men harm. When an Eskimo dies, if he has in life clothed the widows and orphans and given them food, he comes into the good land where the sun shines always and where there is never rain, ice, or strong winds, but always warm weather and countless seal, reindeer, etc., and these are not wild or shy; one can catch them with one's hands. He, on the contrary, who has not had a good character in his life, comes to the bad land which is the complete opposite of the good land. While I was carrying on this, to me, most interesting conversation with these Eskimos whom I was beginning to love, the captain came and summoned me to the boat. I rose and was about to go, but my grey-headed friend, Kenalualik, held me back; he said that I should wait and tell them more, and should live with them. I replied that I could not do this, but must go with the ship to seek our friends who were lost in the ice; at which he offered me a sledge and dogs, with which I could go to the ship over the ice when the next moon disappeared and the sea was frozen; but till then I should remain with him; to which I replied that the ship might go far, and I would be unable to find it; at which he repeated his former offers, and added thereto a tent, so that I was to have sledge, dogs, and tent. I told him firmly that my *angajuga* (commander, captain) was telling me to come and that I must follow and obey. But he began once more to repeat his promises and set before me his daughter with the words "takka unna" ("take her"). In the meantime the captain came to fetch me, and he took us both by the arm and conducted us to the boat where we distributed gifts and re-embarked. To my old friend Kenalualik and his daughter – a girl of very lovely appearance, some sixteen years old – I gave double gifts, and to the latter many needles, because these are of especial value. An Eskimo woman was caught making off with our boat compass. I also missed my pocket-handkerchief, but recovered it from an Eskimo who bore a genuinely thievish appearance. To escape from the throng which was pressing upon us we took to the boat and left

60

these poor folk lining the beach and wishing us a thousand *aksusijy* (farewells). Fifteen *kayaks* and Eskimos in their *umiaks* accompanied us to the ship where the sailors delighted them with many gifts – many were dressed from head to foot in European garb. As it was beginning to grow foggy they returned joyously to their families in their new clothes. The dialect of these people is somewhat different from that of other Eskimos along this coast; they understood me very well; but to me, especially at the first, it was difficult to understand them – they were almost unintelligible. A number of them have brown hair and blue eyes;[1] their clothes, made skilfully out of the best skins, set off well the figures of these small but well-proportioned people. They call Cape Bathurst Nuvoak, the first or nearest island Akkunek, the next Tuppelisoak; the water between the cape and the first island they name *koruk*. The dogs of these people are of the same breed as in Labrador.

1 September 1850 (lat. 70° 36′; long. 128° 48′; temp. 30°)

Fine weather, light wind; we saw today many whales, seals, and very many water-fowl. Yesterday evening at 9 o'clock we set sail and in the night rounded the two islands, Akkunek and Tuppelisoak, and drew near to Cape Bathurst on its other side. In the morning we entered heavy ice and got the ship through only after much toil and labour, and Divine Service for today was cancelled. Towards midday we came into open water where sail could be used again, but soon lost the wind, and after two hours of calm came a fresh headwind. Fifteen Eskimos in *kayaks* and two boats full of men and women came to the ship and looked all over the upper deck; no one was permitted below. Some of them had made our acquaintance the day before, and were as

[1]Stefansson's "blond Eskimos". The type had previously been noted by Sir John Franklin in 1821.

familiar and void of fear as if they saw us in their homes and not on shipboard; they were especially friendly to me, brought me various little gifts, and followed me even into my cabin. The captain took an Eskimo into his cabin and offered him a glass of wine, which he tasted, but would not drink. We tested them with every drink on board; but nothing would these people taste except water, which they drank in great quantities. With food it was the same: they rejected everything except fat pork. An Eskimo told me that the day before yesterday strange Europeans in two boats had been here, and set up tent on land, and had shot a polar bear on the ice near by; they gave an exact description of the boats with their masts, of the men in their various clothing, of their stature, and told me that the captain of the boats, a stout man, would pace up and down the beach; each time he walked twenty paces and then turned about. The captain gave this man a gift in return for this information, which he found much to his liking; but now, instead of the day before yesterday, he placed the incident two years ago, referring to Dr. Richardson, who led a boat expedition from the Mackenzie to the Coppermine River. A woman, who carried her little child in her hood, said that she also had seen Europeans, but that was three summers ago: these had boats of wood and skin with masts, and had given the Eskimos knives, needles, beads, etc.; for confirmation she called upon another Eskimo woman, who also was carrying a little child on her back; she confirmed the story, and while so doing drew her child out of the hood and displayed it – a child of charming appearance with curly hair. It was the captain's opinion that these women were dreaming up stories to obtain a reward. We had other proofs that we were entertaining impostors: a poorly clad Eskimo came in his *kayak*, mounted to the deck, and stood there, shivering all over; a sailor took him below and clothed him in woollen undergarments with his own fur clothing over them; soon the same man was standing aft in his own ragged clothes and trembling with cold in every limb. The captain, coming on deck just then, took pity on this poor wretch, led him to his cabin, and told his steward to provide him with good warm underclothing, at which the man rejoiced greatly. Later the same man was observed in his old get-up and replaying the same act; the underclothing given him was found in his *kayak*: he had taken it off and hidden it. A woman told me that recently she had been collecting mussels and (edible) sea-grass along the shore; her only child was playing with pebbles a short distance away; she heard him scream and ran to him and – what horror! – a polar bear was dragging the child off in his jaws, gripping it pitilessly with his fangs; he swam off to a piece of ice, and the poor bereaved mother saw how the savage beast tore and devoured her beloved and only child. She wept bitterly as she told this story. I told her that a Great Spirit dwells above the stars, that He sees all that we do, and created the first men; and from His lofty dwelling-place watches what every man does, and knows all our thoughts, etc. I told her how she should live, what she should do and not do, and comforted her with the assurance that if she followed these words she would see her child again and dwell with him in a heavenly land where there is no sorrow or weeping, etc. Why has the Lord banished these folk here where no missionary can reach them? This is the question which so often forces itself upon me. All on the ship had now received handsome gifts, and as on account of shoal water we were going into the ice, our friends left us and went home rejoicing.

3 September (lat. 70° 18'; long. 126° 19'; temp. 35°)
Yesterday and today tacking through the ice; contrary winds and tide make us work very hard. Whales, seal, and water-fowl are here in abundance. We had target-shooting; the seamen and marines fired from the stern forward at a

target, and the officers at empty bottles hung in the air. Two polar bears were chased, but neither was killed; both got away. Through the telescope we see many Eskimos. Tents on shore. To the east of Cape Bathurst the coast begins to grow higher.

4 September (lat. 70° 6'; long. 126° 35'; temp. 39°)
Fine weather, no ice, but wind and tide against us. Cape Bathurst is behind us; we are sailing close to the land into Franklin's Bay; towards evening we saw great thick smoke rising on land, and supposed that it was caused by natives. As it grew dark the captain ordered rockets discharged, but no light or fire was seen from the place where the smoke had appeared in daylight.

5 September (lat. 69° 51'; long. 126° 18'; temp. 40°)
Weather fine and warm, wind contrary, little ice. In the night we had passed Horton River. As soon as it was day we perceived thick smoke rising in the same place as yesterday, but because of the contrary wind could not approach it in the ship; it was six to eight English miles away. In the afternoon the ice-master, Newton, reported that from the masthead he had seen by telescope tents[1] and men in white jackets on this and that side of the smoke. The captain asked me what I thought of it; I replied that I did not suppose that any Eskimo would be found where cliffs rising vertically afforded no space for tents, nor was there wood enough on the whole coast to produce those volumes of smoke. The captain ordered a boat to be lowered, and sent Lieutenant Cresswell, Dr. Armstrong, and me with seven sailors to examine this curious phenomenon. Then we saw a column of smoke rising from the ship which said to us: "The ship is on fire!" Slowly, slowly now we went

[1]Mr. Newton was in the habit of "seeing visions", and this was to get him into trouble at a later date. See entry for December 20, 1850.

forward; back we dared not go, for no signal was hoisted: were the ship to sink before our eyes, or to be blown into the air, which might well happen with all the gunpowder she had aboard, we also must miserably perish, for in the boat we had neither food nor clothing. The emotions which overcame us can no man describe, nor could he describe our joy as the smoke ascending from the ship was seen to diminish and finally fade away; and the ship lay there quite undamaged. We now steered for the pillar of smoke on land; several times we had to frighten a whale from our course. After rowing for two hours we finally arrived at this great column of smoke and found neither tent nor man, but a thick smoke emerging from various rents in the ground, and a smell of sulphur so strong that we could not approach the smoke-pillar nearer than ten or fifteen feet. Flame there was none, but the ground was so hot that it scorched the soles of our shoes. There was no rock or stone in sight; the vertical coastline was composed of a fused mass like rubble, neither clay nor sand, but like a very soft pumice-stone, and in colour green, grey, brown, and mostly sulphur-coloured; where the smell was strongest the heated earth resembled a thick or tough dough; long oars were thrust into it, and each time the smell of sulphur was redoubled, but no flame could be seen; we counted thirty or forty smoke-pillars rising from the earth in different places: Alas, alas! that none of us had knowledge of chemistry;[1] the whole place seemed to me like a huge chemical laboratory. We

[1]This is unjust to Armstrong, who had some knowledge of chemistry, and discourses learnedly on this phenomenon. Armstrong evidently disliked Miertsching, to whom he refers never by name, but always disparagingly as the interpreter: in giving the ship's nominal roll, he lists him not in his proper place among the officers, but at the foot of the list, after the A.B.s — and he spells his name incorrectly. Miertsching, who held his head high, no doubt repaid this dislike as heartily as piety and Christian charity permitted. It might be noted that on this occasion where he down-grades Armstrong as a scientist, the surgeon totally ignores him and names Cresswell as if he were the only officer to accompany him on the excursion: "Lieutenant Cresswell and myself were dispatched in the second whaleboat . . . " (p. 203).

took samples of the particoloured dough or earth with us to the ship; but later to our sorrow we learned that our pocket-handkerchiefs in which we brought the specimens to the ship – and also the wood in which we laid them – were scorched. The captain, with whom we shared each type of earth, arranged them on the table in his cabin, and a little later was startled to find his splendid mahogany table burnt full of holes as if vitriol had been spilt on it. We disposed of our samples in thick-covered glasses. On other parts of the coast there was an appearance as of a brick-kiln; whole layers of burnt strata, a half-inch thick and varying in extent; very similar to tiled roofs, in colour reddish and also grey. In such places we found small reservoirs full of water which tasted sour. Cape Bathurst is sixty feet high, and from there to the east the coast grows ever higher; here in Franklin's Bay it is already four hundred feet, and Cape Parry, the easternmost angle of Franklin's Bay, is seven hundred feet above the level of the sea. Sixty English miles west of Cape Parry a river, still unknown, empties into the sea, and there the coast begins to have a rocky formation; part sandstone, and then again sharply defined in clay-slate. Limestone is also of frequent occurrence.

6 *September (lat. 70° 30'; long. 123° 7'; temp. 31°)*
Throughout the night sailed slowly between masses of ice. Today fair wind and very clear bright weather; 8 a.m. we passed Cape Parry, and wished to follow the coast by Dolphin and Union Strait, but the coast seemed to be obstructed with heavy drift-ice; so a more northerly course was set,[1] where also, to be sure, much and very heavy ice

[1]For his success in the autumn of 1850 McClure was indebted in part to his own daring and effrontery (viz., the passage through the Aleutians and his evasion of Kellett), but most of all to luck and the pattern of the ice which shouldered him (against his choice, if Miertsching is correct here) into the unknown strait which was to prove the last link in the Northwest Passage.

was met, but there was so much space that the ship could pass through and wind freely in a broad zigzag. We saw many whales and seals, and three polar bears. In the morning an inquiry was held into the fire that occurred yesterday on the ship, by which a large part of the ship's new tackle had been ruined. At midday land was discovered from the crow's-nest to the north; and towards it our course was set. Three hours later we could see it from the deck. At 8 p.m. we were sixteen to twenty miles distant from it. It was seen to be a lofty, mountainous land.

CHAPTER THREE

7 September 1850 (lat. 71° 8'; long. 122° 48'; temp. 32°)

Bright weather and clear; little wind and much ice. During the night the wind was favourable and strong; the ship struck ice-pieces several times with such violence that I, and others besides, were twice flung from our beds. By 9 a.m. we were within two miles of the newly discovered land. The southernmost promontory is a cliff rising vertically 780 feet above the sea. Behind it is a loftier peak of a height estimated at over two thousand feet. At 10 a.m. we found an anchorage, and the captain with a number of officers and men landed, hoisted the English flag and took possession of the new-found land in the name of Queen Victoria of England, at which we all gave three hurrahs after the custom of the sea. This high promontory the captain named Lord Nelson's Head. We remained on land for several hours, collected plants, flowers, and stones; traces of human beings were nowhere found, but very many of reindeer, foxes, and wolves. Sea-mews without number swarmed around the cliff; many fine specimens were shot; I shot two great birds, white with black heads and very long necks – a species of swan. Because of the heavy ice dashing against the shore we could not sail around this new land to the west, so we set an easterly course along the coast where the ice was neither so thick nor so heavy. In the evening we had thick, snowy weather. We were all entertained by the captain.

8 *September (lat. 71° 20'; long. 121° 5'; temp. 32°)*
All day little or no wind, and such thick fog, often accompanied with a fall of snow, that one can scarcely see the ship's length. The disagreeable weather makes everything on board unpleasant.

9 *September (lat. 72° 1'; long. 118° 53'; temp. 34°)*
Yesterday we did not progress much along the shore, but have left behind us Nelson's Head, which we can still see when the fog permits. Before us is a great bay into which we are sailing; on our right hand also is land and a small island. The entrance to this bay is at least thirty English miles broad; as we sail farther into it, it grows somewhat narrower.

10 *September (lat. 72° 47'; long. 118° 8'; temp. 32°)*
Wind and weather favourable and pleasant; on both sides we have land which is everywhere covered with snow. The bay into which we have now been sailing for two days is here ten to fifteen miles across; on both sides are mountains 600-800 feet high. At 1 p.m. we passed two little islands in the middle of the bay.[1] The depth here is most variable, 40-130 fathoms. This shows plainly that the bay must be very deep. In the evening we came into frightful ice.

11 *September (lat. 72° 53'; long. 117° 50'; temp. 25°)*
Last night was sleepless for us: the strong wind kept both

[1] The Princess Royal Islands.

ship and ice in motion. Collisions occurred all night and were terrifying. Today the weather is fine and very cold. Today the sailors were busy getting the ship free from these frightful ice-pieces, but all their toil and trouble is in vain. There seems to be a kind of irregular eddy-current which keeps the ice so disturbed. On both sides the land seems to consist of continuous pretty hills. Ach! could one only once again set foot on land!

12 September (lat. 73° 5'; long. 116° 46'; temp. 23°)
This night the ice was still. Today fine weather and fairly cold. The current has carried the ice and with it the ship fifteen miles further to the north-east; and yet no end to the bay is in sight. We are only thirty-five miles from Banks Land;[1] depth 6 fathoms. Around us is nothing but ice; we can move neither forwards nor backwards, and are fixed here helpless in the grip of this frightful ice.

16 September (lat. 73° 4'; long. 115°; temp. 25°)
I have spent the last four days chiefly in my cabin and in bed; I had caught a bad cold. This ship is still fixed fast in the ice, and with it by wind and tide carried now this way, now that; all attempts to get her into lighter ice remain until now fruitless. The bay is here fifteen miles wide; the water in the middle 95 fathoms deep. Seals are often seen; the waterfowl are passing from north to south. The captain is growing anxious, and would gladly bring his ship into a good haven for the next winter.

17 September (lat. 73° 6'; long. 117° 11'; temp. 14°)
The weather bright and cold – and no wind. As far as

[1]From the "loom of land" sighted from the north at a great distance by Parry thirty years before. Actually the shore to their left was Banks Land, but the continuity of this shore with Parry's discovery was not yet proved.

man can see there is before and behind us continuous ice, through which no boat could find a way, much less a ship. A number of ice floes were measured, and are twenty-five to thirty feet thick. By night and when the ice-pieces are not being churned up by the tide, they freeze together, but are always broken apart by the flood-tide. Mr. Court asserts that this is not a bay but a long strait or channel in which we find ourselves, because ebb and flow are regular, and often the tide is very strong; here we are eighty English miles from Melville Island. From the eastern shore we are some four miles distant, but can go there neither by boat nor on foot.

19 September (lat. 73° 6'; long. 117° 20'; temp. 9°)
Yesterday the ship's rudder, badly damaged by the ice, was unshipped, and is now being repaired. As the crew now have nothing to do, they are exercised on deck and then shoot at a target. The ice remains in the same condition.

21 September (beset in ice; temp. 7°)
We are frozen in the ice and are being pushed along with it to the north; If only it would keep on going through Barrow Strait to Melville Island![1] on both sides along the shore is open water, but we cannot get there with the ship, and fast-frozen here must await helplessly what the future may bring. This evening again, as is usual on Saturday, uproarious noise and recreation; it seems as if the men must work themselves into a state of absolute exhaustion on Saturday night in order to observe Sunday with the strict

[1]Thus completing the Northwest Passage; Parry had reached Melville Island from the Atlantic in 1819. By Barrow Strait Miertsching means Viscount Melville Sound, the westerly extension of Barrow Strait.

repose which English custom enjoins;[1] the noise grew too much even for the captain, and he let the men go to bed an hour early.

23 September (beset in ice; temp. 11°)

Yesterday we were driven back southwards[2] fifteen miles by a strong north-west wind. As there is now no hope of escaping from this dangerous ice into a safe winter harbour before the onset of winter, the captain proposes to deposit an assortment of food and clothing on land so that, in event of the loss of the ship, those of us who reach land will not perish by hunger, but will have a chance of making our way to the mainland. Today I took a walk with Dr. Armstrong near the ship on ice now frozen into one continuous mass. The officers have built an ice-house. Milner, who for some days had been held in irons, was flogged today.[3]

24 September (beset in ice; temp. 11°)

Weather melancholy; fast frozen in the ice, we have been driven with it southwards; we passed the two little islands, and about 6 p.m. were forced against heavy ice immovably held up by some reef or sandbank. Through the pressure of these opposing masses the frozen surface in which our ship was fixed was shattered; and though we were anchored fast to a great floe with several cables and a chain, yet the ship was so squeezed against the ice that her beams began to give. This lasted for a long time and we were all warned that the ship could not hold out for long. The captain hastily assembled the entire company on the upper deck,

[1] A touch of unconscious humour. As one notices also elsewhere, the Moravians were less strict than English Evangelicals of that era.

[2] To the south-west; hence Miertsching may have meant a north-east wind.

[3] Officers' servant (*Armstrong*, Introduction).

addressed us briefly, and, in anticipation of an extreme crisis, divided us into crews – each crew with its boat, so that we might make our way to land – through that awful ice! ! ! An officer was assigned to each boat – I am in No. 2 cutter. The boats are made ready, each with its tent and some rations. The frightful convulsions in the ice lasted into the night. At 11 o'clock the ship was more than once lifted up by the ice and thrown over on her broadside; but she righted herself as soon as the pressure relaxed. By midnight all was quiet. I had a long and earnest conversation with the captain, and before I wished him good-night I opened my *Losung* and read aloud: "Be ye therefore ready, for ye know neither the day nor the hour when the Son of Man cometh." Help us, Lord Jesus!

5 *September (lat. 72° 49'; long. 118°; temp. 13°)*

From 2 a.m. to 1 p.m. each man of us stood with a bundle which contained the most needful pieces of warm clothing and some biscuit – ready, upon the first shock of the ship on the sandbank between these masses of ice piled house-high, to throw himself on the ice and make his way to land as best he could; with pockets full of powder and shot, and guns in the hands of many, to get food on land – so we stood there. Ach! how long would we live if it came to that – not a week; the merciful Lord and Saviour, who desires not the death of a sinner, but rather that he should turn from his wickedness and live, so guided the ice, and with it our ship, that about 3 a.m. we came near to land in deep water, but still between opposing floes by which the ship was so pressed and squeezed together that the door of the captain's cabin would neither open nor close. At 9 a.m. the ice grew calm. These were anxious hours; Lord, graciously protect us; and if it be Thy will that our journey end here, make ready our hearts. We are all so slack and weary that we yearn for rest.

26 *September (lat. 72° 45'; long. 118° 3'; temp. 3°)*
Yesterday we had only a few hours of repose; we had lain down for a short while only, when we had to rise, and, cold and tired and weary, we stood the night through, and a part of the day, on deck. The blows of the ice on the ship were frightful. The gale drove the ship with the ice again northwards towards the high, rocky, 120-foot, perpendicular south side of the island, which now we have named Princess Royal Island; and in order not to be dashed against this steep mountain wall the ship, after much toil and labour, was moored with six hawsers to a great floe. We came within fifty feet of the deadly crag, and yet were again preserved. The water there was 65 feet deep. The past night was the most horrible that we have yet experienced; we have endured storms at sea when almost all the upper masts were carried away, but, appalling as a storm at sea is, everyone of us vows, "ten hurricanes at sea are not the equal of last night"; these hours of terror I am not able to describe, and store them in my memory where they are so deeply imprinted that never in all my life will the impression be effaced, but will remind me of what I owe to my Lord and Saviour Whose grace and pity are unspeakably great. To His honour was the last drop of my blood consecrated. For seventeen hours we stood ready on the deck where each moment appeared to be our last; great massive pieces of ice three and four times the size of the ship were pushed one on top of another and under continuing pressure forced into a towering heap which would then come tumbling down with a thunderous roar. In the thick of this ice-revolution lay the ship, thrown now on one broadside, now on the other, then again heaved up out of

the water, and, when the towering ice collapsed, the ship came crashing down into the sea. The ship's beams were so sprung apart that the tarred oakum was falling out of the seams; even the casks in the hold began to crack. These casks are stowed so tightly that they cannot budge with the rolling of the ship; two of them cracked, so great was the pressure on the ship. Had we seen a chance of reaching land across this surging ice-field, not a man would have remained on the ship; but neither by boat nor on foot was this possible; so we had to endure, and expect each moment to be our last; yes, so utter was the despair, when every man saw clearly that here was no hope of rescue, that in the very next moment the ship might be crushed like a nutshell, that some sailors, with neither hope nor the fear of God before their eyes, burst open the chamber where the spirits were stored, made themselves and others completely drunk and stupefied their senses, so that in this condition they might escape the agonies of death. Our helplessness and danger had reached the highest point – the ship was flung over on her broadside, and a towering ice-heap was threatening to cover her with rubble, and so in a moment to bury seventy-six [sixty-six] men in a living tomb; then spoke the mercy of God: "Thus far shalt thou go, but no further"; the commotion in the ice died away, and it lay without the least motion; we gazed at one another, and marvelled at this sudden change: one doubted whether it was fact or fantasy. The ship was lying on her side and we stood rigid, expecting a fresh outbreak of this frightful volcanic upheaval; but the good Lord held the ice in His mighty hand; it lay quiet and motionless. A strong watch was set on deck; the rest of us went, tired, limp, and drenched, to enjoy a little rest.

27 *September (lat. 72° 42'; long. 118° 4'; temp. 2°)*
The ice is still at rest, and the cold is binding it into a solid

mass. On board amongst the crew there is a hush; the men behave as if frightened and few words are exchanged; they all seem to have suffered a shock and to have no spirit left; no work was done today; except for the strong watch on deck, all were enjoying sorely needed sleep and repose. The six anchors with which the ship had yesterday been moored to a great floe have been lost through the parting of the hawsers. As the ship is lying on her broadside and no one can walk on deck or on the ice, everyone keeps to his cabin. The ship has been pumped out; 25 inches of water stand in her.

28 *September (lat. 72° 44'; long. 117° 55'; temp. 5°)*

The night passed quietly and every man could have his rest out; yet must every man hold himself ready, prepared at any moment to become a homeless wanderer. The watches on the upper and lower decks have strict orders to be very alert. The wind has wholly died away; and the whole mass of ice, and naturally we with it, have been slowly drifting to the north with the ebb and flow of the tide.

All the time the ice is freezing more solidly together. The ship, which still lay on her side, was righted today, but not all the labour and machinery employed could set her upon a perfectly even keel, for she rests entirely upon ice, and cannot be trimmed as if she were afloat. Everyone worked with a diligence which surprised even the captain; all the officers were willing and carried out their duties without a word.[1] Although it is Saturday, yet there is no singing or dancing; everything is strangely quiet. This evening I passed the time most agreeably with the captain.

---

[1] A remark made all the more impressive by the casual tone in which it is expressed: McClure's harshness was offset — and perhaps made necessary — by a want of evenness and firmness.

29 September (temp. 8°)

Last night and today no movement in the ice. Since yesterday we have remained in one and the same place, four miles north of the Princess Royal Islands, six miles from the coast to the east, eight miles from that to the west. Should the ice continue to freeze together as it has done since the day before yesterday and should no fresh upheaval occur, this place will have to be named our winter quarters. No Divine Service was held today. The mood of the men is very impressive and very strange. A quiet reigns over the ship which is altogether wholesome and a little odd; each man moves, works, does his duty, and attends to his responsibilities willingly and as if with pleasure; every man is very earnest. The captain appears on deck as usual, but seldom speaks a word and that only to the first lieutenant. I dined with the captain today, read him a sermon after coffee, and we talked on various agreeable topics; he told me how he proposed tomorrow to deal with the men who had burst open the wine and rum kegs a few days before, and we talked much about that. The interior of the ship is very damp, for water has leaked in everywhere, and it is beginning also to be cold. Clothes and linen are damp and there is no way of drying them. I often feel depressed in these mournful surroundings. Lord, strengthen me and give me health and courage.

30 September (lat. 72° 46'; long. 118° 12'; temp. 2°)

The weather is and remains fine but cold; everything is freezing into a mass; there has been no wind for some days, and, though the ice stirs, it remains quiet in the neighbourhood of the ship. This morning came the order from the captain that no work was to be done. At 9 a.m. the crew was mustered, and after the captain had inspected the ship, he read an extract from the Articles of War relating to discipline on board ship, and the punishment by which it is enforced. While this was being read everyone stood bareheaded. After this reading the captain addressed the men in terms of vehement rebuke, set before them their disgraceful behaviour, called them a band of thieves, unworthy of the name of Englishmen, and said that he was ashamed that such base robbers, such a thievish rabble, should walk the deck of an English ship, etc., etc. He then pronounced against the offenders the punishment which they had deserved and would receive. After this severe rebuke he began to admonish the men; he set plainly before them the danger in which we had been, still were, and still would be, and showed them that all human strength and skill were ineffective in such hours of need; only Almighty Providence had through a manifest miracle saved us from certain death, etc. Even old sailors inured to danger, with weather-beaten faces, could not restrain their tears, and all to a man promised amendment and gave the captain a cheer. In the afternoon the three ring-leaders were punished.

7 *October 1850 (temp. max. 0°, min. −5°, med. 2°)*

Until today, the 7th, we have had weather fine and calm but very cold; the new-frozen ice is a foot thick; although the ice is in constant movement, yet it is quite still near the ship. Yet we must always be prepared for flight in event of another convulsion in the ice.[1] The topmasts and

[1]Though there is no reason for mistrusting Miertsching's facts, he appears sometimes to be wanting precision in dates — the not unnatural consequence of losing his original journal. He at least implies that the ship was in no danger from the ice after 1 October: Armstrong describes her as suffering fearful buffeting and pressure on October 4, and this appears to be the crisis described by Miertsching in his entry for September 26. Where discrepancies occur the surgeon, who seems to have saved his journal, is the more trustworthy authority of the two.

yards have been taken down; on the upper deck also they are working to make ready for winter. All the work is carried out willingly and cheerfully. The coarse "language of the sea" is also less indulged in. My servant and friend, Farquharson, is much troubled because the sailors cannot read and instruct themselves by means of books and tracts. The captain and his officers are now on the best of terms and the unpleasantness which formerly existed has not recurred since our departure from the Sandwich Islands. Every day I spend some most agreeable hours with the captain: he seems now to realize that he is not the good exemplary Christian which he used to think himself; for some days he has been reading his Bible morning and evening. The health of the crew is very good; now there is no one on the sick list. On every clear day the aurora borealis appears to the south-east from 7 to 11 p.m.

October (temp. max. 0°, min. −6°, med. −2°)

The weather is most agreeable; the ice is at rest and all the time is growing more solid with frost; the ship is now being converted into a winter residence; above the upper deck a covering of stout sailcloth is stretched and fastened at the sides to the now-repaired ship's bulwarks; so that the ship resembles a huge tent, and in snowy and stormy weather the men can walk to and fro with pleasure and comfort on the upper deck which has been cleared for that purpose. When the sailors have no more work to do on the ship they must, morning and afternoon, walk on the ice for some hours or take such exercise as they prefer.

The days are growing so short that already the sun shines for a few hours only; but it seems that it still wishes to do well by us before it leaves us altogether; several times we have seen more than one sun; and daily for the last few days three or four, roughly in this shape:

10 October (temp. max. 4°, min. −8°, med. −1°)

Pleasant bright weather, but cold. The captain intends, as soon as the state of the ice permits it, to visit the land which lies to the east of us, and take formal possession of it; because for several days the ice has been still as far as we can see, and the weather is fine, he resolved today to carry out his plan; at 8 a.m. Captain McClure, Dr. Armstrong, Lieutenant Cresswell, and myself, with four seamen, set out and after two hours of scrambling over uptossed, frost-welded ice-masses, we reached land, mounted a hill a hundred feet high and planted the English flag. The captain named the land Prince Albert Land, and the sailors set up a cairn and in a bottle buried the notice that this land had been taken possession of for England. While the sailors were doing this, we four climbed a 1,200-foot mountain that lay an hour's walk away, in the hope that from its summit we might see whether the water in which our ship was frozen was a deep bay or a strait. We had a fine, extensive view from the summit; on land many high mountains were to be seen, but the end of the bay was cut off from our view by mountains. We ate the bread and butter brought with us – and now frozen like stone – on

80

the mountain-top, and began our journey homewards. At 3 p.m. we reached the sailors waiting for us on the shore and at once set out to cross the ice to the ship. We had scarcely walked for a quarter of an hour when we came upon a channel of water a hundred feet across; it had been lifted, broken off, and separated from the land-ice by the action of the tide. We walked up and down the margin of the water in the hope of finding a narrow place where we might leap across; but the farther we went the wider the channel seemed to grow. So we went back and climbed a hummock 36 feet high from where we could clearly see the ship, and fired off our guns until our powder was spent; all in vain; those on the ship did not hear it; but as it was now quite dark we saw from time to time rockets fired from the ship; cannon also were discharged; but all this did not help us. We had no fuel, and so could kindle no fire, and had no more powder, and so could give no signal. We were suffering from hunger and thirst, for one might say that we had not eaten all day; especially disagreeable was it for myself and Dr. Armstrong, for in the darkness we had slipped on the ice and fallen into the water; the others hauled us out, but now, drenched through, we could barely endure the cold; our clothes were frozen into icy sheets. 9 p.m. we saw three parties bearing torches quit the ship in different directions; we stood together and shouted in unison as loudly as we could, but all to no avail; the ship was too far off, and no one heard our cries. Finally towards 11 o'clock one of the searching-parties seemed to be coming in our direction; we heard their gun-shots and saw their torches; we shouted together with all our strength; and towards 12 o'clock we had the joy of speaking to our rescuers on the other side of the water. These had heard our cries, but, as we had no light, did not know where we were. We were ferried over in an inflated rubber boat, and after we had a little restored our strength with those of the wine-flasks brought along which had not been broken in clambering over the ice, we went as best we could, climbing over the frightful ice towards the ship which we reached at 2 a.m., happy and thankful that we had broken neither leg nor neck on that difficult road. A good meal awaited us; every man had an appetite, and we did it justice.

Such was our visit to Mount Adventure.

Prince Albert Land rises some two hundred feet above the level of the sea. Individual peaks rise as high as 1,800 feet, with rounded tops; innumerable little hills have the same shape. The surface soil is gravel and sand; here and there great round stones occur. Inclined strata of rock and sandstone have we seen only in one place in a tour of thirty-seven English miles. In the valleys one finds grass and much moss. Traces of reindeer, foxes, and hares show the presence of wildlife.

14 October (temp. max. 24°, min. 15°, med. 20°)
Up till now we have had the finest of weather; the ice remains always without motion: since that memorable day when it stood still it has not moved once until now. The ship is, of course, frozen fast, and is now completely fitted out for winter quarters. When there is no work for the seamen on board they walk on the ice morning and afternoon. Around the ship the ice has been levelled; great hummocks have been blown up and carted away and deep holes filled, so that one may now walk around the ship with comfort. Life on board seems to have grown very agreeable; for some weeks there has been none of that frightful noise which used to prevail; and everywhere on the ship one sees cheerful, contented faces. The captain is very busy writing: he is making a good copy of his daily journal.

15 October (temp. max. 18°, min. 8°, med. 15°)
Today we went—the captain, Cresswell, Sainsbury, Piers,

and I – to Princess Royal Island. The flag was hoisted and a good grog drunk. We discovered a few traces of earlier inhabitants of this land: a grave, a few fox traps and caches or depots (*kematolivik*). These remains are very old, for the stones are all overgrown with moss. Both islands, the smaller as well as the larger one, are of rock throughout, and full of fossilized mussels and shellfish.

16 October (temp. max. 10°, min. 7°, med. 8°)
The whole day much snowfall and mild weather. The captain intends next Monday to take tent, sledge, and eight men on a journey of some days: he will search for the end of the bay in which we are frozen. Today I made myself a hunting-bag of watertight drill.

17 October (temp. max. 11°, min. –3°, med. 1°)
Throughout the night keen wind which drifted yesterday's snow; today very pleasant calm weather; everyone enjoys leaving the ship, and outside they find recreation in levelling the ice in order to have a fine promenade and playground. Messrs. Sainsbury, Wyniatt, Ford, and Newton were on Princess Royal Island and brought back a hare and three snow-grouse – the first we had seen. The hare, and the grouse as well, are the same as in Labrador: the hare white with black ear-tips (*ukkalek*), the snow-grouse (*rippen-akkigilek*), white with black tail-feathers – the former seven pounds, the latter one and a half pounds. We entertained the captain – very agreeable.

18 October (temp. max. 4°, min. –3°, med. 1°)
Bright calm weather. The captain and others of us visited the island, found more remains of Eskimo homes, and collected various fossils and little red crystals, half an inch long and edged, which are found only in stone resembling

granite. The distance from the ship to the island, measured exactly, is four English miles, and one requires a good two hours to go there on foot, because he cannot go in a straight line, but must go by a very roundabout way. In the evening we saw not one bright shining moon but three, and in addition a rainbow of the most splendid colours.

21 *October (temp. max. −1°, min. −4°, med. −2°)*

The weather is and remains good; the cold also is quite bearable, and the health of the crew is good. At 7 a.m. all was ready for the captain's departure; the party consisted of the captain, Mr. Court, and seven seamen to draw the sledge on which they carry a tent, blankets, and buffalo-robes for sleeping in. The sledge and its load were carried separately by the whole crew a journey of two hours to the point where level ice begins, for it is impossible to draw a sledge over hummocks. The sledge was then loaded on the margin of the smooth ice, and the captain and his party were sent off with three rousing cheers. We went back to the ship; the captain and his party to the north-east. Sergeant Woon and a sailor went to Prince Albert Land and there on the beach found a number of large pieces of driftwood. Mr. Cresswell and I walked to the island and there saw two white foxes. At 9 p.m. quite unexpectedly Mr. Court appeared and told us that the smooth ice extended a few miles only; they had broken their sledge and had sent for a new one.

22 *October (temp. max. 6°, min. −1°, med. 3°)*

At 7 a.m. Mr. Court left with a new sledge; Mr. Wyniatt and seven men accompanied him. The weather is most unfriendly. Today some more spoiled meat thrown overboard; already seven hundred pounds of this preserved meat have been thrown away as unfit.

23 October (temp. max. 0°, min. −9°, med. −6°)

At 9 a.m. Mr. Wyniatt and party came back; they had lost their way yesterday and passed the night a half-hour's walk away without knowing that they were so close to the ship. Every day I am busy with my chart and comparison of old Eskimo words with new ones recently acquired.

. . . .

29 October (temp. max. −8°, min. −14°, med. −10°)

This morning Messrs. Paine, Sainsbury, Newton, and I went to Prince Albert Land, taking with us coffee, bacon, and various tasty items such as sardines, to have a picnic on that snow-covered land. A good walk of two hours over the rough ice brought us to land where we gathered drift-wood and kindled a roaring fire. After we had drunk a good kettleful of coffee, we sought the higher ground in quest of hares and snow-grouse, and did find and shoot a hare. On our way back to our fire we saw some distance off a company approaching over the snow-covered ground, and wondered what it might be; we took it for Eskimos. I rejoiced at meeting Eskimos here, and formed a splendid plan for spending the winter with them, should they live near by, etc. The group came ever nearer to us, and we, full of curiosity and expectation as to how these people might behave, almost stared our eyes out. And then we perceived with astonishment that these were no men but five big black animals. We could not determine what kind of animal they might be: black or brown bears are not met with at so high a northern latitude; nor were they reindeer, for they had no antlers, and all other known animals in the north are white in colour. The first thing that we did was to load our guns with ball instead of birdshot, and then we awaited whatever fortune might bring. Mr. Sainsbury was not in a condition to load his gun, for his finger was frozen stiff, white as an icicle, and quite without feeling. It was for the

85

three of us who remained to receive these five strangers with coolness and determination. As they were coming straight for us without seeing us, we lay flat on the snow twenty feet from one another on the side of a smooth-sloping knoll. We saw now that these wild animals, not suspecting what lay before them, came ever nearer; they were the size of an ox – with frightful horns curved like those of an ox – and their bodies were covered with hair so long that it brushed the snow, and their feet were scarcely visible; sixty paces off, and they were aware of us; they stopped suddenly and stood there, snorting, stamping on the ground with their fore feet, and tearing up the ground with their horns: we in the meantime lay quite quiet, but ready for battle. The beasts huddled together with their heads towards us; one, the largest ox, now came alone towards us slowly, snorting, while the rest stayed motionless in one place. Some thirty paces off he also stood still, stamped on the ground, and received our first ball in his head, somewhat too low, as we later found, four inches above the nostrils. He was turning away bleeding when a second ball was sent through his ribs. He went back to the herd and stood still with his bleeding nose turned towards us. We crawled forward on elbows and knees fifteen paces nearer and opened fire with three double-barrelled guns. The mortally wounded animal was now mad with rage; and well it was for us that we three were not together, but so spread out as to fire from three sides; while one of us was attacked the rest had time to reload. Three animals lay dead on the ground; another charged blindly at me; I pulled the trigger; my gun missed fire; the priming had fallen off; I leapt aside, tripped, and fell flat on the ground. The ox, no less frightened than I, dashed by me and with-out looking around ran on, leaving a trail of blood behind him. In a moment I was on my feet, adjusted my weapon, and ran along the blood-stained trail of my fugitive. The

86

other two hunters were having lively sport with the fourth ox which was savagely infuriated. The most unpleasant feature of so cold a hunt is adjusting one's priming with fingers stiffened by cold. After a short run I found my fugitive standing deep in snow and bleeding from several wounds; one more ball, and that stretched him lifeless on the ground. I ran back to aid my two comrades with the other enraged ox, but found him also breathing his last. Our joy was indescribable; the five huge creatures lying there were ours and would provide many good beefsteaks, etc., for our table. But amidst our joy at our good fortune in obtaining so rich a booty we now first realized in what danger we had been; to the Lord Who had so graciously protected and guarded us everyone freely acknowledges that this is a Divine Providence and above all a gracious gift of God; for now we have a prospect of enjoying more *fresh meat* in the course of the winter. We had read in James Ross's *Travels*[1] that he had met with the musk-ox on Melville Island; we had never seen them but thought that there must be such creatures. The five oxen now lay dead, and, because we had seen traces of wolves and polar bears in the snow near by, Messrs. Sainsbury and Newton, who had both frozen their fingers completely, went back to the ship; we two, Mr. Paine and I, remained to guard our booty. We kindled a fire and again prepared a good cup of cocoa. It was already growing dark when a sledge came from the ship bringing us a tent, blankets, and food. We dragged our kill close to the tent on the sledge, and Mr. Cresswell, who had brought six men with him, organized a watch to be kept all night. After a good supper, a pipe of tobacco, and much talk about our lucky hunt, we turned in.

[1]Presumably a reference to Sir John Ross's *Narrative of a Second Voyage*, etc., which contains extracts from the journal of his nephew, James. The Rosses, however, were exploring in Boothia, and were never within hundreds of miles of Melville Island.

30 October (temp. max. −1°, min. −11°, med. −5°)

At 8 a.m., after a good breakfast with cocoa, one of the carcases along with the tent was loaded on the sledge to bring it to the ship. While we were thus employed, there arrived from the ship seventeen men with two sledges, and they also took two carcases. The journey over the rough ice was difficult for the heavy-laden sledges – one of them was broken in fragments; and its load lay on the ice until the following morning. At 3 p.m. we reached the ship and met the entire crew who had come on to the ice to cut a smooth road to land. As soon as the road was ready, Lieutenant Cresswell went with three sledges and brought in the two remaining carcases from the land and the one from the ice. The sailors received us hunters with three loud hurrahs and were delighted to see these five oxen lying on the ice near the ship. Now there was a great festival of victory in which all participated: it was a genuine celebration; how astonished the captain will be when he sees so much fresh meat hanging from the yards! How he will rejoice, etc.! There are four bulls and one cow. The largest of these oxen furnished 420 pounds of meat, and altogether these five musk-oxen gave us 1,296 pounds of good meat, not reckoning the heads. . . .

31 October (temp. max. −5°, min. −23°, med. −16°)

Yesterday morning at 8.30 the captain came back from his expedition, and came on board without being observed on the ice. He had left behind his crew and sledge nine miles from the ship at 10 o'clock yesterday, thinking to reach the ship by 2 p.m., but it began to snow, he lost his way and wandered the whole night and could not find the ship; he had no rest, sleep, food or drink; he was twice in danger from polar bears, but had seen them before they saw him. He fired off all his powder to draw the attention of the ship's watch, but probably was too far from the ship for this to be heard. Finally, after he had been wandering for twenty hours, the sky cleared, the sun rose, and he found himself in the midst of hummocks a half hour's walk from the ship. He came aboard more like a corpse than a living man; his limbs were stiff with cold; he could not speak a word. He was carried to his cabin, where both doctors, Armstrong and Piers, took charge of him. At midday the captain's sledge-crew came aboard in great anxiety to learn whether the captain had arrived before them. After the captain left them they had set up the tent and prepared a good meal. Soon after, snow began to fall and they thought it necessary to remain in the tent and spend the night on the ice. Now they were in excellent condition after an absence of ten days, rejoicing at the success of their journey. On 26 October they had reached the end of the water in which we and the ship were frozen, and found themselves at the east end of the land Captain Parry had sighted thirty years before from Melville Island and had named Banks Land. To the north they saw ice only; to the east the shore of Prince Albert Land fell away: so the problem of the Northwest Passage, disputed for 300 years, was solved.[1] Here, where our ship lies, the strait is ten miles across; where it opens into Barrow Strait [Viscount Melville Sound] it is thirty-five English miles from the east end of Banks Land – named Point Russell – to where the easterly trending coast of Prince Albert Land forms a cape which our captain has named Point Peel. For hundreds of years men have sought this passage; many ships have been lost in the quest, and many more lives; and now it has been the fortune of the ship *Investigator*, Captain McClure, to discover it. At Point Russell a cairn was erected and a record

[1]Sir John Franklin, or members of his company, had discovered an alternative passage two or three years previously; but as not one of them lived to report this success and as the fact of their achievement was not proved until 1859, posterity has perhaps been guided by sentiment rather than by justice in assigning the honour of discovery to Franklin and not to McClure.

deposited. The strait in which we find ourselves will from now on bear the name of Prince of Wales Strait. Our ship is frozen in at lat. 73° 31′, long. 114° 30′ [1] west of Greenwich. . . .

This new ice of this season was measured in five places today; it was twenty English inches thick.

2 *November 1850 (temp. max. −16°, min. −27°, med. −23°)*

Today the captain gave the crew a good dinner to celebrate the discovery of the Northwest Passage. In the morning the captain mustered the crew and gave a speech in which he expressed his satisfaction with their conduct and exhorted them to behave well in the future and preserve cheerfulness and good humour. Sports and recreations would be organized, and to these he would contribute as much as he could; for they were the surest means to good health, and also through them could the long, cold, dark winter be made agreeable. He promised that when they returned to England he would not forget to recommend his crew to the Admiralty as favourably as he could.

[A note on other ships in the Arctic in 1850 may be of interest at this point.

Collinson's *Enterprise* reached Bering Strait a few days after the *Investigator*, and after an unsuccessful effort to penetrate the ice to the north pulled out and wintered at Hong Kong.

No fewer than eleven ships (two from the United States) came in by Lancaster Sound and gathered at Beechey Island, where Franklin's winter quarters for 1845-6 were found, but no indication of his intended course. The main rescue squadron under Captain Austin in the *Resolute* with the *Assistance* (Captain Ommanney)

---

[1]This should read 118° 30′. See entry for June 10, 1851.

and the steam-tenders *Pioneer* and *Intrepid* sailed west from Beechey Island, were frozen in at Griffiths Island, offshore from the modern post of Resolute Bay, and there spent the winter of 1850-1, some four hundred miles to the east of Banks Land.

Austin was particularly fortunate in his officers. Leopold McClintock, the pioneer of arctic sledging, was first lieutenant of the *Assistance*; those capable travellers, Lieutenants Mecham and Osborn, also served under his command. The future geographer, Sir Clements Markham, was mate on the *Assistance*.]

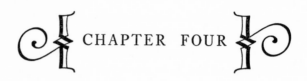

CHAPTER FOUR

9 November 1850 (temp. max. −6°, min. −11°, med. −8°)

The weather is for the most part bright and clear, but the cold is very biting: men often come on board with noses, ears, and fingers frozen, and are confined to the ship by the doctor.

Daily experiments are made of the effect of explosives on ice. On Princess Royal Island various kinds of stones and fossils are found, collected, and brought to the ship. A vein of metal also seems to have been discovered.

11 November (temp. max. −15°, min. −26°, med. −22°)

Today and in clear weather we saw the sun at midday for only one minute, and for the last time this year. Oh, how joyfully will we greet him at the beginning of February, should we live so long! The snow lying on the ice has been cut into two-foot cubes with saws and cutlasses, gathered up, and brought to the ship to provide a snow wall which will ward off the cold to some degree. On either side of the ship is an ice stairway – ten feet from the upper deck to the ice, which has been carefully levelled near the ship so that we will not stumble.

The long-cherished wish to have a school for the sailors is now fulfilled: this evening order was given that all winter, five times a week, the sailors will be taught reading, writing, and arithmetic. Mr. Paine is chief instructor.[1] Mr. Court has four students in navigation. There are sixteen scholars in reading, thirty-seven in arithmetic, five in spelling. The school is held from six o'clock to half past seven; after that, frequently, recitations, dancing, or a concert last until half past eight; but now the bounds of decorum are never exceeded. . . .

16 November (temp. max. −7°, min. −15°, med. −10°)
Weather clear and cold. The ship is now encircled with a snow wall eight feet thick. On the upper deck snow has been spread a foot thick, and then covered with a newly invented "polar cement", which is a mixture of snow, sand, and water, and throughout the winter is as good as a plate of granite. Two ravens pay us a daily visit – the only creatures besides ourselves in this frightful region of ice. Since his return from discovering the Northwest Passage, the captain has not been in good health, and today he became so ill that he was forced to stay in bed; his body also is covered with sores. . . .

. . . .

30 November (temp. max. −23°, min. −32°, med. −28°)
The weather is now unpleasant every day; violent storms – snow storms – are making it very cold. Since the ship was surrounded and covered with snow it has not been so cold on board; but on the other hand it is so moist in the cabins

[1]It is little to the credit of the senior officers (who were now without regular daily employment) that this important and burdensome task should have been thrust upon a junior too low in rank to object, and, apart from the cook, perhaps the only man on board whose duties had in no way been lightened during the months of inactivity.

that moisture runs down the walls; likewise our beds are damp and have a distinctly mouldy smell. I have rheumatic pains in all my limbs and am cold continuously. There is no chance of being thoroughly warm or of drying one's clothes because the ship's stoves are not heated;[1] for the captain is convinced that heat is injurious to the men, and says that the Eskimos have no stoves and no fire and yet are the healthiest of men. The captain is somewhat better and to-day walked on deck for a quarter of an hour. In the stove in his cabin he burns daily thirty-two pounds of coal and *lignum vitae*. On the ice not far from the ship the sailors have levelled a great space where they play ball (football) daily. The school seems to please them very well. It is amusing to see how these great bearded men exert themselves to learn their letters, and to write letters and figures. A number of men are on the sick list, chiefly from rheumatism. . . .

6 *December 1850 (temp. max. −3°, min. −10°,*
med. −8°.)

The weather is raw and cold with strong wind. Today the captain, convinced of the dampness in the ship and of the mouldy smell in the sleeping quarters, gave orders for all stoves to be kindled in order to dry out every corner; at the same time a ventilating system was set up to bring fresh air in and foul air out. I have two glowing-hot cannon-balls hanging continuously in my cabin today. A great change has come over us: the frightful, dissolute "spectacle" has been done away with; one hears less and less frequently the abominable profanity [*Schifferworte*]; instead,

[1]It is difficult to understand this and the following sentences: Armstrong, certainly no flatterer, expresses himself as satisfied with McClure's provisions for the health and comfort of the men, and gives sixteen pounds as the captain's daily coal allowance. Probably Miertsching complained that the stoves were not sufficiently heated and took seriously some jesting reply made by McClure.

1. Johann August Miertsching

2. "Critical position of H.M.S. Investigator on the North Coast of Baring [Banks] Island – August [29-31] 1851"

3. "Sledge-party leaving H.M.S. Investigator in Mercy Bay – April 15, 1853"

4. "Sledging over hummocky ice [on Melville Sound] – April 1853"

there is now much reading; and though the men still have their amusements – often a sea song and even a dance – yet all is done in a decent manner.

13 *December (temp. max. –17°, min. –27°, med. –21°)*
If we are to have all winter the sort of weather we have had up to now, it is going to be a very tedious affair. There is little snow, but the wind makes the cold unendurable. Daily, men come to the doctor with frozen faces, fingers, and toes, so that he is kept very busy. The captain, now fairly well recovered, takes a daily walk of an hour's length on deck. . . .

For some time no one has gone to the land; for in the perpetual darkness it is impossible to make one's way over the hummocks of ice. We take walks nowhere but on the level space near the ship. Two ravens used to come daily to the ship; but for some time only one has come. This bird has grown quite familiar with us: he is given food and then flies away to the west. School goes on with regularity. It is interesting to see a polar school: some of the bearded scholars writing on paper, others on a blackboard, others forming letters; some mending their clothes, while others in a half-reclining posture smoke their pipes of tobacco and play the silent spectator; at one table they play checkers, at another cards, and much tobacco is consumed. All this is done quietly and in an orderly fashion.

20 *December (temp. max. –34°, min. –37°, med. –36°)*
For several days the weather has been very pleasant; although dark and cold, for there has been no wind. As far as one can see, nothing is visible except snow and ice; no tree, bush, or stone to lend relief to the expanse of white. Nature is dead, and such a stillness reigns that one hears his watch ticking in his pocket – indeed some assert that they can hear their hearts beat. Yet there are objects of great inter-

est here; for example, one sees the stars night and day and around the moon there is often a coloured ring; and often shooting-stars, and meteors, and such-like objects. Yet a few days and the sun begins his journey back to us. Yesterday when Mr. Newton had the watch he conversed with the captain when he was on deck, and the brazen fellow was inspired to make mischief in an extraordinary way, or rather to make his own stupidity known beyond all doubt. He asked the captain why the piece of mast and the ship's plank which had been seen lying among the driftwood on the shore of Prince Albert Land had not been brought to the ship, for they might well be wreckage from the vessels of Franklin. The captain, astounded at the news, asked who had seen them; Newton described how he had found and examined them: one piece was a topmast, the other a fragment of ship's planking; three men who were there with him also knew of this; he had come to the ship and reported in due form to the first lieutenant; but now eight weeks had flown by and the wreckage had not been picked up; so he took the liberty of communicating with the captain himself. The first lieutenant, who was promptly summoned, could not remember having heard anything of the discovery; the three men who had accompanied Newton on that occasion knew nothing, because they had seen nothing, nor had Newton mentioned the matter to them. Consequently this morning the first lieutenant, Newton, and the three men were sent by the captain to look for the wreckage seen and reported by Newton.[1] They came back at five in the afternoon with faces and hands frozen, so that they were all put in the doctor's care. They had hunted for several hours, and had found plenty of driftwood, but no

[1]For McClure thus to equate his second-in-command with a warrant officer, a man of proved unreliability (see entry for September 6, 1850), whose story was by implication contradicted by his companions, shows insufficient respect both for his first lieutenant and for the Queen's Commission. The matter should have been investigated by that reliable neutral, Stephen Court.

mast: a piece which Newton designated as a ship's plank was a stout piece of driftwood five feet long, and this Newton was compelled to drag to the ship. Now convinced that this was a pure fabrication on the part of Newton which could easily have disagreeable consequences on his return to England, the captain degraded him from his post and required him to offer public apology for the lies he had told.

21 December (temp. max. −15°, min. −31°, med. −23°)
Praise and thanks to God, this is the shortest day; now we have fresh hope and a revival of spirits. At midday, though there was no moon, the sky was bright − so bright that one could read large print; we brought books printed in various types on to the ice, but only the very largest type was readable. . . .

24 December (temp. max. −12°, min. −27°, med. −19°)
Today is Christmas Eve, and the best of weather, but unhappily no Hosanna resounds in this wilderness of ice. How and in what manner this day and above all the Christmas festival were here celebrated I do not think fit to insert in my journal, but it will abide in my memory as long as I live. I spent most of the day away from the ship and thus alone could give myself up to enjoy various agreeable meditations appropriate to Christmas. Tired and chilled through, I came back to the ship, locked myself in my cabin, but got little sleep in the whole night because of the noise and the "spectacle" which was kept up by a few men, and those very drunk, all night. Two officers kept watch, one on the upper, and one on the lower deck, to ensure that the drunken seamen did not wander on to the ice and there find a speedy death.

25 December (temp. max. −7°, min. −18°, med. −13°)
Today is the joyous festival of Christmas, but nothing

could be less enjoyable to us. The captain, who could not sleep all night because of the noise, is greatly annoyed; at the usual 9 a.m. muster he administered a sharp rebuke. No Divine Service was held, for the heads of several sailors were still swimming, and certainly a religious service seems misplaced in this sort of life. In the afternoon the officers were guests in the captain's cabin and spent a few hours after the meal in pleasant and instructive conversation. In the evening we shared a good punch with the captain.

31 December (temp. max. −35°, min. −39°, med. −38°)
The last days of this year have gone by in routine fashion; unhappily our conduct on Christ's Holy Day was most uproarious and un-Christlike; but the captain admonished and warned the crew, and seems not only willing to be converted but to perceive that it is not at all the act of a Christian so to defile the Holy Day of Remembrance. Ah, would God only send His Spirit with fire and sword upon us to kindle in us a new life. . . . Praise to the Lord Jesus for His grace, mercy and truth. In all these trying and often very disagreeable circumstances, surrounded by enemies of the Gospel, and above all, of missionaries, yet I have passed comforting and holy hours when, more than before, I have had grace to enjoy the nearness of the Lord and of a few friends. He has preserved me in health all the time; also I am treated with friendship and courtesy by every man on board. . . .

1 January 1851 (temp. max. −26°, min. −35°, med. −29°)

Jesus, for thy faithful leading, which throughout
    our course we trace,
We adore Thee, still proceeding onward in the path
    of grace;

While another year we enter, we renew our vows
    of love,
All for Thee resolved (to) venture, our benign
    Conductor prove.

The weather is very pleasant, except for a fairly strong wind and consequent severe cold. The ice was measured at 3 feet, 6 inches. The health on board is very gratifying; five men are in hospital, but suffering only from frozen hands or feet. Today is a great festival for the ship's company. Extra rations and grog were issued this morning. A 9 a.m. the whole crew was mustered on deck and the captain admonished the sailors to enjoy themselves in an orderly fashion, and thereby really have pleasure. After the muster we went, led by the captain, to the men's quarters, and were astonished to find a hall elegantly decorated with flags, pictures, sea-paintings; the tables laden with excellent puddings and roast beef, all arranged in a clean and appetizing manner; the sailors, neatly and tidily dressed and with friendly faces, received us with three cheers as we entered. A proof of their skill as cooks was offered us by each mess. . . . To see a sailors' banquet of this sort is especially interesting to a novice such as I, who had never seen one before here, where there is no daylight, and perpetual darkness demands ample lighting. Assuredly no flowers were there, but Jack loves only flags and anchors painted on paper. . . . After coffee we were invited by the sailors to an oratorical display: a sailor representing Lord Nelson, and another as a French admiral, fought anew the battles of Gibraltar and Alexandria; after this there were more sea songs and finally "God Save the Queen"; upon which the festivities were ended and the signal "Hang up hammocks" given. I went promptly to bed, for I had slept little the night before, yet happy and well. In spirit I was in the Community, and heard the trumpet proclaim the advent of a New Year. . . .

6 *January (temp. max. −19°, min. −28°, med. −24°)*

The weather in the new year is growing much more pleasant; very cold it is, but calm so that daily without interruption the crew can organize games on the ice and obtain the exercise so necessary to their health. Now that the new year is past, people begin to make plans how to pass the time while the ship is still frozen in the ice, and until the break-up, for monotony is very irksome in the long, dark, polar winter. Life on board ship is, so to speak, a sort of machine: one day is like another; every task is done every day at the same time in the same way.

An exact picture of the daily life on board will show it to be simple but exacting. The lower deck and all cabins are lighted by lamps and candles. Every opening through which cold can enter is protected as much as possible; entrances are secured with double doors, to ward off the cold drafts to the best of one's ability. At 5 a.m. a signal given by the watch tumbles the men out of their hammocks, which are lashed together and piled. For the officers and the captain this reveille is a signal that they may enjoy two more sweet hours of rest. Before breakfast the ship is swept and cleaned inside and put in perfect order.

At 8 o'clock breakfast. The members of each mess – eight men apiece – line up at a steaming kettle from which each receives his appointed portion; with healthy appetite he now consumes his cup of cocoa and a half a pound of salt pork. The steam from the kettle and the vapour generated by so many coming in from the cold air causes a thick fog. From this atmosphere of 50° one mounts a short stairway to reach the deck, whither by the opening of the door a thick cloud of fog accompanies him, and finds himself passing into quite a different climate, from 50° above immediately into 50° below zero. Breakfast with its witty remarks and short yarns is over at a signal to which instant obedience is given: each man draws on his warm clothing and goes on deck, only a few remaining behind to clear the tables, wash up, and bring everything to perfect order. 9 a.m. brings the signal to muster, whereupon all form up with precision in rank and file and are inspected by the captain and officers; then they are hunted out on to the ice where they shorten the time as best they can until 11.30; six men gather clean snow or ice for the ship's cook; this is melted.

At midday is dinner, which consists of salt beef or pork, and peas, dumplings, or dried cabbage as vegetable. The officers dine at 2 p.m. At half past one the signal puts the men back on the ice where one sees them pacing back and forth alone or in groups of four to six men discussing past events or future prospects. At 4 p.m. they come aboard, most of them shivering with cold, and have a supper of black tea and salt pork and then a grog, issued by the Master-at-Arms, and a pipe of tobacco. From 6 to 7.30 is school and then until 8.30 free time, and then the signal proclaims "to bed". This monotonous life is the same every day: those who have no private occupation such as reading, writing, sketching, knitting, etc., are in evil plight and are much to be pitied. My cabin is open to all, and to my great joy I often see men coming, to whom I read aloud and then amuse myself and them by holding a discussion on what has been read. Such men as pass their lives entirely without God might well be aroused here, for I think that here especially the want of something higher makes itself felt. The lack of worldly pleasures on the one hand, and on the other the need of help and powerlessness to help one's self, makes this want felt....

31 *January (temp. max. −40°, min. −45°, med. −43°)*
A month of the new year has passed and, thank God, we are all healthy and well. The dark period of winter is almost over: yesterday for a minute we saw for the first time the

returning sun; daily now he will come nearer with rapid strides. Everyone on board seems filled with new life; for, though lamplight still prevails on board, outside, despite the cold, is the friendly sun. The weather in this month was for the most part clear and pleasant; at times the wind was strong and bitterly cold. . . . The ice, measured in five different places, is 4 feet, 9 inches thick.

5 *February 1851 (temp. max. −29°, min. −35°, med. −32°)*

We are having glorious weather and sunshine daily. I spent the whole morning walking on the ice with the captain, but in spirit I was at home, sharing in the birthday celebrations of my dear mother. The captain noticed my absent-mindedness, and when I told him the reason he shared with me an after-breakfast snack on our return to the ship, and invited me to lunch and coffee. I had a punch-tea with Mr. Paine in the evening. In the last few days I have made myself a pair of boots, and when the days grow longer will go hunting in them; also I have begun a new pair for the captain. These boots are made of felt with cork soles.

12 *February (temp. max. −25°, min. −36°, med. −32°)*

For the past week I have been very busy repairing my undergarments: I have relined my sealskin coat. A few days ago two seamen who had been for a walk on the ice came running in and reported that a great grey wild beast had followed them for a long way. In the evening the beast actually came to the ship; it was a wolf; the ship's dog, Mongo, was turned loose and drove him off. Yesterday the wolf came for another visit, and played for some time with our Mongo, but kept beyond the range of firearms. . . . Williams, Griffiths, and Willioks [Wilcox] come to my cabin every evening. Oh, how much pleasanter it is now on the ship than formerly, when grossness still had the upper hand.

19 February (temp. max. −38°, min. −45°, med. −42°)
... I have gone to Prince Albert Land with the captain several times; we have seen foxes and ptarmigan, but have shot none. Messrs. Haswell and Piers and I were on the island and shot a white fox and three ptarmigan. Dr. Armstrong, who is not the best of comrades, was properly humiliated[1] by the other officers today. The captain was informed of the whole affair, but took not the least notice of it. ...

28 February (temp. max. −45°, min. −51°, med. −49°)
The sun now rises at 8 a.m. Barrels and chests have been taken from the ship and placed on the ice in order to convey them later to Princess Royal Island. The captain fears a terrible disturbance when the ice breaks up in Prince of Wales Strait,[2] and as a precaution will place clothing and provisions for the whole crew for three months on the island, and also a large boat, so that in case of disaster all will have a chance of escaping and reaching the shore of the mainland. ...

8 March 1851 (temp. max. −35°, min. −42°, med. −39°)
For the past week the weather has been extremely fine. The men are daily freighting supplies to the island on sledge. ... I accompanied the captain to the island and saw two hares.

[1]One would like to know just what Miertsching's "gehoerig gedemuethigt" implies. It must have been something fairly drastic to merit, in his opinion, the captain's notice.

[2]The ship lay not in a sheltered harbour but in the middle of the strait, a situation of much danger if the ice broke up in a strong gale. McClintock's *Voyage of the Fox* contains a graphic description of the actual occurrence of the danger McClure feared (pp. 102-5, Philadelphia, J. T. Lloyd, 1860).

15 March (temp. max. −38°, min. −44°, med. −41°)

The depot of provisions, etc., is now fully secured so that no fox or bear can do it any injury. The island has been placed out of bounds to the seamen lest they should attempt to tap the barrel of spirits. Next month the captain intends to send three sledges along the coasts of the unknown lands near by to search for traces of Franklin's ships. Should the ice by chance break up before the return of the sledges a boat will be placed on the shore of Prince Albert Land to give the sledge-parties a means of escape. Now with the spring tides one often, especially in the evening, hears the ice crack with a noise as loud as a cannonshot.

22 March (temp. max. −22°, min. −34°, med. −29°)

Wolves often approach the ship, but are so shy that we are unable to capture any. The captain, Cresswell, Court, Piers, and I, with two seamen, were on the Westland, which until now has had no name; the flag was hoisted, and the captain took possession of the land in the name of Queen Victoria, and named it "Baring's Land";[1] we remained for several hours, tramped around in various directions and found traces of wolves, reindeer, foxes, and hares, and saw a few ptarmigan but shot none. I have accompanied officers several times to Prince Albert Land, and have shot five hares and seven ptarmigan. Forty sailors loaded a boat on two sledges and dragged it to Prince Albert Land; they spent two days on the task. The weather continues to be very pleasant, and, at times when there is no wind, quite warm; but it is both painful and injurious to the eyes when the bright sun shines on the white snow, and so dazzles the eyes that one must wear very dark glasses or goggles.

[1] Actually McClure had known since October 26 of the previous year that this "Westland" was identical with the Banks Land of Parry.

27 March (temp. max. −16°, min. −29°, med. −24°)
The officers and crews assigned to the journeys to be made next month were named today. Lieutenant Haswell with eight men to draw his sledge is going to Wollaston Land; Lieutenant Cresswell is to go in a north-westerly direction along Banks Land; and Mr. Wyniatt is to go to the north-east in the direction of Cape Walker.[1] The men are busy making ready the sledges, and those appointed to travel are working on clothing and boots. The armourer is also busy preparing lamps, kettles, and apparatus for cooking with fluid on the journeys. The travelling sledge-parties will be away from the ship for four weeks.

31 March (temp. max. −15°, min. −31°, med. −23°)
The weather fine; the glare of the snow is blinding; a number of sailors have been suffering from snow-blindness for days. . . . A few white foxes have been taken alive, and to have a little sport the crew formed a great circle on the ice, spaced two yards apart, and each man armed with a stick. Two foxes and the ship's dog were let loose within the circle, and the dog gave chase to the foxes for half an hour but could catch neither; at last all three were exhausted and lay down to rest. The circle then closed in narrowly, but both foxes luckily made their escape back to freedom. . . .

3 April 1851 (temp. max. −15°, min. −26°, med. −21°)
Growing daylight, declining cold. . . . The weather is con-

[1]Wollaston Land was the south-western shore of Victoria Island, sighted and so named in 1826 by a detachment of Franklin's second land expedition under Richardson. In 1839 Thomas Simpson was on the south-eastern shore of the island and, in ignorance of its continuity, named it Victoria, and this name has supplanted both the Wollaston of Richardson and the Prince Albert of McClure. Cape Walker was on a small island on the northern shore of Prince of Wales Island, important from its prominence in the sailing orders of Sir John Franklin on his fatal expedition.

sistently pleasant, and a windless calm prevails. Although it is a walk of two hours to the nearest land, those who are not tied to the ship by regular daily duties go there almost every day to hunt, but they bring back little in the shape of game because they follow the English method of hunting – the best in the world – even in these strange wilds. If pheasants and moor-hens abounded here, our English sportsmen would probably be successful;[1] but with these northern ptarmigan and white hares no skilled sportsman is as renowned as I. I have gone hunting three times, and have shot twenty-one ptarmigan and three hares.

The sailors are engaged in pulling down the ship's snow wall and carrying it away on sledges. Today the snow which all winter long has covered the deck a foot thick has been removed; and it gives one a sense of comfort to be able to walk on wood again instead of on snow. In the sun the thermometer stands at 25° above, in the shade at 25° below.

10 *April (temp. max. −6°, min. −21°, med. −13°)*

The day before yesterday I went with Dr. Armstrong and Mr. Sainsbury to Prince Albert Land, and saw many ptarmigan, but got not a single one; yesterday I went again, alone, and shot fifteen; came back very tired, and was invited to dine with the captain. Today I went with the captain to Baring's Land: we saw fifteen hares in one herd and shot two.

12 *April (temp. max. −15°, min. −31°, med. −23°)*

The ship's inventory was taken today; every article on board that was not private property, but belonged to the government, was taken from below, laid on the deck, and painstakingly checked by the appointed officers. . . . Today I strayed alone to the land and felt very happy: in spirit I

[1]This criticism would have delighted the late Dr. Stefansson.

was with my Eskimos in Labrador and sang with them: "O Bethanien du Friedenshuette". Towards evening we saw the first clouds to appear in the sky for several months.

13 April (temp. max. −13°, min. −32°, med. −20°)
Today is Palm Sunday, but here are no palm trees for us: from early in the day until evening snow fell so thickly that already it is two feet deep, and we are very thankful that we have a housing over the ship, and sheltered by it can walk back and forth on deck. In the afternoon I was with the captain and read him a sermon for Palm Sunday delivered by an old bishop in Scotland in 1685.

17 April (temp. max. 38°, min. 17°, med. 22°)
Bright sunshine has succeeded yesterday's storm; the new-fallen snow of the storm which raged yesterday and last night has entirely disappeared. The sun shines so warmly that snow near the ship is growing moist. Around the ship, ice three feet deep has been hacked out and carried away in order to caulk as far down as possible the sides of the ship, which have become leaky in the dreadful ice; that is, to stuff tarry material between the ship's planks. Today all is astir with preparations for the three crews that are to set out tomorrow morning. Lieutenant Haswell, with supplies for nine men for 42 days, will do his utmost to reach Wollaston Land which is supposed to be joined to Prince Albert Land. Lieutenant Cresswell is to solve the problem of whether to the west Banks Land is joined to Melville Island; and Mr. Wyniatt in Barrow Strait will try to reach the Cape Walker of Parry's chart. Each officer has eight men to draw the sledge on which is carried the travelling equipment. Travel by land here is truly far more difficult than in Labrador. There the sledge is drawn by dogs: here it is to be done by men; and therefore one must take pains to keep the load down as much as possible, and to make

sure that all travelling equipment is in perfect order. The equipment of a travelling party is as follows: First a sledge 10 feet long, 30 inches wide, 12 inches high, fastened with iron and weighing 64 pounds; and canvas tent 9 feet long and 6 feet wide. [There follows a detailed catalogue of clothing, bedding, tools, cooking equipment, weapons, etc.] The total weight of such a sledge load for forty-two days exceeds a thousand pounds. Therefore a man must draw 125 to 130 pounds. The officer goes in advance of the sledge to find the easiest way through the rough ice, and carries a double-barrelled gun, telescope, compass, and a notebook for recording the observations made with the instruments.

18 April (temp. max. 28°, min. 17°, med. 22°)
Today on Good Friday we had Divine Service in the morning, after which the travelling parties were warned to be ready to set out at 4 p.m. They made their preparations with strange feelings, for everyone of them seems to feel that they will not find the ship here on their return, but that she will have been swept away or utterly wrecked;[1] it was therefore a mournful parting for a sailor to make. All partook together of the midday meal, and then at 4 p.m. the travelling crews assembled on the quarter-deck and were addressed by the captain. The ensign was hoisted, the sailors harnessed themselves to their sledges, and with a triple hurrah from those who remained behind they set off, each party in its appointed direction. We accompanied them for an hour. The weather was most pleasant, yet the rough surface, though levelled somewhat by the last snow, made the sledges draw heavily; they will find smooth ice near the land. I spent a pleasant evening with three friends in my cabin. . . .

[1]Because the ship was not in a harbour, but liable to be carried away in moving ice.

20 April (temp. max. 7°, min. 7°, med. 2°) [*Probably minimum intended to be −7°*]

All day today strong wind, gloomy sky, and much snow. In the morning Divine Service was held; I dined with the captain, and, since the sailors were not put off the ship in the afternoon because of the snow, I held a private gathering which many attended, and when it was over they begged me to hold another soon. This was not the first meeting of its kind; and although neither the captain nor the officers attend them they seem in no way opposed to them. . . .

6 May 1851 (temp. max. 21°, min. 3°, med. 12°)

At 1 a.m. today Mr. Wyniatt came back unexpectedly with his sledge-crew – all in the best of condition; we supposed that they must have found traces of Franklin, but the cause of their return was that when thirty-two German miles from the ship, travelling east on rough, uneven ice, the officer, Mr. Wyniatt, fell from a hummock and broke the chronometer that he carried, without which he could not make correct reckonings, so he thought it best to return. The captain gave him no friendly reception when he came on board, but reprimanded him so bitterly for his foolish conduct that he went back covered with shame. The captain allowed him and his men twelve hours of rest on the ship and then they were to be off again, and furthermore *without* a chronometer,[1] and to complete their

[1] Wyniatt's conduct in returning when he had progressed more than a hundred miles from the ship was without excuse: he could not miss his way back as long as he obeyed orders and kept close to the shoreline, and his primary purpose was not to make charts but to search for Franklin. But his mistake was irremediable, and if, as we are to assume, a spare instrument was available, it was an act of senseless fury on McClure's part to withhold it, and wantonly rob his officer's observations of their value. One wonders if Wyniatt's act was not in part due to the reluctance and fears of his men – aggravated by loss of the chronometer – and McClure's furious rebuke intended to impress them as much as their leader.

appointed journey as far as Cape Walker: "Before chronometers were in use men found their way all the world over and discovered new lands." Some sailors were on Prince Albert Land and saw two reindeer. Mr. Piers, Stubberfield, Bow [respectively cook and private of marines] and I were on Barings Land, saw much wild life, and shot five hares and nine ptarmigan. The captain has determined to send a hunting-party to land for a period of several days. At 6 p.m. Mr. Wyniatt with his sledge-crew started off to repeat his journey and then press along the coast towards the east – without a chronometer. At the same time Mr. Sainsbury left with four men, sledge, and tent to spend a week on Baring's Land and hunt the numerous hares and other wild creatures; for the same purpose Mr. Newton has gone with two sailors to spend a week on Prince Albert Land.

7 *May (temp. max. 29°, min. 8°, med. 16°)*
I went with Whitefield, Bow, and Kerr to Baring's Land; we encountered high wind and drift on the hills; we saw a herd of thirty hares, but could not shoot in the driving snow; went back and visited Sainsbury's tent where we drank a warm grog; the sailors could not remain still, but went out in contempt of the storm to look for the herd of hares; two hours later they came back empty-handed – all except Whitefield; we waited another two hours, but no Whitefield returned. We set out in different directions to look for him, but did not find him, and thought that he must have gone out on to the ice. Finally at 10 p.m. as we lay in the tent he came crawling on hands and knees to the entrance. We found him speechless and dazed, and so took off his frozen garments, rolled him in woollen blankets, gave him warm tea with rum, and left him in the tent. I went with Bow and Kerr to the ship and reported to the captain and to the doctor.

8 May (temp. max. 15°, min. −2°, med. 6°)

At 4 a.m. Mr. Piers accompanied a sledge to fetch the disabled Whitefield from Baring's Land, and we came back at 10 a.m. Whitefield seemed somewhat better, but had not fully recovered his reason: he told his story very incoherently: how he had lost his way and after wandering about on the land for four hours, had fallen weak and exhausted and had no strength to get up again. He lost consciousness, and after he had lain on the snow for a long time the weather cleared, and to his great joy he saw the tent, and, still unable to rise, had crawled to it on his hands and knees. . . .

8 May (temp. max. 27°, min. 10°, med. 21°)

. . . The crew is busy repairing cables, sails, etc., and painting the ship and boats. Whitefield has recovered so well that he goes for walks on the ice near the ship. Yesterday both hunting-parties came back to release other men, and brought fifty-six ptarmigan to the ship. . . . At 6 p.m. Mr. Court took three men to the tent on Baring's Land, and I took Woon, Bradbury, and Nelson for a week to the tent on Prince Albert Land. About 10 o'clock we came to the tent, heated some cocoa, went out to the hills, and shot three ptarmigan. We adopted the system of remaining in the tent by day on account of the blinding glare on the snow, and of going out to hunt by night.

3 May (temp. max. 31°, min. 13°, med. 24°)

At 11 a.m. we were aroused from our sleep in the tent by Messrs. Piers and Newton, who had come from the ship with the news that Lieutenant Cresswell had come back from his journey to the north-west because his people were suffering from sickness and frozen limbs; he had reached the western [eastern] end of Banks Land,[1] whence the coast trends not towards Melville Island but to the south-west [north-west]. . . . Mr. Cresswell was promptly made ready with six men and supplies for twenty days to follow the coast from here as far as Nelson's Head.[2]

24 *May (temp. max. 30°, min. 15°, med. 24°)*
At 12 midday as we were eating we heard twenty-one guns fired from the ship to pay homage, even in this new polar land, to Queen Victoria on her birthday. . . .

28 *May (temp. max. 34°, min. 19°, med. 26°)*
Yesterday I went with the captain to the island; we did not see a drop of water, but for the first time this year met with a gull flying by. On our way back we saw two wolves chasing a reindeer over the ice. Today a bear was shot on the ice, and in the afternoon we saw several gulls flying around the ship.

29 *May (temp. max. 33°, min. 18°, med. 26°)*
This morning at 11 o'clock Lieutenant Haswell came back from his journey of forty-one days, with his crew in the best of trim. This party had made a round trip of 720 English or 180 German miles; on a cape they had found Eskimos living in five tents. The natives received them in friendly

[1]He had done more — he had followed the shore of Banks Land eighty miles beyond Point Russell.

[2]According to Armstrong (p. 331) those of Cresswell's former sledge-crews who had not been disabled on the first journey were promptly detailed to participate in the second; and set out after a rest of two days only. This seems like an ill-natured expression of the captain's resentment at their failure to complete their first commission. Cresswell was fully justified in turning back when he did — as it was, two of his men underwent minor amputations. He might be considered at fault for not better securing his men against frost bite, but his sledge-mates were blameless, and ought not to have been given a laborious second assignment when plenty of their shipmates were fit enough for the vigorous pursuit of hare and ptarmigan.

fashion, but unfortunately they could communicate only through signs. As these Eskimos were encamped only a hundred miles from the ship on a newly discovered land, and were also newly discovered Eskimos, the captain resolved to pay them a visit in which I should accompany him, in order to learn from these people how the land lies, especially the coast to the south-east of here. After brief consideration and a discussion of the journey with me, he ordered a sledge, six men, and rations for twelve days to be made ready. In the evening at 6 p.m. we quitted the ship to the sound of three cheers. The crew accompanied us as far as Princess Royal Island. At midnight we made a half-hour halt, ate bacon with grog, and smoked a pipe of tobacco. After we had rested, we went on in bright daylight at midnight.

0 May (temp. max. 44°, min. 22°, med. 33°)
From 6 p.m. yesterday to 5 a.m. today we travelled at a rapid pace near the shoreline and found the ice smooth and flat with little snow on it. We had covered twenty-six English miles when we came to a low sandy cape lined with driftwood; we set up the tent, kindled a good wood fire, cooked and ate a good warm meal followed by a double-grog. Ptarmigan were flying close by the tent; we shot six. Tired but happy, we lay down to rest. At 12 midday the captain made and worked out an observation of the sun. Seawards, not far from the tent, was high, uneven ice on which we observed four bears; they did not come near the tent. Throughout the night and today the weather was most agreeable and not cold, 28-30° Fahrenheit, and yet one of our people, Hewlett [Hulott, according to Armstrong], a mulatto, through wearing canvas shoes which were too tight, so froze his feet that subsequently on the ship he lost seven toes. At 4 p.m. our breakfast was ready, and about 6 we resumed our journey, but did not go so fast;

we all felt somewhat tired and stiff. Every three hours we halted, took a grog with biscuit, and rested for half an hour. In the afternoon the weather became very stormy, and soon so thick was the fog and drifting snow that we could not see ten paces, and moreover the wind was in our faces. The captain felt indisposed all day, and, as we could not see land and the compass is most unreliable here, we halted and set up the tent, glad and grateful that we were under a roof. We travelled eighteen miles today. The ice measured 7 feet, 1 inch.

31 *May (temp. max. 47°, min. 23°, med. 33°)*
We awoke at 2 p.m. the weather was very fine and warm; not a breath of wind. After a good breakfast of cocoa, biscuit, and roast ptarmigan, we made a pleasure trip to land where the snow was almost melted away, and here shot ptarmigan which were flying north, and collected geological specimens. At 6 p.m. we resumed our journey, and with very fine weather, perfectly level ice with little snow on it, made many long strides, and –

1 *June 1851 (temp. max. 47°, min. 29°, med. 37°)*
– at 6 a.m. made a halt: we had gone twenty-six miles. Set up the tent on the sandy shore, gathered driftwood, and prepared a good meal at a blazing fire. After a refreshing sleep we took to the road again about 6 p.m. The road was well marked and the weather good: in twelve hours we put twenty-seven miles behind us. At 6 p.m. [a.m. must be intended] the tent was again pitched, and after a good meal we tried to sleep as quickly as we could.

2 *June (temp. max. 45°, min. 29°, med. 35°)*
At 6 p.m. we were again ready for the road, and started on our way lively and in good humour hoping to reach the Eskimos in the morning. The captain and I followed the

snowless shoreline, the sledge following us at a short distance on the ice. We had put some ten miles behind us when to our joy we discovered before us five tents standing on a small hill; we came nearer and saw a handful of men standing by them. I was in joyous excitement at the prospect of soon again seeing Eskimos, and could scarcely wait until I could speak to them. We drew ever nearer wondering whether these people would understand me and I them. The Eskimos stood clustered near their tents, and when we were near enough I shouted to them that we were visiting them as friends and bringing rare gifts. They stood as if petrified and with a heavy heart I drew near and took it as already certain that they did not understand my words, because they uttered no sound; then they raised a universal cry: "Sivoravogut! erksidlarpogut!" ("We are afraid!") These were the first words which I heard from these folk and to my no small joy I also understood them. These poor folk made no gesture of resistance to our approach – indeed they had no weapons at hand; but they were full of fear and anxiety; never yet had they seen a stranger, and they took us as supernatural beings. By many words and a few gifts useful to them they were brought into a somewhat more tranquil state of mind; they understood me and I them very well; and because I wore Eskimo clothing they readily accepted me as an ordinary being, and gave full proof of that by feeling my arms, features, and hair, etc. Their language, nature, features, dress, and tools, etc., and, as it seemed, also their character, are just the same as in Labrador. Their harpoons, knives, hatchets, arrow-points, sewing-needles, etc., are all of good copper which they obtain pure from Eskimos dwelling farther east in exchange for seal-oil, walrus tusks, etc. The women tattoo their faces; also they have long tails to their jackets, as in Labrador; while on the contrary the Eskimo women of the American coast wear their coats with the broad, short hinder part as in Greenland. The dress of the Eskimo male I have found one and the same as in Labrador. Unlike the Eskimos of Cape Bathurst these people have *not* pierced the under lip for bright stones, which apparently have the same purpose as the pierced ear-lobe in Europe, from which stones, glass, metal, etc., are hung. These very poor, simple folk, not yet corrupted by civilized man, have disfigured neither their ears nor their under lips. Yet the women here seem not entirely pleased with the work of their Creator, for they try many blue and red lines and figures to make perfect what the Creator, in their opinion, has neglected.

These poor Eskimos of Prince Albert Land were much astonished to learn that there were other lands inhabited by human beings; for they supposed that they were the only men; a great land to the south which they see in clear weather they call Nunavaksnaraluk; probably this is the continental shore. In winter they dwell in great snow houses, and in summer in tents of sealskin; for tent-poles they use the tusks of the narwhal.[1] Through the summer, probably from May to October, they move their families and tents along the coast from place to place. I could not learn whether they have their winter quarters at one and the same place every year. After these people had gained confidence and we had satisfied their curiosity by answering many wondering questions, we laid a large fold of paper on a great outstretched sealskin. On this I indicated the position of the ship, the coast, and our route as far as their tents; and requested them now, after much explanation, most trying to the patience, to trace the coast from there on to the limit of their accurate knowledge. After about an hour the sketch was finished, and by the men as well as by the women who knew the coast it was declared good and perfectly correct. The shorelines indicated reached as far as

[1]The narwhal does not occur in this area: perhaps some form of whale-bone is intended.

Point Parry on Victoria Land; also the two longest known islands of Sutton and Liston in Dolphin and Union Strait were marked quite correctly; according to their assertion, many Eskimos dwell on the coast to the south and southeast, and this they confirmed by naming capes and the families living there. The captain and the sailors examined the country round about and the tents while I occupied myself with the Eskimos who remained near me. These people know nothing of a universal Creator. They have the same theory of the stars as the Cape Bathurst Eskimos: namely, that while they rest at night the sun looks down on the earth through little openings. Of a life after death they have the same idea as the Eskimos of the mainland shore, of Greenland and Hudson Strait: that there are two different lands – a good and a bad. These people know also by tradition of a high mountain on the land where long ago their ancestors of this cape dwelt in tents during the time of the great flood. It grieved me to part after so short a time from these simple folk who were so dear to me, and I asked the captain – when he had already given the command to start on the homeward journey – that in this fine weather he would prolong his stay for half a day. He would have been willing to do so, but could not consent because of the ailing Hewlett, whose frozen feet were growing worse and more painful, so that he sat on the sledge in stockings and had to be carried in and out of the tent.[1] I distributed the gifts which we had brought, which consisted of red and blue flannel, knives, saws, needles, beads, and various other trifles; especially fascinating to them was the small look-

[1] Here we have an example of the malice with which the officers of the *Investigator* pursued one another. Armstrong states (p. 337) that on this journey McClure disabled several of his men by excessive rapidity of travel, which, he insinuates, was intended to answer no other purpose than to demonstrate the captain's superiority to the slower-moving Haswell as a sledge-captain. It appears here that McClure's haste, however unwise, was inspired by the humane wish to get the earliest possible medical attention for Hewlett.

ing-glass. These people could not comprehend the idea of a gift, and when I gave something away the recipient would ask what was its value and would offer all sorts of articles, home-made out of copper, as an equivalent. As we were taking our departure from these kindly folk and were already on the move, the captain was so grieved at leaving these loving people helpless in this frightful region of ice that he could not refrain from tears; he took off his thick red shawl and wound it around the neck of a young Eskimo woman who was standing near by with a child on her back. She was much startled at this and said that she had nothing to give in return; then she drew her little child from her hood and, in great distress and still covering it with kisses, offered it to the captain as payment for the shawl, which she had not ventured to touch; only after I had declared to her clearly and emphatically that it was a gift, she looked at the captain in a very friendly manner and laughed, delighted that she could keep her child. With her curiosity aroused she began to inquire what sort of animals had these red skins, by skins meaning the shawl, for these people are familiar only with clothing of skins and are quite unacquainted with cloth and similar materials; our canvas tent, our woven garments, handkerchiefs, paper, etc., they supposed to be the skins of different animals; to explain all this to them clearly and in language which they could understand – for this the time was too short.

Most of the Eskimos whom we have hitherto met have been, in some instances, greedy and childish; but here, on the contrary, we did not detect it: these people seemed to be honesty itself. As we were starting on our way back, three Eskimo men appeared, returning from a reindeer hunt; they told us that inland there were numerous herds of *tuktut* and *uningmak* (reindeer and musk-oxen) to be found, but so timid and wild that one could not get near them. These Eskimos hunt wild animals with bow and arrow and with throwing-spears. After a good march of eight hours we had put eighteen miles behind us; we pitched the tent, lit a fire, ate and drank, and lay down tired enough to sleep; this was at 11 a.m.

3 June (temp. max. 43°, min. 30°, med. 35°)

At 6 p.m. after a good breakfast we were off again. So far we had always kept close to land, but now, to take a short cut, we had to cross a bay twenty-three miles across. The weather was good, the wind rather strong, but that was an advantage to us; the farther we drew away from land the stronger it blew, and after a few hours it became a regular gale with rain and snow, which so drove us on that we did not walk, we had to run. The storm was setting the ice in motion. At 1 a.m. we came to a cleft in the ice four feet across; we leapt over and then had to work the sledge across. The weather was such that we could not see ten paces; the compass was utterly useless so we could steer by the wind alone, and went, or rather ran, straight on in the hope of stumbling somewhere on land; at 5 a.m. we arrived suddenly at a cleft in the ice 11 feet across and filled with water which –

4 June (temp. max. 43°, min. 30°, med. 35°)

– we could not cross without a boat; we were lost; we had been steering only by the wind, and might have gone astray and travelled right out to sea; according to our reckoning we should have been on land long ago. In short, we did not know where we were. The blizzard was so strong that we could not stand erect. With much labour we managed to pitch the tent on the ice near the cleft; while sitting in the tent we had to hold it down, or it would have been torn away by the wind; stiff grog and biscuit were twice distributed. After 3 o'clock the weather cleared, and to our great joy we saw right before us land some five miles away; so

119

far had we gone in the wrong direction during the storm. We found a place where the cleft narrowed, and made our way across. In two hours we reached land where we set up the tent, cooked a good meal and then sought everyone of us to sleep as soon as possible. Our wet clothes were spread on a stone to dry. After some six hours of good sleep we made off again to reach the ship with all the speed possible, for the sick man Hewlett was growing worse from hour to hour. From here to the ship, which was a long day's journey, we often suffered from violent squalls of rain, and often waded knee-deep in water; we reached the ship at 9 p.m. (5 June). The doctor examined our sick, and straightway took them under his care. Short as our stay had been, it was yet a great pleasure to me to have seen and spoken to the Innuit who live here, separated so far from the rest of mankind. Perhaps the time is coming when these friendly people also, now dwelling in heathendom on Prince Albert Land, will be taught the Gospel, the glad tidings of a Saviour.

7 *June (temp. max. 48°, min. 34°, med. 39°)*
Today the weather is again fine and warm; through the intermittent rain much water has gathered on the surface of the ice. Three polar bears came near the ship, were wounded, but got away. The ship is now made ready for sailing in the open sea; the boats are freshly caulked and repainted. The captain caught a severe cold on his last journey, and now lies confined to his bed; also two of our travelling sailors, Dawn [Gauen?] and Caroll, are quite ill. This morning Mr. Wyniatt came to the ship from his journey to the north-east with his crew in good health; he had not reached Cape Walker owing to shortage of provisions. On the way, once or twice, foxes had emptied their provision sack while they were sleeping in the tent, and polar bears had walked off with shoes and clothing. Many

remains, very ancient, of Eskimo dwellings were seen. No driftwood had been found; hares and ptarmigan very scarce. The coast of Prince Albert Land is flat as far as its junction with Barrow Strait; on the other hand, from Point Peel eastwards it is high, rocky, and steep. In the evening came Mr. Piers from Baring's Land and Mr. Sainsbury from Prince Albert Land with their hunters, and brought as a week's booty: fifteen hares, forty-five eiders, and nineteen ptarmigan. They have found many old Eskimo remains on Baring's Land. On one moss-covered plain were the ruins of thirty-two houses built of stone, and in many other places isolated old Eskimo dwellings were found; stone lamps, arrow-heads, broken stone knives, etc., testify that Eskimos have lived here; one finds evidence of the same on Prince Albert Land. Ten miles inland beside a cache lined with stone was found a very old Eskimo sledge shod with bone.

10 June (temp. max. 45°, min. 36°, med. 40°)

Now that both crews sent to explore Prince Albert Land to the south and the north-east have come back and have found no trace of the Franklin expedition, the boat appointed for their rescue in case the ship should no longer be here on their return has been brought back to the ship. Near the shore there seems to be much water in which countless eiders are swimming. Today, also, men were sent to the island to paint the boat placed there, and to put it into a seaworthy condition; they are leaving this boat with three months' supplies for seventy men. In the afternoon Mr. Cresswell came back to the ship in good health from his journey with his men; he had not only reached Nelson's Head, but had gone beyond it to Cape Lambton, and naturally had seen nothing of Franklin or the *Enterprise*. On the coast, ruins of old Eskimo houses were found, whence one may be sure that this region was once well populated.

Our ship is in lat. 72° 46′ north, long. 118° 12′ west. Lieutenant Haswell was absent on his journey for forty-one days, and travelled along the coast of Prince Albert Land to lat. 70° 38′, long. 115° west of Greenwich. Mr. Wyniatt was fifty days absent and – as closely as he could reckon with no chronometer – was east along the south side of Barrow Strait as far as lat. 72° 6′, long. 107° west. Mr. Cresswell reached lat. 74° 16′, long. 117° 40′ on his first journey, and lat. 71° 10′, long. 123° 4′ on his second.

[In the spring and early summer of 1851, Collinson in the *Enterprise* was on his way up from Hong Kong to begin an arctic cruise which lasted for three years, while Dr. John Rae of the Hudson's Bay Company, starting from Great Bear Lake, made a journey along the south shore of Wollaston Land (Victoria Island), during which his track came very close to that of Lieutenant Haswell descending from Prince of Wales Strait. Extensive surveys were made by detachments from the four ships of Captain Austin at Griffiths Island. Lieutenant Sherard Osborn took a party down the south-western shore of Prince of Wales Island, and his farthest on May 23 was only sixty miles east of the journey's end of Wyniatt, who turned about on the 24th. Lieutenant McClintock made the 800-mile round trip from Griffiths Island to Parry's Winter Harbour, a landmark where Franklin's men would have been certain to leave a record had they been anywhere in that region. Dr. Armstrong justly censures McClure for omitting to send a party across Viscount Melville Sound to Winter Harbour in April, as a likely way of establishing communication with Captain Austin and making the position of the *Investigator* known.

It was in this season that McClintock developed the system of advance depots and supporting sledges later employed by Peary to reach the North Pole, and by Scott to arrive at the South Pole.]

CHAPTER FIVE

19 June 1851 (temp. max. 38°, min. 32°, med. 34°)

The weather is continuously fine and pleasant, but one thing is most trying – we cannot go to land any more and shoot hares, reindeer, and water-fowl. The ice is broken, and on its uneven surface are many ponds of snow- and rain-water; neither by boat nor on foot can one hope to reach land. From the ship by telescope we can see reindeer moving about on land; on the island all is fully provided for: yesterday a copper cylinder containing the history of our cruise and a map of the newly discovered islands was placed in the great stone cairn built on the cape of the island. The snow on the low-lying sandhills on both coasts has almost disappeared. The captain still lies on his sickbed, and is very impatient at remaining so long under the doctor's care. For some three weeks we have often seen mirages, as I had seen them before in Labrador; only here they are much more vivid. Yesterday morning was one of the most striking I have ever observed, and we were deluded in the most ridiculous fashion: the watch on deck reported that not far from the ship a bear was lying on a piece of ice; we studied it through a telescope, and, sure enough, there lay a bear frequently moving his head; we made out his black eyes and nose quite plainly. Guns were snatched up, and forth we went, wading through ice and snow to shoot the bear. We were barely 150 paces from the supposed bear, when he rose in the air and flew off, while we stood knee-deep in water, realizing that a white owl had made fools of us. These comical deceptions are of frequent occurrence.

24 June (temp. max. 38°, min. 32°, med. 34°)
. . . The captain is still quite sick, though yesterday he seemed to be somewhat better. I pay him long visits twice daily, and often read to him or else we talk. Often waterfowl are shot near the ship. The ice is beginning to break up in every direction, but as yet one can detect no movement. The ship is fitted with new sails, and all is ready for our voyage to England. If only we could have open water – soon.

30 June (temp. max. 36°, min. 33°, med. 34°)
Nine months have already flown by since we were fixed in this spot, and yet we are still as fast in the ice as in the deepest winter. As no movement at all has yet occurred in the ice the captain hopes to break loose at the beginning of August, and put an end to our banishment. . . . Today the sick Hewlett had seven toes amputated. Facey and Griffiths have lost a few fingers by frost-bite.[1] One and one-half feet of ice have melted away this month.

July (temp. max. 40°, min. 34°, med. 36°)
. . . As now everything on the ship is made ready and in the best of trim the sailors have no employment; all sorts of games and recreations have been devised to shorten the

---

[1]Facey and Griffiths were casualties of Cresswell's journey up the Banks Land shore. The former was a sail-maker, and highly esteemed by Armstrong, who was later his ship-mate on the West Indian station.

time. Two hours are daily spent at target-shooting. Because the sun, which never sets, makes night day, one sees as late as midnight twenty or thirty men on the ice busy flying paper kites of various form and colour; each one naturally asserts that his own is the best. Others again are busy sailing their little home-made boats of cork or light wood. . . .

. . . .

10 July (temp. max. 45°, min. 35°, med. 37°)

Waiting is beginning to grow tedious; the ice remains immovable; it is full of rifts; but we wish yearningly to see it move. There is no hope of hacking our way out of the ice, for here it is over 5 feet, and the thickest places 15-25 feet thick. Only by a gale can it be moved, and enough channels be opened to afford a passage for the ship. All around seals lie on the ice in great numbers, but they are so alert that no one can get a shot at them.

14 July (temp. max. 47°, min. 34°, med. 40°)

Yesterday we noticed the first stir in the ice, and a number of large openings were made in it by the exceptionally high spring tide; from the masthead open water is sighted to the south and west. Today occurred the highest spring tide: early in the morning wide leads appeared through the movement of the ice; towards noon the frozen sea was shattered into fragments, and the ship was afloat, pushing between the ice-pieces as they fell apart. A feeling of joy mastered each one of us at the thought that after being ten months imprisoned we were once more free. Even the seals seemed to rejoice at the break-up, for numbers of them were playing near the ship, chasing one another across the floes, enjoying regular romps, and then tumbling back into the water. The whole scene was most interesting; and now suddenly all is alive with activity after our long habitual repose and regular routine. The various commands of the officers are answered by the labouring sailors from the deck, the ice, and the mast with an "Ay, ay, sir", and no one can form a picture without having lived through it; the ship drives with the ice slowly to the north-east. The captain, who is sufficiently recovered to come on deck, mustered the crew and spoke to them earnestly: he bade each one to be ready, in the event of disaster, to leave the ship; the boats were to be kept ready, and supplied with necessities; and each man was ordered to have ready a travelling-bag containing wollen underclothing, two pairs of socks, gloves, scarf for the neck, needle, thread, and biscuit.

16 July (temp. max. 41°, min. 37°, med. 38°)

The weather is very fine. Yesterday the ship was secured with five anchors to a great floe and moved with flood and ebb, first to the north and then to the south. At 11 p.m. there was a terrible disturbance in the ice: three anchors sprang loose and a five-inch hawser parted. Today we are beset on all sides with heavy ice; a strong north-east wind has driven us southwards close to the Princess Royal Islands. There is a hideous fascination in watching how floes driven by the tide toss about great masses of ice; pieces of more than fifty tons are pushed up one on another, until with a loud crashing sound the heap topples over; the shocks of this rock-hard ice against the ship are pitiless and most unpleasant. A copper sheet on the ship's side measuring 36 inches by 13 was grazed by the ice and folded back so that now it is only 9 inches long.

17 July (temp. max. 40°, min. 35°, med. 37°)

Rain and snow all day today. Soundings, this morning 68, this afternoon 10 fathoms; in the morning we were thrust by the ice almost to the steep rocky wall of Princess Royal

Island, but there was a little wind; sail was hoisted; with the aid of that and by blasting away the ice with powder, we made our way in the afternoon to lighter ice where the ship lay peacefully anchored to a floe. Fresh water for the ship is obtained daily from the floes.

18 July (temp. max. 38°, min. 35°, med. 36°)
The north-east wind remains strong, and is driving heavy ice down upon us, and the ship is in a critical position. The pressure is so severe that beams and planks are creaking; to protect the ship in some measure from violent shocks she was moored with six ice-anchors to a floe, but no anchor would hold; they sprang loose or broke; so we were at the mercy of the ice. But the faithful Watcher over Israel watched over us also, so that we passed safely through all the dangers of the night.

19 July (temp. max. 44°, min. 36°, med. 37°)
We find ourselves today in the same position as yesterday; the wind is the same, and the unyielding ice makes the ship creak and quiver. We tried today to get rid of the threatening ice-blocks by blasting, but it helped us little, for other pieces just as big pressed in to replace them. . . . Soundings 15-24 fathoms; south from us all is full of heavy ice; on the other hand to the north the water appears to be open.

20 July
. . . In the morning we were driven seven miles to the north and in the afternoon five miles to the south.

21 July (temp. max. 43°, min. 34°, med. 37°)
Today for the entire day the ship lay still and undisturbed, anchored to a great floe, except that we drift now north, now south, according to the flow and ebb of the tide. I took a walk with the captain on this floe; he ordered it to be

127

measured: length five miles and breadth two English miles. The thickness of the floe was measured in twenty-five places: the thinnest was 7, the thickest 64 feet. . . .

. . . .

23 *July (temp. max. 50°, min. 40°, med. 45°)*
Very warm weather; all through the night until this fore-noon we were held fast among the floes; about 11 o'clock we heard the roll of distant thunder which soon aroused us; but it was below, not above us – it was the ground-swell; and in its wake the great ice-fields were broken into smaller fragments. Soon the ice as far as we could see was in great commotion; pieces were thrust one upon another to a height of 34 feet, then collapsing like a house of cards. Suddenly the ship heaved up in the air and lay for a long time on her side. The gigantic turbulence of the ice-pack was diminished by the rising of a strong wind from the south-west which began to scatter the loose ice. The ship was refloated, sails set, and the farther north we sailed the more open water we found. . . .

24 *July (temp. max. 50°, min. 38°, med. 41°)*
Today weather fine, but no wind; to the north lies open water; but with no wind we can do nothing. We found our-selves near Point Armstrong, and through the telescope discovered on the snowless beach a considerable quantity of driftwood. Six sailors took me ashore in a boat, gathered wood, and found traces of Eskimos and their dwellings. The land here is of a heavy, clayey soil mixed with little round stones; other places, and especially the smaller hills, consist of coarse sand; here and there on the surface lie great rounded stones. There is no rock to be seen; we saw four rivers, but in one only was there any water, a sign that there was not much snow on land, or else little warm

128

weather. Near the beach I found many patches of level ground bare of snow and overgrown with grass and moss. White and yellow flowers stood proudly in full bloom. I gathered plants, flowers, and moss and found a few mussels, of which, however, the captain and the doctor – in the friendliest manner – robbed me, with the promise that at the first opportunity I might go ashore again and make a fresh collection. . . .

. . . .

August 1851 (temp. max. 38°, min. 36°, med. 37°)
Before the month now beginning reaches its end it will have answered our great question: whether this year we will free ourselves from this frightful sea-ice and get back to Europe, or whether to the bitterest disappointment of all we must spend another long dark winter in these polar regions. The prospect of reaching Europe this year is dim, but everyone hopes just the same. We are so beset with ice that the ship cannot move: daily from the masthead one searches for open water with a telescope; but the report is ever the same: no water, ice everywhere; and today it was added that light ice is being driven down on us by great island-like masses beyond, which shows that more and heavier ice is coming down upon us from the polar sea.

9 August (lat. 73° 3'; long. 116° 2'; temp. max. 45°, min. 40°, med. 42°)
We are in exactly the same situation as at the beginning of this week: on all sides thickly hemmed in with ice; in the distance water is visible, whence the ship could sail north, but we cannot reach it; yet we have drifted somewhat farther north in this week. . . . A fresh attempt was made to move the ice with powder and bring the ship to more open water, but all labour is in vain.

13 August (lat. 73° 13'; long. 115° 32'; temp. max. 48°, min. 37°, med. 37°)

The last four days we have been in a damp fog so thick that one can barely see one end of the ship from the other. The ice remains quiet. Today the captain told the crew that he hoped to be in Lancaster Sound with the ship by the 15th of September. . . .

14 August (temp. max. 38°, min. 33°, med. 35°)

For a long time we have had only light winds, and for the most part even calm. Today there arose a very strong wind from the north-east which dispersed the ice, so that immediately around the ship we had much free water. What the conditions are farther north or south we cannot, by reason of the thick fog, determine. The rudder was shipped today, and because the compass is also useless, due to the nearness of the Magnetic Pole, we set sail for the north, groping with the lead; we had soundings – 25, 17, 11, then 20 fathoms; the next sounding gave 4 fathoms, and before the ship could be put about she took the ground in 2 fathoms on a level bottom. But here again, as so often before, the Gracious Saviour took pity on us and brought our ship without any mishap or injury back into deep water.[1] At 11 p.m. we came into very heavy ice and were compelled to anchor the ship to a great floe.

15 August (temp. max. 36°, min. 31°, med. 33°)

We passed a quiet night – in the morning a thick fog which

[1]Here, as in other crises, Armstrong's phlegm is in amusing contrast to the excitability of Miertsching: "We immediately tacked," says he (p. 371), "but while the ship was in stays, she struck on a shoal, stirring up mud plentifully around us. The headsails were at once backed and filled – the ship hung in the balance for a moment – in the next she floated, and we had the pleasure of seeing her again standing off the shore through a thick fog towards the ice."

130

was partially dispelled about noon, but grew thick again in the afternoon. We saw Prince Albert Land close aboard; open water to the south, but to the north, as far could be seen from the masthead, an unending mass of very heavy polar ice. The ship was brought into deep water, and we sailed south with a strong north-east wind, suffering some fearful shocks on ice-pieces, on one of which the ship broke her spanker boom, 14 inches thick; finally we could go no farther and we came to anchor on a floe, and with it kept drifting to the south. The captain has given up hope of taking the ship through Prince of Wales Strait into Barrow Strait.

16 August (temp. max. 45°, min. 30°, med. 34°)

Early in the morning at 2 a.m. the fog disappeared completely and we found ourselves to the astonishment of all very near the shore of Baring's Land; since midday yesterday we had drifted south with the ice fourteen miles. To the north much open water was visible; so we set sail and steered north;[1] but at 8 a.m. we encountered fearful ice which stretched slantwise across the strait from shore to shore and entirely blocked our way. From the masthead no water was visible to the north, but frightful ice coming down from the polar sea. The captain made up his mind in a moment: he put the ship about, hoisted all the sail he dared, and away we went to the south, ploughing through so fast that the water foamed around the bowsprit and washed back over the foredeck. On this backward course we found Prince of Wales Strait wholly free from ice, passed the Princess Royal Islands at 4 p.m. and at 10 p.m. reached Nelson's Head. It is now the captain's intention to reach Melville Island by sailing around the west side of Baring's

[1]With revived hopes of breaking out to Barrow Strait.

Land.[1] In the clear weather we had a magnificent view of both shores, Prince Albert and Baring's Land. Both lands consist of gently sloping hills with a proportion also of high mountains rising 2,000 feet above the level of the sea. These lands remind me much of the hill-studded county about Herrnhut, only one must think away all the villages, woods and cultivation, and try to imagine a lifeless landscape covered with ice and snow; at best one finds a little moss and grass in low spots or on the south side of a hill. Rocks are few; the land consists of coarse brown gravel or sand.

17 August (lat. 71° 34'; long. 119° 54'; temp. max. 50°, min. 41°, med. 45°)

Throughout the night we had good wind and fine weather, and have put 180 miles behind us. Off Nelson's Head the ocean swell caused several cases of sea-sickness. We passed Cape Lambton without being hindered by ice; north-west [a little south of west] from us towards Cape Bathurst the sea was covered with heavy polar ice; we were sailing along the west coast of Baring's Land in a northeasterly direction at 6-8 knots.

18 August (lat. 71° 55'; long. 124° 56'; temp. med. 45°)

Fine clear weather and good wind; an open channel as far as we can see. After rounding Cape Lambton we set course

[1]And so sail through the Passage and circumnavigate the Americas after all — a questionable choice: the continental shore lay not far to the south, offering reasonable assurance of a safe exit by Bering Strait, and at the worst a safer refuge than the islands if the ship came to grief; on the other hand the extent of Banks (Baring's) Land was quite unknown, its northern shore likely to be infested with "the frightful polar pack"; as it proved, the venture failed and cost the crew many months of privation. McClure, then, showed insufficient regard for the men placed under his command, but deserves credit for daring and persistence; indulgence to is due to an officer who takes excessive risks for his country's honour as well as his own. Armstrong, ever ready to censure, seems cordially to endorse the captain's decision to try his fortune to the limit.

to the north-east along the coast of this newly discovered land. The coast running exactly north-east is like a wall. This wall, in places sheer, is from 60 to 100 feet high, and prohibits any attempt at landing; above is a flat snow-land backed by high mountains. The geological composition of this coast we had no opportunity of determining; probably it is lime or sandstone. More than once rivers combine to form a deep channel reaching to the sea, and form a fine, safe harbour. Water-fowl, especially white snow-geese, were seen in thousands along the shore. Two curving capes running out into the sea form the safest of harbours for a great fleet; the entrance, a quarter of a mile across, is 7 fathoms, and the harbour 12 fathoms deep. This harbour is named Captain Kellett's Harbour[1] in honour of the last person seen on passing through Bering Strait. On a cape was planted a barrel containing a bottle with notice of our visit.

19 *August (lat. 73° 55'; long. 123° 52'; temp. max. 50°, min. 43°, med. 47°)*

From Cape Lambton to Kellett's Harbour the coast, running in a north-easterly [north-westerly] direction, is a perpendicular wall from 40 to 100 feet in height; but from there on it becomes quite flat, so that when some two English miles from the shore we found bottom at 3½ fathoms. The weather is fine, the wind good, and before us lies open water, so we sailed for another whole day in a north-easterly direction along a very flat coast, passed an old river bed, small sandy islands, and the mouth of an apparently deep bay. We saw reindeer on land, seal in the water, and many snow-geese on the beach today. This afternoon three hours were spent in warping the ship off a sandbank with the capstan: she often touches on the sandy bottom.

[1]The *cape* was named Kellett: the harbour is the Sachs Harbour familiar to readers of Stefansson's *Friendly Arctic*.

20 *August (lat. 74° 29'; long. 122° 49'; temp. max. 50°, min. 36°, med. 44°)*

Throughout the night we sailed very slowly because of shoal water; we passed two small islands;[1] both were surrounded with thick ice. The farther east we came, the higher and bolder grew the coast, and the water also became deeper: from 7 fathoms we came suddenly into 60 fathoms quite close to the shore. On the left we had the frightful polar ice covering the sea with a solid mass, on the right an abrupt shoreline: the channel between grew ever narrower. About 4 o'clock we came to a high cape named Alfred where the ice lay so close, and between it and the rocky wall there was so little space, that the ship was towed through. For some time thereafter we sailed slowly along the shore and so close to it that in many places a sailor standing at the ship's rail hove the lead on to the dry beach. For two hours we sailed along this narrow canal where projecting angles of the heaped-up ice-masses often had to be blasted away before the ship could pass; then we came to a regular ice-labyrinth which brought the ship to a full stop. This seemed to be the end of the water and the beginning of eternal ice. Here is the true polar ice of which no one can form a conception without actually seeing it; to describe it one must write archives full, and then those who have seen only European ice in rivers, ponds, and the sea would find it unintelligible and beyond belief. Suffice it to say that the level, floating floes – with thousands of little pieces the size of a house between them – rise 8-10-12 feet above the water, and remember that for one part above the water there are seven beneath it. Here the labour of driving the ship forward came to an end; she was anchored to a great stranded floe in the hope of pressing on to the east when the next friendly land-wind pushed the ice back from the shore.

[1]Norway and Robilliard. Stefansson reached land about here after his journey over the ice of the Beaufort Sea.

134

The captain, Dr. Armstrong, and I landed and climbed a mountain 875 feet high from the summit of which we could view a sea buried in ice to the west, north, and east; we collected plants and moss, but the samples were very small and poor, and shot two ptarmigan. There were no rocks to be seen; the land was composed of brown earth, coarse sand, and a sort of pulverized stone. Broad, dry river-beds wind their way deeply into the land. We saw a great many little lakes – or large puddles – from this height.

.   .   .   .

22 *August (lat. 74° 27′; long. 122° 48′; temp. max. 36°, min. 32°, med. 34°)*
The weather is pleasant and bright, but here in the ice and so near to high land it is very cold. The great, very massive floes with which we are surrounded as far as the eye can reach seem to be pushing the ship slowly ashore; we are already 12 feet nearer to it than yesterday. Should this be our winter quarters, it will be for the ship, and for us too, probably our tomb. We found today two mountains which consist of trees in layers – trees 2½ feet in diameter. Those on top were partly or wholly petrified; those which lay somewhat deeper, buried in sand and clay, resembled lignite which I had seen in *Mirke bei Kleinwerke*; burnt in the stove, they gave a similar odour. A tree-trunk 9 feet long and 14 inches in diameter was brought to the ship as a specimen for the Botanical Museum. Fir cones and petrified oak were found. Sailors were detailed to bring this lignite to the ship for fuel.

23 *August (temp. max. 34°, min. 31°, med. 32°)*
Today there was a great fishing excursion; a half-hour from the ship are two small patches of open water; to keep the sailors employed the captain sent thirty-seven men with a

large net to fish; after five hours they returned, cold and wet, with four small fish. These fish were of a species quite unknown to us. Only in one pool were these little fish found; in the other was discovered a wholly unknown little round green fruit which seemed to grow in the water on the ocean floor. These fruits resemble very much the round seed-pods hanging from ripe potato-tops. Thousands of these were swept up in the net and brought to shore.[1] The smallest are like peas, the largest a good inch in diameter.

25 *August (lat. 74° 28'; long. 122° 32'; temp. max. 39°, min. 29°, med. 34°)*
Yesterday being Sunday, every man had leave to go ashore, but without fire-arms.[2] The captain and I measured two mountains with the barometer. The men went hunting inland, saw two musk-oxen, but had no means of capturing them. The captain, Dr. Armstrong, and I went four hours inland, shot two hares and nine ptarmigan, and arrived at the ship late at night. For the most part the land consists of gravel and earth of a baked brown; neither rock nor large stone are to be found. The valleys are scantily clothed with moss and stunted grass. Reindeer antlers and skulls with antlers firmly attached we found in abundance; small pieces of petrified wood one finds in every sandhill. Also in the river-beds one finds everywhere pieces of this wood, large and small.

26 *August (temp. max. 46°, min. 35°, med. 40°)*
The land is white; last night snow fell, six inches deep; early

[1] Armstrong, a competent scientist, was unimpressed by these. "Possessed of no particular interest beyond the fact of their being found there", says he. (p. 413)
[2] Not, we may suppose, as a part of Sabbath observance, since the officers were armed, but as a precaution against accidents so liable to occur if the whole crew were ashore lethally armed and eager for game.

this morning the ice was three-quarters of an inch thick. From the highest mountain, 900 feet, ice only and not a drop of water can be seen in the sea. The captain, Mr. Cresswell, and I were out hunting, and saw *nothing* living. In the afternoon fourteen men, hunters, went out; they came back at 11 p.m. with a bag of two ptarmigan; Mr. Kennedy had the misfortune through mishandling his gun to give himself a dangerous wound in the abdomen.[1]

28 August (temp. max. 31°, min. 23°, med. 26°)
Yesterday there was a strong west wind and very disagreeable snowy weather; no one went ashore. With the appearance of the new moon, when tides grow daily higher, one must be alert for movement in the ice. Today I was ashore with Dr. Armstrong, Sainsbury, Paine, and Wyniatt; we shot *one* ptarmigan, and found some apparently very ancient Eskimo ruins consisting of five huts, crumbled and overgrown with moss; around these ruins lay nineteen musk-ox skulls and many bones overgrown with moss.

29 August (temp. max. 29°, min. 25°, med. 26°)
Today the Brotherhood choir assembles for a feast of joy, but for me it was a day filled with anxiety and terror such as neither I nor anyone aboard has yet experienced. From 2 a.m. until 10 p.m. we stood, warmly clad and with our bundles ready on the deck, while the ship was tossed this way and that by the pitiless ice. Through the high spring tide and the very strong west wind the ice was put in motion with a violence that we had never before seen. The ship lay, now on her left side, now on her right; soon the piled-up masses of ice came tumbling down and threatened to dash

[1] The boatswain: he had put a charge of powder in his gun, and was resting his stomach on the muzzle while groping for a ball. The powder exploded, burning his clothing and scorching his stomach. The injury, however, was not "dangerous", but was a cause of mirth to his shipmates, even the sour Armstrong condescending to make a joke of it.

her to pieces; then she was heaved up and down and thrown on her side on the floe to which she was anchored. The ship's beams cracked; cabin walls and doors were sprung; about 7 o'clock it was at its worst, so that the captain himself acknowledged: "This is the end; the ship is breaking up; in five minutes she will be sunk!" In order that the ice might cast her ashore where she could still afford us food and shelter for the coming winter, the captain, giving up his ship, with a trembling voice gave orders to cut the five cables. Before this order could fully be carried out – in the most awful moment of our lives – the ice became silent and motionless. This memorable moment was almost too much for us; each man rested against the bulwarks of the listing ship, and, pale and trembling all over, stared at his comrade, who stared back at him; not a sound or a word could be heard, so that on the ship there reigned a death-like calm; many a sigh had been heaved in that moment of expectation and decision. The captain bade all men remain at their posts, and went to his cabin for a few minutes; the ice was, and remained at rest. Preparations were made to get the ship from the ice back into the water.

30 August (temp. max. 29°, min. 23°, med. 24°)
The prolonged danger and wakefulness have made all so slack at their work that the blasting away of the ice goes forward very slowly. The ice is perfectly still, and even so the mood on board is remarkably hushed: no one speaks any more than necessary; an unusually serious frame of mind is noticeable everywhere. Ah! would that such an impressive lesson and warning might bear much fruit among us. Today much blasting has been done, but the ship still lies high and dry upon the ice.

31 August (temp. max. 26°, min. 21°, med. 23°)
Today they succeeded in getting the ship from the ice back

into the water; only by blasting away the ice was this made possible. As soon as the ship was properly afloat the water she had taken in was pumped out, and the damage done to her repaired. The ice is everywhere motionless, but there is no water to carry us back out to sea. Since this occurrence I have had long and pleasant conversations with several of my ship-mates: the captain told me yesterday and again – openly – today that he has arrived at the genuine conviction that a Higher Power, an Almighty Providence, is watching over and shielding us, and that under this protection none of us will lose our lives, but all will safely reach our fatherland; of this he felt certain. . . .

1 September 1851 (temp. max. 27°, min. 24°, med. 25°)
The ice is without motion and is beginning to freeze into one solid mass; the land is decked in the white of new-fallen snow. The captain spoke to the assembled crew at some length today. He reminded them of the gracious protection granted the ship and with much kindness and the deepest sincerity admonished them to keep this miraculous deliverance in mind, and not to be despondent or lose heart at the outset of another winter season: it had been his wish to bring the ship into a safe winter harbour; no one would have expected that after only four days of open sailing water to be frozen in here as early as 20 August, etc. In conclusion he said that he would do his utmost to make life happy for every one of them. The very high hummocks near the ship have been blown up and a broader road levelled to the shore.

4 September (temp. max. 32°, min. 20°, med. 24°)
For the last three days heavy snow-storms. From today the sailors will be busy every day on land gathering stones and bringing them to the beach; early next year they will be brought on board as ballast. A hundred tons (at twenty

hundredweight) must be collected. Little birds, snow-buntings or *amanlikat* are often seen. A bird of prey (gyrfalcon) was shot today. The ice is continuing to freeze into a solid mass; the young ice is 4 inches thick. We are making our cabins ready for winter....

. . . .

8 *September (temp. max. 31°, min. 20°, med. 24°)*
The weather is becoming bitingly cold: the ice is freezing together more and more, so that one can hardly hope to break out with the next high tide. We go ashore daily to get game for our winter supply, but in these icy regions there is little or nothing to be found. The climate must have been milder here formerly, for everywhere one finds very old bones and skulls of wild animals, and the ruins of houses; tenting-places and caches are proof that this region was once populated. By what sort of people? That is difficult to answer; for the old ruins partly covered with moss and earth are too much decayed for anything accurate to be learned from them. Probably Eskimos dwelt here also, and were driven south by the ever-increasing severity of the climate.

10 *September (temp. max. 39°, min. 25°, med. 34°)*
Yesterday I was ashore with the captain, found a great stone knife, and shot – nothing! Returning to the beach we followed a fresh bear-track, and near the ship came upon a bear with two cubs; but before we got within range the men on the ship frightened them off. On the beach are fifty-seven tons of stone for ballast. The strong south-westerly gale blowing last night and today has put the ice in motion out to sea; from the 800-foot mountain near by one sees broad leads of open water out to sea. Near the shore the ice is quiet and immovably fixed, but, should the gale continue

and the high spring tide occur, we are not yet entirely out of danger. I walked up and down the beach with the captain and had a pleasant talk. Piers and Sainsbury shot a bear.

11 September (temp. max. 42°, min. 31°, med. 34°)
Yesterday evening, with everything quiet as usual, and pleased that another day was by, we went each one to bed, not suspecting that soon we would again be afloat. As winter routine had already been established, the watch consisted of only three men – the officer, a man on the lower deck, and a man on the upper deck. About 1 a.m. the ice, heaved up by the high tide, broke away from the shore and was driven by the gale, which still blew, out to sea, where the storm had put the sea-ice in motion and opened up long, broad stretches of water – there was room enough to sail. We were quickly out of bed and on deck; but what could we do? The whole mass in which our ship was frozen was drifting from land to sea and threatening the ship with destruction, nor was there the least hope of saving ourselves when so far from land. All the means at our disposal were employed to free the ship, but to no purpose; several hundredweight of powder were expended without success. Finally when the monstrous ice had withstood all the skill and strength of man we perceived again that a Higher Power was on our side: the ice split, threw the ship on its side – whereby five sailors were thrown from the ship on to the ice; the ship slid down slowly, stood upright in the water, and was *free*! As the rudder had been unshipped, she was brought by sail only through great pieces of ice near to land, where about 10 p.m. we anchored ourselves to a great floe which lay with one corner resting on the level beach. We were fifteen miles to the east of the place where the stone for ballast had been gathered, and as a lasting memorial of our visit to that place it will bear from now on the name of Ballast Beach.

12 September (temp. max. 38°, min. 30°, med. 33°)
The weather is pleasant, but very stormy. Ice set in motion by the current pressed hard against the ship. She lies thirty-five paces from the shore secured to a great floe with five 7-inch, two 9-inch, and one light cable, with eight anchors. A mass of ice which drove against the ship in the afternoon was blasted away with 180 pounds of powder. The thickness of this ice was 67 feet.

14 September (temp. max. 42°, min. 29°, med. 35°)
. . . Today the ship is more at rest; the ice itself is still. The captain and I climbed a mountain near by to obtain an extended view: to the east there was less ice along the coast, and a good south-west wind could drive us far in that direction. The vegetation on land is very scanty. We saw snow-owls, foxes, and crows, and very many mouse (lemming) holes.

15 September (temp. max. 30°, min. 14°, med. 23°)
Today we were left at rest all day; the ice was freezing together. Messrs. Court and Newton were sent to a cape nine miles distant to ascertain whether there is much ice inshore farther east. They returned in the evening with the report that beyond the cape the coast takes a south-easterly trend and is beset with heavy ice. The captain has long believed that this Baring's Land must be an island between which and Melville Island a broad channel leads into Barrow Strait; should this prove true we have discovered *two* Northwest Passages.

17 September (temp. max. 21°, min. 11°, med. 16°)
Weather bright and cold; the ice is freezing fast into a mass. Should this be our winter quarters, next spring – humanly speaking – will be the end of us and of the ship; for any considerable pressure will either crush her or drive

her up on the beach. From here also it is impossible to reach on foot the food-depots which we have left behind. Two polar bears were wounded but could not be pursued amongst the hummocks.

18 September (temp. max. 31°, min. 22°, med. 27°)
Last night it was very stormy, but the ice was quiet. At 7 a.m. it began to blow hard, and so lasted all day, in consequence of which the ice began to churn up, and we had the joy of seeing open water in the distance. All day long the ice around the ship was being blasted away, and by that, along with the strong wind, a way was opened. By evening the ship lay in open water securely moored to an ice-floe.

19 September (temp. max. 32°, min. 26°, med. 29°)
At 4 a.m. the ship was cast off from the floe and drove with the ice eastwards at two miles an hour between the solid pack and the shore. At 11 we came to more open water, saw two whales and began to sail at six knots along a coast beset with thousands of small icebergs. At 6 p.m. we were stopped by ice, and as there was no suitable berth near by where the ship could lie safely in the darkness of the night, we sailed back six miles to a huge grounded floe, which, however, instead of protecting us from the onset of the moving ice, nearly pushed the ship on to land, high and dry. A strong charge of powder luckily shattered this into several pieces; we put about and sailed forward again and found a small corner into which the ship was worked, and there we spent the night undisturbed by the heavy ice-pieces that lay around us.

20 September (temp. max. 30°, min. 25°, med. 27°)
The night passed by without mishap. The weather is foggy, and the wind very light; the ship is sailing slowly along the

143

coast at two knots. For some days the land has been veiled in fog, and today the ice-covered sea is obscured. The ship constantly takes hard knocks from the ice. Whither we are actually going, not one of us knows, except that it is in an easterly direction. The captain really is not well, sailing thus along a coast which is absolutely unknown, with the lead in his hand and with winter at the door, knowing of no place where we can safely pass the winter; but the Heavenly Pilot, Who has shown us so many miracles and has brought us so far, will continue to care for us and will provide a haven. In the evening we came to a promontory which rises perpendicularly to a height of 300 feet. This headland was named Crozier by the captain. We spent the night beneath this wall of rock.

21 September (temp. max. 34°, min. 27°, med. 31°)

Though surrounded by heavy ice, we passed a quiet night anchored to land-ice at the foot of the wall of rock. Early in the morning there was, as far as we could see for fog, an open channel eastwards along the shore, so that we could immediately sail a good stretch; but the captain said that we must have Divine Service before getting under way – and I for my part could have wished that this rite, however simple and natural, might have been omitted – but today Divine Service made a great impression, not lightly to be forgotten, on everyone. About 11 a.m. a passage was won for the ship by blasting; and until evening she was towed by four oared boats through loose ice. In the evening she found herself close inshore and was anchored securely to land-ice for the night.

22 September (temp. max. 37°, min. 25°, med. 32°)

After a peaceful night the ship was got clear of the ice at the first glimmer of daylight and under easy sail we steered

144

a course slowly along the coast again to the east, not knowing in the least what lay ahead. Before us we saw nothing but ice, but the ship kept in motion, frequently making a sluggish response to hard knocks. In the evening she was anchored close inshore, fifteen paces from the beach with the ice towering up around her. I went [ashore] and from the rock, a sandstone formation, gathered some interesting specimens.

23 September

Again a very peaceful night; about 3 a.m. the ship was towed from her icy night-haven in light ice, and after 4 o'clock, when it was growing grey with dawn, sail was set and we moved off slowly amid ice-pieces through which the poor ship must regularly bore her way. As daylight advanced, the captain himself went up to the masthead, but by reason of the thick fog could barely see half a mile. The wind was growing stronger, all sails were set and four men were stationed at the lead with orders to take a sounding every two minutes. In addition to the fog, there began in the forenoon a heavy snowfall which lasted until evening.

At the top of the foremast, as is usual in ice-navigation, a man was stationed named the ice-pilot, who from his lofty post determines the best course for the ship through the ice-pieces and communicates this to the officer of the watch on the deck through a long gutta percha trumpet; and the latter directs the ship accordingly. But today none of the men taking turns at this duty could offer any guidance: to repeated questions they invariably answered, "Ice everywhere!" So frequently the officer himself would go aloft to ascertain the truth of this "ice everywhere" – for the ship was going ahead at five to six knots; but he would find that it was actually so, for the ship was speeding ahead in a short stretch of water beyond which lay impenetrable ice as far as one could see. The captain confirmed this extraordinary phenomenon with his own eyes.

The steersman was given no fixed course, he held the ship so that the sails received the fullest impulse from the wind. The seamen had nothing to do: they walked back and forth on the deck, or formed groups discussing eagerly this amazing and inexplicable passage, in full expectation of seeing the ship next moment dashed against the appalling ice which hemmed her in. This period of long anxious inaction was interrupted by the roar of the ice-pilot, "Heavy ice ahead!" At the command of the officer of the watch the sailors flew each to his appointed post to take in sail. The captain rushed up to the crow's-nest and confirmed the order to take in sail with all possible speed; but before this, a task of two minutes, could be accomplished, the ice-pilot cried: "Hold on; the ice is splitting and opening a way for us." And actually, to the astonishment of all, it was so. Without the least obstruction the ship sailed into this narrow gorge, hemmed in on both sides by lofty walls of ice; on both sides the ice was so high that the ends of the ship's yards kept on knocking against it. After sailing for half an hour through this ice-canal which God Himself in His omnipotence had opened for us – as for the Children of Israel He had opened a way through the sea – we came into lighter ice and more open water. One overheard various exclamations and comments among the sailors on this strange miraculous passage. For instance, a great bearded sailor observed to a comrade who stood near him: "My old mother used to tell me that it stands on record in an old book that in ancient times many wonderful things occurred – men were suddenly turned to stone, the walls of a fortress fell down at the blast of a trumpet – and because then there were no ships, therefore thousands of people left France by a lane into which the waters divided themselves, and settled in England. But such marvels, said my old mother, happened only in very ancient times; since the age of Richard Coeur de Lion they have occurred no more; but the old woman does not imagine what I will tell her when I get home of what I have seen with my own good eyes." This unschooled but very brave seaman was born in Christian England, there baptised, and there grew up; yet what is the difference between this Christian and the honest friendly Eskimos dwelling in heathen ignorance on Prince Albert Land? After we had passed through this very heavy ice, which had parted to let us through, we went on under full sail through fog and thick, falling snow along the shore, not knowing how or whither, except that we knew that before us to the east lay the land sighted by Captain Parry from Melville Island and by him named Banks Land, and felt sure that it must be a part of the Baring's Land discovered by ourselves. The sea before us and on all sides covered with ice was still opening up ahead. Finally the ice-pilot, quitting his post aloft without leave, apologized to the officer of the watch and said that he could no longer endure to be aloft: all was ice ahead and not a spoonful of water to be seen, and yet the ship was speeding on without hindrance, as could be plainly observed from the land features which we were leaving behind us; he could not bring himself to ascend again to his post aloft. In addition to fog and snow it was beginning to grow dark, and the captain gave orders to take in sail and anchor for the night as soon as we found a suitable large floe. About 6.30, as we sat drinking tea, the ship, to the surprise of all,[1] struck on a sandbank. The captain took charge, and everyone laboured with all his might to get the ship afloat and bring her into deep water before the heavy ice, ever edging nearer, pushed her right ashore or crushed her; for if the ship was wrecked here we must perish with her. To lighten the ship, heavy articles were brought up and loaded into

[1]"Surprise", because the leadsman had sounded in 15 fathoms a minute before.

boats; but all toil, sweat, and skill seemed wasted: the ship remained fast in the sand; instead of 16 feet there was a depth of 5 feet only under her bow. When the captain perceived that all exertion was in vain and that the men, exhausted and drenched to the skin, could endure no more, he bade them take a period of rest. As I was going down the companion ladder the captain told me to come and drink a cup of tea with him as soon as I had changed my clothes. He met me as I entered, with an open book in his hand, crying: "See how Holy Writ mocks me; in this crisis and extremity, when all our lives are trembling in the balance, I opened the Bible to find words of comfort, and thus it answers me in Psalm 34, verses 3 and 4 – in flat contradiction to our present situation." I read the two verses aloud,[1] at which he said: "I thank God that my mind and understanding are unclouded, and I well know what our situation is." We discussed these verses, and I told him that it had also happened thus to me, that I could not find the answers of Scripture appropriate, but in the passage of time they had been confirmed. As we were drinking our first cup of tea there came a mighty shock which made the whole ship quiver. The captain was up on deck like lightning; I followed, and as I came on deck felt the vessel roll: she was afloat in deep water; a flat piece of ice impelled by the current had struck the forward part of the ship violently and pushed her off the shoal into deep water.[2] One can neither describe nor conceive how this first joyous moment affected everyone, especially the captain and me.

[1]"O magnify the Lord with me and let us exalt His name together. I sought the Lord and He heard me and delivered me from all my fears."

[2]Armstrong more plausibly asserts that the ice struck the ship on her broadside and swung her clear. Miertsching often appears casual and imprecise in his treatment of details. Had McClure had the good luck to miss the sandspit he might have overshot Mercy Bay in the darkness and gone on, perhaps to disaster, but not improbably to the supreme achievement of navigating the Northwest Passage under sail only.

> All glory to the Sovereign God and Father of compassion,
> To God, our help and sure abode, Whose gracious visitation
> Renews His Blessings every day,
> And takes our griefs and fears away:
> > Give to our God the glory.

With the singing of these verses I awoke the captain this morning at 7 a.m. after he had slept two hours. After all cargo had been taken in from the boats and again stored in the ship, and a fair degree of order had been restored, it was the captain's intention to sail from here through the ice to Melville Island and there winter in the very bay where Captain Parry had wintered thirty years ago. But as soon as it was daylight and the fog had been driven off by a strong west wind, he perceived the impossibility of advancing even a mile through the ice that was driving against us. In the clear light he now saw for the first time that we were in a bay near the west end of Banks Land;[1] to the north we had a clear view of Melville Island. As there was no possibility of going farther by any means, the ship was anchored in a cove of this bay, where she lay in perfect security, sheltered by the great sandbank from the drifting pack outside.[2] The entire crew, except for a watch of two

[1] An inexactitude: McClure had arrived at about the mid point of the Banks Land north shore, and must have known it, as he had taken observations at Point Russell in the previous autumn.

[2] Providing a dismal anti-climax to an adventurous and (considering the circumstances) an amazingly successful voyage; the men of the *Investigator* were now condemned to nearly two years of isolation and semi-starvation. Armstrong, an amateur but shrewd observer, wholly denies the need for berthing the ship in Mercy Bay. He contradicts Miertsching's statement that impassable ice lay close to the ship, informs us that a few days later Mr. Court found open water on the other side of Point Back, and states — with the support, he says, of other officers of the ship — that she might have reached Winter Harbour or some berth farther to the east that autumn. Sherard Osborn in his *Discovery of the North-West Passage*, based on McClure's journal, is far more cautious than Miertsching in his appreciation of the

men, were told to sleep until further orders. Here might we
sing with truth:

> The cruel ice came floating on, and doused beneath our lee;
> 'Twas ice around, behind, before, — and there is no more sea.
> The night is neither bright nor short, the singing breeze is cold;
> But ice is not as strong as hope: each seaman's heart is bold.

25 September (temp. max. 24°, min. 21°, med. 22°)
The weather bright, clear, and calm. After a rest of twelve
hours and a sound sleep, the whole crew, again prompt and
cheery, went briskly about their work; but not to get
under sail again, for the ship is already so frozen in that
the captain and I walked to land and back over the young
ice. The captain assembled the crew on deck, thanked them
for their good conduct and prompt discharge of duty in a
time of difficulty and danger, encouraged them to be bright
and active, and stated that here would be our winter quarters. He named the great sandbank, or rather the long
sandy cape, Point Providence, and the bay in which we
are to winter, the Bay of God's Mercy, in grateful acknowl-
edgement of the Lord's wonderful help.[1] The ship and the

---

situation: the ice, he says, lay too close to Point Back (on the opposite side of
the bay) to afford a passage to the east. But this is pure rationalization: it
was impossible for McClure at Point Providence to judge accurately the
conditions at Point Back, seven miles away. But though Armstrong was probably right in his facts, one need not endorse the censure he passes on his
captain. For weeks McClure had hoped for nothing better than a secure
wintering-place, and he seized the first that offered, probably without even
considering the alternative; and the more readily because officers and men
must have been in a frightful state of physical and nervous exhaustion. This
was one occasion when McClure put the well-being of his men before his
own honour and reputation; and it is one of the ironies of life that had he
not done so he might have completed an epoch-making voyage and spared his
men many months of misery and privation.

[1]"Some amongst us not inappropriately said, it ought to have been so called,
from the fact that it would have been *a mercy had we never entered it.*"
(Armstrong, note to p. 465)
    The cape opposite Point Providence, which marked the eastern limit of the
bay, was named Point Back, after Sir George Back under whose command
McClure had made his first voyage in the ice in 1836-7.

boats have all been washed and cleaned, inside and out; and directions given to fit the ship as our winter residence. In the afternoon I accompanied the captain up a mountain from which we had a clear view of Banks Land and Melville Island. The sea was covered with ice as far as the eye could reach.

[By the autumn of 1851 all ships engaged in the search for Franklin had withdrawn from the Arctic except the *Investigator* and the *Enterprise*. Collinson had passed through Bering Strait in the summer, had followed the continental shore, and, like McClure, had been steered by the ice into and up Prince of Wales Strait. Failing to break out into Viscount Melville Sound, he also attempted to circumnavigate Banks Land, but, more prudent than McClure, sheered off from the heavy ice on its western shore and wintered on the coast of Prince Albert (Victoria) Island at the lower end of Prince of Wales Strait.

Collinson's story may be finished here. In the summer of 1852 he took his ship through Dolphin and Union Strait and he passed the next winter at Cambridge Bay. In the spring of 1853 he searched the west side of Victoria Strait and came very close to the scene of the Franklin disaster. He spent three whole years in the Arctic (1851-4), kept scurvy at bay throughout by fishing with great success, and brought ship and crew safely home after a cruise of over five years. He quarrelled with his officers more bitterly and persistently than McClure but kept up the morale of the seamen with amazing success. Noel Wright (*Quest for Franklin*, pp. 201-3) sketches his character in a lively and entertaining manner. Posthumously, Collinson was highly honoured by Amundsen's testimony that he was perhaps the ablest navigator Great Britain ever sent into the Arctic.]

CHAPTER SIX

26 September 1851 (temp. max. 20°, min. 15°, med. 18°)
Already the ship is frozen immovably. Today, since the weather was fine, the sails were dried, rolled up, and laid away – to serve next year, if the Lord so wills it, on our voyage back to Europe. Many sea-fowl were seen flying south.

30 September (temp. max. 8°, min. 1°, med. 5°)
In the last few days we have had strong winds and much snow. The ice is already 6 inches thick. The ship is now completely adjusted to winter routine: the upper masts have been taken down, and the housing spread over the ship. The ice is quite smooth around the ship; the beach is 400 paces away, and the nearest iceberg, whither a sledge goes twice daily to fetch fresh ice for cooking and drinking, is 600 paces distant. The country hereabouts consists of high mountains separated by broad, flat-bottomed valleys, covered in places by moss. Rocks (limestone and clay-slate) are found in some places; for the rest, the soil is a sort of baked clay – this clay and limestone is common hereabouts – and small deep gorges cut across the land in every direction. Many of the deep, narrow valleys are filled with everlasting snow; countless skulls with the horns of

musk-oxen are found lying there; also a few antlers of reindeer. The Bay of Mercy is nine miles long and four miles across; the greatest depth is 26 fathoms. From Ballast Beach to here the coast is lofty and extremely dangerous, because deep water comes up to the very shoreline, and heavy ice can drive in without being grounded. . . . Today the ship's inventory was taken.

1 October 1851 (temp. max. 8°, min. –4°, med. 4°)
The weather is bright but bitingly cold. The ship has been dried out with iron stoves and red-hot cannon-balls; winter routine is in full swing. The result of the inventory has been that for the next two months we shall no longer receive the full seaman's ration, but two-thirds only; and should examination of supplies show that more of them have been spoilt through damp – as is suspected – our future portion will be even smaller. A great source of comfort and well-being is that the ice near the ship is so smooth and flat, and also the land is near, so that one may shorten the long and weary hours by walking. I was shoemaker today, and re-soled my own and the captain's boots.

7 October (temp. max. 21°, min. 13°, med. 14°)
The weather is changeable: snow falls a good deal. Today Mr. Court came back with six men and a sledge from a five-day journey; he had been sent to look for the cairn which Mr. Cresswell and his men had set up in the late spring with a record stating that they had come so far from Prince of Wales Strait, and because of sickness could press no farther west. Mr. Court did not find this cairn and record because there had been a landslide on the part of the beach where it stood.[1] . . .

[1] It may be significant that Miertsching, who was much attached to the captain and no friend of Armstrong's, omits to mention that immediately beyond Point Back (only eight miles from the ship) Court found open water extending east as far as he could see, a confirmation of the surgeon's assertion, previously noted.

11 October (temp. max. 14°, min. 5°, med. 9°)

The weather has been for the most part raw and windy; at times, snow. Messrs. Haswell and Piers and I went to a high cliff six miles from the ship, which had not yet been visited; there we saw twenty or thirty white hares and shot three. Sailors had seen a number of reindeer more than once on land; the next day I went with the captain on a hunt with twelve men; after three hours of circling around we came on their tracks and soon after caught sight of a herd of at least thirty reindeer, old and young; but these were so wild that we shot only one deer of 160 pounds. Four officers were at the Hares' Cliff, and brought back three hares. Mr. Court with seven men was sent out on a week's hunting journey. Mr. Cresswell with six men was also sent on a reindeer hunt. I was at the mountain today, and shot two hares. The wolves howl all night.

18 October (temp. max. 9°, min. −21°, med. −4°)

Very unpleasant weather we have had for the past week — much snow, strong east wind, and at times a raw fog. Mr. Court came back with his hunters bringing six hares and a deer, 110 pounds in weight. In his place Mr. Wyniatt went out for a week. Mr. Cresswell's party came back with two hares and three deer. Mr. Piers went out with seven men, and Sergeant Woon with six men and a tent for a week's hunting. I spent the whole day with the captain away from the ship at the mountain; we shot a few hares and ptarmigan; we saw a single reindeer more than once, but the wolves who followed us scared it away. Today I went to the mountain with Dr. Armstrong; I shot a deer, my first – 96 pounds.

25 October (temp. max. 7°, min. −18°, med. −3°)

The weather was so bitterly cold that all the hunting-parties came back, bringing their tents with them. Mr.

Wyniatt brought three reindeer, 322 pounds. Mr. Piers and Woon brought in twenty-four hares and twelve ptarmigan. Four men on land lost their way in the fog, and finally got back to the ship with some of their limbs totally frozen. This week the captain and I shot five hares and two ptarmigan.

31 October (temp. max. −5°, min. −22°, med. −12°)
Because of the weather, which has been cold, foggy, and snowy, it has been impossible to go hunting. The 26th was a day of festivity for all hands: the captain authorized extra rations and grog to celebrate the day on which, a year ago, the Northwest Passage had been discovered. . . .

I was ashore with Mr. Haswell today; we pursued six wolves for five hours without getting a shot at them; I shot a hare. . . .

7 November 1851 (temp. max. 8°, min. −18°, med. −8°)
The weather is consistently most disagreeable; for the most part so bad that one cannot leave the ship, and the ice necessary for cooking and drinking is obtained with difficulty. Every man tries to make himself comfortable for the winter; tailors and cobblers are here in abundance, for each man must repair his own shoes and clothing. Today all received a blanket for the winter as a gift from the captain. Yesterday the sun shone for three minutes, and so made his last appearance for the year. . . .

. . . .

22 November
. . . Throughout the ship, as in the cabins, everything is moist and damp: continuous dripping from the deck, and the beds damp through. Ah! could I only sleep one night in a dry, warm bed. I made the captain a warm pair of bed-shoes. . . .

29 November (temp. max. −24°, min. −39°, med. −32°)

In the last days of this month the weather has been some-what better than previously; although a cold, cutting wind whines continuously, yet the sky is clear; daylight is at an end, and we see stars continuously. The Northern Lights are too feeble to spread brightness, and only when there is a full moon can we enjoy a bright light by night and by day. About a week ago, day and night, many meteors were seen. This winter we have the advantage of smooth, level ice around the ship, and the land is quite near, yet no such games have been arranged as in the previous year; the order is the same; here too the crew must daily spend five or six hours off the ship,[1] and employ themselves as they please, but, as it seems, the two-thirds ration is the cause of their apathy. Of hunting there is no thought, as day and night it is too dark to pursue game or to detect traces of their foot-prints in the snow; therefore one sees the men walking to and fro on the ice in small groups, where they earnestly discuss the past and the future; at the first stroke of the bell at 11.30 a.m. or 4 p.m. they come on board stiff and shivering with cold. . . .

6 December 1851 (temp. max. −40°, min. −44°, med. −43°)

. . . The captain made it known that as a great amount of provisions must be discarded as spoiled and injurious to health, utmost economy must be practised, and he had decided gradually to reduce the two-thirds daily ration to one-half, which admittedly small portion would be main-tained only for those months when the ship was frozen in, and no work, heavy or light, was demanded of the men, and as soon as the ship was under sail, or any strenuous effort required, the full daily ration of food would be restored.

[1]Collinson provided a skittle alley and a billard-table under the housing on the upper deck, giving entertainment not only to the players but to num-erous spectators.

For the last three days we have had frightful wind and heavy snowfall; on one side of the ship is a snowdrift 11–15 feet high and 165 feet long, which with its weight has so pressed down the ice that salt water is oozing through the rents; the snow wall around the ship is completely flattened. . . .

13 December

. . . The previous winter we received weekly three tallow candles per man, and this winter we receive three for fourteen days; with the light neither of sun nor of day one must exist for fourteen days with eighteen hours of light; these are truly dark and gloomy times. Near by the wolves make themselves heard almost daily; their howling makes this already rigid and lifeless region even more melancholy. . . .

27 December (temp. max. −24°, min. −32°, med. −28°)

We have once more celebrated a joyous Christmas; but what sort of joy prevails here? Not such as a good Christian could share in; if it is observed in England as it is here and on other English ships, one should call it a festival of gluttony and wine-bibbing. . . . The captain himself took part in the sports of his boisterous crew. . . .

.   .   .   .

1 January 1852 (temp. max. −48°, min. −51°, med. −50°)

No Divine Service was held today, and because of the stormy weather the sailors were permitted to stay on board and take a holiday. This morning after mustering the crew the captain spoke to them, congratulating them all on the New Year; he thanked them for their good conduct hitherto, encouraged them to be of good and cheerful heart, and promised them extra rations and grog. We invited the captain for lunch, and everyone was glad when it was over on account of the disagreeable relations between the captain and the doctor: yesterday the handle came off the jug; for the deceitfulness of the doctor which had long imposed on the captain was brought to light and openly revealed;[1] and today at muster there was also bitter contention between the captain and the clerk-in-charge [Paine]. These disagreeable relationships aggravate the wretchedness of our life on board. . . .

31 January (temp. max. −5°, min. −9°, med. −7°)
Pleasant weather have we had all week, and also the sky is growing brighter in daytime. The hunt has been resumed with vigour; two reindeer have been shot. The daily ration seems to grow smaller and smaller; the men are complaining of hunger. Three sailors have been severely punished for stealing and devouring the dog's food. . . .[2]

4 February 1852 (temp. max. −21°, min. −35°, med. −28°)
With the continuously bright and cloudless sky we have an hour of daylight which grows daily in brightness and duration. Each one insists that in a few days he will be the first to see the beams of the returning sun. We hunt daily when the wind is not too cold and strong. Last week two

[1]This is the only instance where Miertsching takes sides and betrays a personal dislike. The quarrel may have related to the reduced ration to which the surgeon was opposed, though on grounds of prudence McClure could make out a good case. If Armstrong's "Falschheit" lay in suppressing for two years his antipathy to the captain, he made handsome amends later in his *Personal Narrative*. One wishes that McClure had not fallen out with Paine in the presence of the crew. The officer administering a reduced ration had a cruelly difficult task.

[2]The flogging of three half-starved men for taking the portion of Mongo, the ship's mascot, seems revolting; but McClure dared not, in this crisis, overlook a breach of regulations, whatever the circumstances. By this apparent ruthlessness he was spared the necessity to which the American arctic traveller, Greely, was reduced, some years later, of ordering his sergeants to shoot a thieving comrade in cold blood.

reindeer were shot. A number of hunters set out this morning, and in the afternoon at dusk all came back without having shot anything, except for Sergeant Woon and the Negro, Anderson, who did not appear at the appointed time. As these two did not return at 6 p.m., and the heavy fog that comes every evening was beginning to descend, a cannon was fired every five minutes and rockets were let off. At 8 p.m. three parties, each consisting of an officer and six men, set out in different directions to search for the missing men. At 1 a.m. the parties came back bringing the two lost hunters; both had frozen limbs and faces, and poor Anderson had in particular suffered terribly. He was carried in as stiff as a board and without the least sign of life; after three-quarters of an hour he gave signs of animation, yet the doctor was still doubtful of his recovery. Sergeant Woon tried to explain how they lost their way, but so unintelligibly and incoherently that no one could understand him;[1] not only their limbs and their faces had suffered, but their minds had been terribly affected by the bitter cold. . . .

27 *February (temp. max. −25°, min. −33°, med. −26°)*
. . . For a week we have had the finest weather, and the glorious sun has created an entirely new life in and around the ship. Our ship has been literally disinterred: the drift had so covered it that only the masts were visible above the level snow. The hunters go out daily; the only game is provided by stray reindeer: three have been shot in these days. Health aboard has been very good this month; once each week reindeer flesh has been issued instead of salt meat. One cannot satisfy oneself with the miserably small ration, and hunger is growing painful. The few white foxes

[1]The story of the lost men, when it *was* made known, was one of singular heroism and self-sacrifice on the part of the sergeant of marines (Armstrong, pp. 499-503). It is worth noting that Anderson, to Miertsching wholly "Gottvergessenen", is praised by Armstrong as "very good" and "well-conducted".

and lemmings that are caught or shot on land, and are not assigned to the ship as game, are devoured with the greatest relish. . . .

1 March 1852 (temp. max. −35°, min. −52°, med. −46°)
The inactive life aboard is going smoothly on its appointed way; in fine weather men go hunting every day – the only occupation we have for the daytime – and in the evening they talk of their adventures to pass away the time; many who have never before fired a gun are here, to judge from the stories they tell, the greatest of heroes. Our worthy captain does his utmost to revive the drooping spirits of the men, hushing with kindly words the complaints of those who are suffering from the small ration, comforting and cheering them with hopeful promises for the future. I go hunting with the captain daily, but until now we have not been particularly lucky. Two sailors, Brown and Gibbs, went out hunting yesterday, but failed to return in the evening. Three parties from the ship searched all night without finding them, and next morning other parties went out, but these also came back in the afternoon without having seen a trace of them. The captain now resolved to send out the entire crew at one time and to search in every direction, but before this was done we saw them in the distance, staggering in drunken fashion across the level ice. They were brought aboard by sledge, but the power of speech and mind were too far gone for them to give any account of themselves. Today one of them related that they had lost their way on land, and had not slept since leaving the ship, but had slowly wandered about; a hare which they had shot had been devoured raw.

31 March (temp. max. 2°, min. −24°, med. −8°)
The weather has been most pleasant for the whole of the past month, and there had been little wind; but every day,

especially towards evening, there has been a very thick fog. Because there is no employment for the men on board ship they all go over the mountain to hunt, in consequence of which the few reindeer we see are frightened and made shy by unskilled sportsmen, and seldom wounded, whereby the more experienced hunters are bitterly provoked. Nine small reindeer have been shot this month, three of which were eaten by wolves while the hunter was fetching a sledge from the ship. The housing which all winter has covered the ship like a great tent was removed today, and snow two feet thick was taken away, so that now, instead of lamplight, we shall have a few hours of daylight.

The school, held all winter for the sailors, but very poorly attended, was closed today. When one tramps around all day on mountains, snow, and ice, with an empty stomach, he feels exhausted in the evening and has not the least desire to learn. Far rather would he, in a circle of intimate friends, share and discuss the hunting events of the day with a pipe of tobacco in his mouth. So, for instance, one man reports that he had shot three legs off a hare, but after a pursuit lasting two hours the hare made its escape; another with a well-aimed charge of small-shot took all the fur off one side of a hare, but it got away and is now travelling around half naked; such interesting narratives do much to shorten the long evenings. The doctor has found that everyone is losing weight owing to short rations.

7 *April 1852*
. . . Mr. Kennedy wounded a reindeer yesterday, but could no longer follow it; early today I accompanied him to find this animal; by following its tracks we finally came upon seven wolves who had devoured every remnant of the animal and left us only the bones. A number of sailors have become snow-blind: a more emphatic order from the captain: "wear dark-coloured glasses."

11 April (temp. max. 8°, min. −6°, med. 2°)

... The captain has long been resolved to make a journey over the ice on foot to Winter Harbour on Melville Island where Captain Parry once wintered with his two ships *Hecla* and *Griper*. The captain, Mr. Court, and six sailors made ready for the journey; food, tent, and sleeping-bags were stowed on a sledge; and at 4 p.m. the captain after addressing the crew in farewell left with his party, carrying rations for thirty-two days, in order to make sure that here is a second very broad Northwest Passage; which unhappily, like the first, is quite useless for shipping, and its discovery is worthless and will so remain as long as this sea of ice is here.

30 April (temp. max. 3°, min. −18°, med. −4°)

In the last half of the month the weather has been consistently foggy; often the returning hunters must be shown the whereabouts of the ship by the discharge of cannon and rockets. This month I have twice experienced what a man's emotions are when lost in these regions of snow. Had not the Angel of the Lord guided me in wondrous fashion to the neighbourhood of the ship, where by repeated firing of my gun I drew the attention of the crew, I would have been lost in this land of ice. Today Mr. Wyniatt came back from the hunt quite exhausted; he had lost his way and been absent twenty-nine hours from the ship; he had shot five hares, one of which he had eaten raw in his wandering.

The reindeer and hares seem this month to be migrating from west to east. As now the sailors are busy on board, only the best shots are sent out to hunt — those who, instead of frightening or wounding, kill. So fresh meat comes daily to the ship; in a short period thirteen have been shot....

9 May 1852 (temp. max. 10°, min. −25°, med. −8°)

This afternoon the captain returned to the ship with his

party in the best of condition. The outward journey lasted sixteen days owing to bad weather, the return journey eleven days.

The captain had hoped to find a ship from England, or at least a depot of provisions, but neither was to be found. We had heard in the Sandwich Islands that a ship was to be sent there,[1] and held it as certain that a ship or at least a good depot would be there; indeed many bets were laid; some that ships would be there, others betting what actually happened. All our expectations of news from there have ended in utter, bitter disappointment. The captain himself said that when, after long search, he had convinced himself that neither the one nor the other was there, he had wept like a little child: the dismal plight of our ship stood plainly revealed.[2] So our state of complete ignorance of the rest of the world from which we were separated was unaltered. The captain found a written record in a metal cylinder planted on the famous sandstone described in Captain Parry's *Journey*. This record stated that in 1850 seven English and two American ships had sailed in through Lancaster Sound, and Captain Austin with his four ships—*Resolute, Assistance, Intrepid,* and *Pioneer*—had been frozen in at Griffiths Island. In the spring of 1851 Lieutenant McClintock had been sent with six men, sledge, tent, and supplies for seven men for eighty days from the ship *Resolute*[3] to Melville Island; and this party had reached Winter Harbour and left this record. Whether these ships have gone back to England or, just as we, have been fast frozen somewhere, is naturally unknown to us; we only know that not one of them reached Melville Island.

[1] Captain Austin's squadron, which had tried to reach Melville Island, but had been stopped by ice.
[2] By now McClure realized that his ship was trapped in a sheltered backwater, where the ice did not necessarily break up every summer.
[3] The *Resolute* was Austin's ship; McClintock was first lieutenant of the *Assistance*.

We are now as before left to our own resources, and all hope of help from the east has faded away.[1] I am grieved for our sorely tried captain: he must force himself to wear a cheerful look. . . .

31 *May (temp. max. 26°, min. 12°, med. 20°)*
These last days have been very snowy; so much fell that the land was covered as in the depth of winter. Today we saw three seagulls flying by. One cannot often go hunting in the bad weather and intermittent fog, and to send hunting-tents ashore in this damp weather is equally out of the question, for it is most damaging to the health to lie in a damp tent without the means of drying wet clothing. The health of the crew is unhappily not as good as formerly: unhealthy weather, short rations, and gloomy prospects for the future are the principal causes. . . . Most of the reindeer shot in these months are with young and have little flesh. . . . In the month of June these deer migrate, presumably inland, and come back at the beginning of winter with calves not unlike young goats. . . . Many sign-posts have been set up on land to point out to hunters lost in the fog the direction in which the ship lies. . . . The ice was measured at 7 feet, 1 inch.

6 *June 1852 (temp. max. 28°, min. 11°, med. 20°)*
The weather is very agreeable these days; the warm sun is melting the new-fallen snow from the sand-hills. In daytime the glare from the snow is so strong that dark glasses are insufficient protection for the eyes; fourteen men have become snow-blind, and incapable of duty for at least a week; hence an order from the captain that hunting should

[1]McClure's error in not sending a party to Winter Harbour from Prince of Wales Strait in the spring of 1851 in order to leave a record — which Mc-Clintock would have picked up — was now evident. The notice McClure did now plant at Winter Harbour — discovered that autumn by Lieutenant Mecham of the *Resolute* — was to be the means of his ultimate preservation.

be done not by day but at night only, when the rays of the sun are not so strong.

16 *June*

... We hunt every night, but bring always less and less home. The reindeer have all disappeared, and the few hares are so shy that the hunters cannot get within range. ...

22 *June (temp. max. 35°, min. 29°, med. 32°)*

The weather is very warm, but eternal thick fog covers the land. Hunting has been forbidden, partly because of the scarcity of game, and partly because of the fog. The land is beginning to lose its white covering: the little sand-hills are free of snow. Water-fowl are flying by from west to east. As yet no vegetation has appeared on land. ... Our stock of provisions will last to August 1853 on the present half ration. ...

30 *June*

... As yet there is little sign of the approaching summer; only the snow-free sand-hills bid us hope that soon we shall be freed from this repulsive winter prison. ...

3 *July 1852 (temp. max. 37°, min. 33°, med. 34°)*

On the shores of the polar sea, wherever we have hitherto had opportunity to observe, we have found ruins or huts, caches, and circles of stone, as the Eskimos are accustomed to lay them; for when they set up a tent they weight down the borders with stones. These are undeniable proofs that these coasts were once inhabited. Even here at the west end of Banks Land in the 75th degree of latitude, one finds many such remains. With the captain I visited a small island where we found houses built of stone; the inner measurements were 8 feet by 5. The roof, made of whalebones, had fallen in; near by also were these stones, laid in a circle, with two circular receptacles of stone, which probably served to protect food from foxes and wolves. Also on the mountains of the mainland one finds traces of a one-time population; most of all one lights upon cones put together with stone which often serve as signs and pointers to the hunter who has lost his way. Water-fowl, especially snow-geese and a species of duck, fly by in great numbers, but few find their way to our kitchen.

9 July (temp. max. 42°, min. 31°, med. 33°)

In these days we have had the pleasantest summer weather. As soon as a patch of land is bare of snow the little white and yellow flowers are in bloom even before the leaves develop. I have up till now gathered and dried 3,785 specimens of plants, grasses and moss from various lands, and this month I will reap a good harvest. Last night Sergeant Woon went to the mountain to hunt and shoot foxes. These creatures are not required to be turned into the common stock. Unexpectedly he encountered two musk-oxen, and had only three rounds of ball with him; with the first he only wounded an ox, and so came into great danger, and was compelled to shoot one of the wounded, blindly charging oxen with the screw of his ramrod, and with the iron ramrod itself, and both beasts became his prey. This splendid news caused great joy on the ship; when cut up the two animals weighed 647 pounds, and with the head and hair 1,252 pounds.

17 July (temp. max. 36°, min. 32°, med. 33°)

Just as in Germany showers often occur in summer, here too there are storms almost daily, but of snow, not rain; the winter snow has now disappeared from the hills and from the flat land at higher levels; the new-fallen snow vanishes almost as quickly as it falls, and this makes the

166

clayey ground so soft, and causes so much water, that at every step one sinks in two or three inches, and on many snowless stretches it is quite impossible to walk; for the snow-water cannot sink into the frozen ground; and one little stream flowing over the ground enlivens this silent and barren Nature in the most charming way with the chatter of a little waterfall. . . . Along the shore the ice has been broken away by the flow and ebb of the tide, so that at high water one cannot reach land without a boat; the ice seawards in the bay is still as it was in the depth of winter. Today we saw the first seal in the Bay of Mercy; it lay on the ice and disappeared through its breathing-hole in the ice. A number of snow-geese and ducks have been shot in these days. Mr. Court and two sailors broke through the ice close to the shore and lost their three guns.

22 *July (temp. max. 46°, min. 32°, med. 38°)*
Today two great Northern Divers were shot; one weighed 13, the other 15 pounds. Hunting on land seems to be over: there is no game to be seen, and the water-fowl are so shy that one seldom has the luck to shoot any. Today I caught fourteen beautiful bright butterflies on land.

31 *July (temp. max. 38°, min. 31°, med. 34°)*
Today Mr. Piers and I shot two seals, and as the seal is not rated as game, and therefore is not turned in to the clerk-in-charge, we invited the captain to indulge us in our personal tastes; this was granted, and we had at our officers' table a number of really good meals; at least we tasted them with a tremendous appetite. The weather this summer is consistently bad and very foggy; in the cold, dark winter months we had a cloudless sky all the time; now in summer we have for the most part impenetrable clouds over us instead of the sun; also by day a thick mist rises from the land. We cannot yet expect the break-up of the

167

ice, but we live in lively hope of witnessing the ice-revolution that an ordinary seaman sings about in these words:

> Beneath the threatening ground-swells rise,
> And undulating wave[s] the sea of ice;
> Then burst its barriers, that disrupted roar
> Battery on battery — on every side
> Yawn the deep gulfs, the plain in chasms divide;
> Gathers the storm and rises now the wind,
> The icy masses, dashed, disrupted, grind.
> In horrid crash on every side are seen
> The bellowing waves that foam and dash between.

I am on land every night, and collect plants, grasses, moss, etc., and whatever I can find of interest. Various types of small birds are found in the moss-covered swamps which were known to me in Labrador.

2 August 1852 (temp. max. 39°, min. 33°, med. 35°)
Daily someone goes to the 800-foot mountain near by to examine the ice-covered sea and Barrow Strait [Viscount Melville Sound]; always he comes back with the same unpleasant report: "No break-up; no movement in the ice."

Our worst trouble for the moment is that it is impossible to find employment for the seamen; for neither on land nor on the ice is there anything to be shot, and though sea-fowl seeking open water are often seen near the ship, every time a dozen men rush out, not to shoot but to scare; and sports on the ice are not carried on as last year, for hungry stomachs take all the joy out of the men, and even the desire to live. In my lonely wanderings on land I found a small plant with round leaves tasting a little sour — a kind of sorrel. I found it yesterday growing in abundance on the south side of a sandy hill. I brought a whole handkerchief full to the ship, washed it, seasoned some food with it, and presented this salad to the captain and the officers. The doctors said that it was very good for the health and also both a cure and preventive of scurvy. . . .[1] The perpetually bad weather and our dreadfully uncertain future are producing a sorrowful and gloomy frame of mind. Ah, how much better it would be if it could produce a really godly sorrow.

0 August (temp. max. 44°, min. 38°, med. 40°)

In the last few days the ice around the ship has been blasted away, so that its fragments may be carried out of the bay with the tide as soon as the ice breaks up, and open a way for the ship. A seaman, Taylor, stole a loaf from the oven and received in punishment three dozen strokes of the cat. Today for the first time there came a report from the mountain that out to sea the ice was in motion; in the direction of Melville Island a streak of open water is visible; in our bay the ice is as solid as in the depth of winter. . . . Twelve to fifteen men are daily sent to land to gather sorrel; they usually bring eight to twelve pounds to the ship; this is issued by turns to the members of the crew and eaten as uncooked vegetable at the midday meal.

1 August (temp. max. 38°, min. 30°, med. 32°)

So far no change is noticeable in the ice; and also in the bay it remains fast and undisturbed; only along the beach is there a strip of water 50 feet across, so that in order to land one uses a rubber boat. This very handy boat, named Halkett's boat, is made of waterproof rubber, is 10 feet long and 3 feet wide, weighs twenty-five pounds, and carries six men; it is rolled up and carried under the arm until one comes to water, and then it is inflated with a pocket pump. . . . To give employment to the downcast

[1]Armstrong enlarges on the value of this sorrel in the men's diet (pp. 538-40) but makes not the least reference to its discovery by Miertsching.

crew, they were sent to fish in a small pool near by; in four days 173 little fish of an unknown species were caught. . . .

29 *August (temp. max. 32°, min. 21°, med. 27°)*
The circumstances attending our present critical situation I cannot describe. Until now one hoped from day to day for the break-up of the ice; and even now there is a hope, unhappily a feeble one, that we may reach England this year. The water along the beach is covered with young ice 3 inches thick; for the last two days men have been skating on it. The land is white; the new-fallen snow is 3 inches deep and seems likely to remain. The daily plucking and gathering of sorrel – the only employment that the men could find – is ended for the present by the snow. No immediate work can be found for these men, who creep around with drooping heads and empty stomachs. Neither animals nor water-fowl are met with or seen. The captain, oppressed with anxieties, seeks comfort by wandering alone on the hill. . . . A young sailor, Bradbury, has been under close watch for three days: he is quite distracted, and makes a terrible noise at night. Oh that help might come out of Zion, and the Lord send deliverance to us captives! I often have pleasing and edifying meetings with individual sailors; also the private gatherings in which I read aloud from the Bible, expound it simply, and close with prayer, are, it seems, attended with real earnestness; and to God all things are possible: He will add his blessing to my feeble words. . . .

3 *September 1852*
. . . The little water we saw last month is all frozen again. From hour to hour we watch and wait anxiously and hope that some disturbance will break the ice in the sea, and grant us passage at least to Melville Island: everyone has despaired of reaching England this year.

9 September (temp. max. 27°, min. 19°, med. 23°)
Lately the captain himself has gone to the mountain to observe the ice in the sea; but he also, like so many others, brings back a gloomy report. He always, especially in the presence of officers and men, assumes an air of cheerfulness and hope; but in his innermost self it is far otherwise; as a voyager of experience in the frozen seas, which he is now sailing for the third time,[1] he knows and grasps our situation better than anyone on board; his many prayers and sighs uttered in his cabin or on lonely walks on land declare much more than he reveals in words. Today he assembled the crew on the upper deck and addressed them in a solemn and impressive speech: he declared frankly that after careful observation it was his conviction that the ice would not break up this summer, and therefore they would be compelled to pass a second winter in the same place; he would do everything in his power to make their lives throughout the long winter as pleasant and comfortable as possible, and he urged them not to lose heart, but with firm faith to trust in God, under Whose protection they all were, to discipline themselves and behave like British seamen, whose steadfast courage never yet had failed; for himself, he had a firm, unshakeable conviction that not one of us would be left behind, but that all would safely reach their fatherland. In conclusion he said that for a year we had received rather more than half a daily ration; and still through God's good favour found ourselves in good health; and now, to make our small reserve of provisions last until next summer he felt compelled to make another small reduction in the daily ration that we might in a period of complete inactivity remain in health: he had some food, his personally, and this he would share in common on ap-

[1] In Frozen Strait, Hudson Bay, with Sir George Back (as mate, 1836-7), and as lieutenant with Sir James Ross in Barrow Strait in the first Franklin rescue expedition in 1848-9.

propriate occasions. . . . The captain added that next spring we would send forty men away: a sledge with eight men to the Mackenzie River, and four sledges with thirty-two men to Port Leopold at the entrance to Prince Regent's Inlet, where a hut and a plentiful supply of food and clothing were to be found.[1] One could observe many gloomy and anxious faces, but in this situation there was nothing to do but submit. . . .

14 September

. . . It is snowing today: the winter is coming on fast. Waterfowl and land-fowl have migrated southwards, and sorely against our will we must stay in this melancholy wilderness of ice until it pleases the Lord to lead us out of Egypt. . . .

30 September

. . . The doctors have examined all members of the crew, and report that the general health is fairly good, but warn the captain that the daily ration is insufficient and must have evil consequences. Nine men are sick. The new ice is 9 inches thick.

2 October 1852 (temp. max. 4°, min. −15°, med. −4°)

Our reserve of food and also of coal has been checked and weighed; it is found that it will last to November 1853, at the present daily ration. Whether all will be able to survive on so meagre a ration, the future will show; even now one notices symptoms of grumbling and discontent among the men; one even sees hungry sailors burrowing in last winter's garbage-heap, which still lies on the ice, in the hope of finding some discarded morsels to still their nagging hunger. As long as there was little snow on the ground one could stuff his stomach with sorrel, *tripe de roche*, and other plants and

[1]Placed there by Sir James Ross in 1848-9 — in the hope of furnishing aid to the Franklin castaways.

grasses, but that is now at an end. Also, an order has been given that all small game, such as hares and ptarmigan, brought in by the hunters, shall be turned in to the common stock; half will be reserved for the sick and half returned to the successful hunter; larger game, such as reindeer, are all appropriated and issued in place of regular rations. Some have found a way of evading this strict order: they often eat ptarmigan or even hares raw and uncooked before returning to the ship, and so avoid the necessity of giving them away.[1]

7 *October (temp. max. −3°, min. −11°, med. −6°)*

Weather consistently raw and cold. The whole week I have suffered great pain from rheumatism in all my limbs and have been plagued with violent tooth-ache; the doctor drew two of my teeth yesterday on account of a bad ulcer. All day long I shiver with cold, and must then at night lie in a damp bed, where I find little repose because of pain; I will speak of it to the captain tomorrow. Ah! when will this miserable life on board ship come to an end?

14 *October*

. . . For a short time we have noticed in one of our officers, Lieutenant Wyniatt [mate], strange actions that have puzzled everyone. Yesterday they took shape in complete madness, and he, like Bradbury, must now be watched day and night lest he do violence to himself or to a ship-mate. He passes the night with frightful shouting and raving, today he slept a few hours and then began again to jest, laugh, weep, sing, and whistle; neither threats nor kindly admonition have the least effect on them. I went to him

[1]It is to the credit of the starving hunters that the order was not frequently evaded; the captain could not punish the hunters on whose voluntary exertions he depended for caribou meat, especially since, as Armstrong tells us, the good hunters were, with one or two exceptions, officers.

and begged him in the most affectionate terms, as one who occupied the next cabin to mine, to sleep a few hours at night, or at least to remain quiet that others might be permitted to sleep, but he seemed not to understand or to grasp the meaning of my words. My limbs and tooth-ache still cause continuous pain, but not so severely as formerly.

18 October (temp. max. −3°, min. −12°, med. −10°)

For three days the weather has been so frightful that no one can leave the ship. Today at midday the entire crew gathered on the upper deck and demanded, through the officer of the watch, a few words with the captain. As he appeared, four sailors approached him, requested his pardon for their unauthorized assembly, and stated that the crew had resolved to present a collective request for a small increase in rations: they could not exist on the present allowance; they could not sleep for hunger, etc. The harassed captain listened of necessity to this petition, and after an earnest conference dismissed the men with a promise to grant their request.[1]

26 October (temp. max. −1°, min. −23°, med. −10°)

. . . Our two distracted comrades are no better yet; they sleep by day; by night they weep and rave. Today I again visited Mr. Wyniatt; he kissed my hand and wept without speaking a word to me. Today in memory of the discovery of the Northwest Passage the captain out of his own stock

[1]Armstrong in his terse account of this incident (p. 548) gives it, perhaps deliberately, a malicious twist. The men, he says, "came on the the quarter-deck in a body to ask for more food — to their application, Captain McClure refused to accede". The civil and orderly procedure which Miertsching attributes to the men appears more consistent with the good conduct of the crew of the *Investigator* as a body under hardships of unusual duration and severity. Nor is it probable that McClure replied with the harshness his surgeon implies — he did not lack tact in dealing with men in a group. Presumably occasional gifts from his private stock were accepted as a fulfilment of his promise; the organized protest was not repeated.

gave a meal and extra grog to the whole crew; the officers were invited to dine with the captain; unhappily the poor stricken Wyniatt could not be one of us. A quite unwonted animation prevails on board; everyone is cheery and good-humoured.

31 October

... The men are building new sledges for those who are to travel next spring.... The deranged seaman, Bradbury, has grown quite peaceful; he speaks little and sleeps much; Mr. Wyniatt, on the other hand, raves and jests as frantically as ever. I visit him in his cabin daily, but he listens to no advice, takes no medicine, and says that not until the captain and Dr. Armstrong are dead will he cease from his raving....

5 November 1852

... The poor sick Wyniatt is causing much trouble with his raving and babbling. I am the only one besides his servant whom he allows to approach him, but his mind seems utterly unsettled. As often as the weather permits, I go abroad, just to escape from the ship; but unhappily I come home hungry, eat, am still hungry, and go hungry to bed. I have at times, especially in Labrador, seen hungry people, but not until now had I personally felt what real hunger means – perpetual hunger; but I feel it now, and may it leave a deep and lasting impression on me....

.   .   .   .

23 November

... Mr. Wyniatt has grown a little more quiet, he often visits me, but his thoughts are hopelessly confused.

26 November (temp. max. −33°, min. −43°, med. −41°)

For some days the weather has been very pleasant and

clear; stars are again seen day and night. This winter there is no school; the men employ themselves by reading books from the ship's library and other private books, and by sewing, knitting, crocheting, etc. The officers do the same; everyone has learnt knitting or crocheting to shorten the fearful long hours. . . . The captain supplies an extra ration and grog weekly to the whole crew, and this is received with gratitude and greedily devoured; every man is thus made happy and good-humoured.

30 *November (temp. max. −37°, min. −42°, med. −39°)*
Yesterday I was very lucky in the hunt – I shot a reindeer, a hare, and two ptarmigan; the hares and ptarmigan I must turn over for the use of the sick; in return I received from the deer the head, the feet, liver, lungs, heart, and kidneys, as well as a pound of meat, which I may retain for my own use. Everyone who shoots a deer receives these parts of the kill. Today I was again ashore and got five ptarmigan, which I retained because I had made a contribution to the sick the day before. This winter the cook prepares our vegetables in the most original manner; the beans are broken up with a hammer, ground in a coffee mill, converted into a dough with water, then they are cooked in water in a bag, like a pudding, and this mass is brought to the table without fat or butter, and the portions distributed by lot to the hungry crew. . . . The salt beef or pork issued by the clerk-in-charge as a day's ration is in like manner impartially divided and distributed by lot, whereupon each man puts his little portion in cold water to draw out the salt, and, in order not to shrink it by cooking, devours it raw with as much zest as if it were the best roast. . . .[1] The crazed Bradbury is quiet but oppressed with melancholy and weeps

---

[1]Armstrong protested that raw salt meat aggravated scurvy, but McClure declined the risk of again exerting his authority which had already been challenged once (p. 546).

perpetually. Mr. Wyniatt is quiet when on board, but often walks about the ice and bellows insanely. The ice is 3 feet, 1 inch thick.

6 December 1852 (temp. max. −23°, min. −40°, med. −35°)

The weather is very clear but cold. When hunting a few days ago I wounded a buck reindeer with very large antlers; he charged at a sailor who stood by, but the latter struck him a blow on the forehead with the butt of his gun and dashed him to the ground; the gun broke into three pieces, but we shared the proceeds of the deer. Yesterday I shot a hare for the sick, and in so doing fell from a cliff of snow into a deep hollow, whence I clambered out with much difficulty, am now lame and must renounce hunting until my sprained foot is better. Amongst the officers there is no one who goes out hunting – because it is too cold – and so we get no extras, but only our bare diminutive portion. . . .

15 December

. . . The weather outside is fine and clear, but it is quite otherwise on board, there we are all the time gloomy and full of foreboding. My face and fingers have so often been frozen, and on healing have grown so tender that in the cold I can scarcely bear to handle my gun, so usually one of those sailors who are much attached to me carries my gun, and when a deer is killed they share the blood and the contents of the first stomach. A reindeer has two stomachs. . . .

24 December (temp. max. −22°, min. −37°, med. −30°)

Today again the weather is so unfriendly that no one can leave the ship; but it is more friendly on board; one sees genuinely happy faces, for the clerk-in-charge is issuing to-day large portions for tomorrow of meat, flour, raisins, cocoa, tea, and suet, to celebrate with joy the last Christmas we shall have together; for the captain has declared that every man shall eat his fill. Mr. Wyniatt is unhappily in the same lamentable condition; on board he is peaceful, but he is left on the ice daily where he gives free vent to his rage against the captain. Thrice already he has made murderous attacks on him. Messrs. Paine and Sainsbury, who have already often been sick, are very ill again.

25 December (temp. max. −20°, min. −40°, med. −34°)
Today is the joyous festival of Christmas; is it also joyous for me? I alone think that it is not as it should and could be. In the morning was Divine Service; then the midday meal was served and eaten with passionate appetite; from then until 10 p.m. the sailors enjoyed a holiday with all the lights they needed. . . .

31 December (temp. max. −15°, min. −35°, med. −26°)
. . . It has been a very long year for us, imprisoned in the ice and condemned to utter idleness. The Lord has granted us, and especially me, good health; He has also granted me that I should, especially in these times of trial, enjoy sacred hours of His grace and immediate Presence; and He has so inclined the hearts of my ship-mates that they gladly listen to my weak words spoken for the good of their immortal souls; and show by their conduct that they have found the better way and seek to walk in it. The Lord will bless with His Holy Spirit these feeble labours and reveal to us the wages of sin. . . . I feel that I have not been forgotten in my home nor in the Community, but am had in remembrance before the Throne of God; and that it is by no deed of my own but through the will of God that I am here – this assurance has often revived my drooping spirits. . . .

1 January 1853 (temp. max. −57°, min. −65°, med. −62°)

The New Year's festival was not celebrated today with the wonted boisterous rejoicing, but was observed in a very quiet, orderly fashion. In the morning was Divine Service, and in the evening a private assembly. The midday meal today was somewhat better than usual. Thoughts of the future and of what the Lord has in store for us this year have caused a very serious frame of mind among the men, for soon the captain's decision will be known as to which men in the coming spring are to quit the ship and journey for months over the ice, and who will remain on board with the captain, perhaps for another year, to bring her out, by Barrow Strait when the ice breaks up, or, if the worst comes to the worst, to wait until help is sent from England. It will be my lot, along with a party consisting of Mr. Cresswell and six very sick seamen, to travel around Banks Land and through Prince of Wales Strait, southwards from the coast of Prince Albert Land across Dolphin and Union Strait, and thence west along the mainland shore to Mackenzie River, and then 120 miles inland in the hope of reaching the Hudson's Bay post, Fort Good Hope. From there with the help of the Anglo-Indians our journey will take us through the Canadian lakes to Montreal and Quebec, and should we arrive too late in the season and the St. Lawrence be closed to navigation by ice, we shall go to New York and take the first steamer for England, that a ship may be fitted out and in the next spring (1854) sent to the rescue of the *Investigator*. When I contemplate the proposed journey, its difficulty, and ourselves, humanly speaking according to my understanding, there is not the faintest possibility that any one of us should reach England. To God alone is all known that has been decreed for us in the future, and to Him alone is that possible which seems impossible to us.

A medical examination has shown that the men are growing weaker and weaker; also, scurvy is spreading and appearing in a more threatening form; a sailor, MacDonald, has the disease so severely that while he was asleep all his teeth fell out;[1] and now his legs are beginning to turn black and blue. Everyone was weighed on New Year's Day 1852, and again today; I have lost thirty-five pounds. The captain is continuously busy and much concerned to provide what best serves the health and comfort of the crew; and his care is acknowledged by many with thanks. . . .

11 January (temp. max. −50°, min. −60°, med. −58°)
. . . In consequence of the bitter cold the reindeer seem to be coming down from the high land to the low-lying level shore; small herds of five to eight are often seen; but the cold is so severe that the ordinary double-barrelled guns crack when discharged, and the spring of the lock snaps. Dr. Armstrong's double-barrelled gun cost 12 pounds, Piers's 9, Paine's, 7, and Sainsbury's 15 pounds sterling; and all have become unusable; only the best English firearms stand up in this climate. . . . Mr. Wyniatt has become much quieter, but is closely watched because he threatens to murder the captain and the officers, and to set fire to the ship.

19 January (temp. max. −47°, min. −55°, med. −52°)
For some days Mr. Wyniatt has been so frantic that of necessity he has been kept bound. The ship's baker was reported to the officer of the watch for thieving; when his

[1]Miertsching is prone to quote unfounded gossip. Four months later when MacDonald had been carried on sledge 160 miles to the rescue ship *Resolute* an observer noted that "his teeth could be moved to and fro in their gums by the slightest movement of the tongue" (Geo. F. McDougall, "The Eventful Voyage of H. M. Discovery Ship *Resolute* . . .").

chest was searched, meat, flour, and dough were discovered; after stubborn denial he finally confessed to the offence and received two dozen of the cat on his naked back. Since we are again obtaining reindeer meat, the small game, hares, and ptarmigan are the property of him who shoots them. Every bit of a reindeer is used and made eatable; even the entrails and the hide are eaten, though not with the best appetite, under the compulsion of hunger. The hair is removed from the hide by boiling, the latter is then cut into strips and eaten as *Sauerfleisch*.

25 January

. . . Our two mental cases howl and make a maniac noise day and night. A sailor, coming aboard stiff with cold, fell on the gangway and broke his arm; Messrs. Sainsbury and Paine are sick unto death; and the report made by the doctors has reduced the captain to utter despondency. . . .

31 January (temp. max. −26°, min. −47°, med. −37°)

This morning the weather cleared, and many went hunting; but because all went in an easterly direction where deer had been seen, and because usually little or nothing is shot where so many sailor-sportsmen congregate, I went to the west alone, found reindeer, and shot two which weighed 170 pounds. In the afternoon a frightful storm and blizzard arose suddenly, so that one could scarcely go fifteen paces from the ship; and five of the unlucky hunters lost their way and strayed about until late at night, when the discharge of guns and rockets guided them to the ship, bringing nothing back except frozen features and limbs. . . . There are seventeen patients in hospital; most of them suffering from pains in the head and back along with lameness in the legs; in addition, many on leaving hospital are afflicted with body sores and diarrhoea. . . .

9 February 1853 (temp. max. −47°, min. −54°, med. −52°)

Once again the weather permits us to go hunting, and the sun, visible today, is coming nearer with great strides, prolonging the brightness of day. The poor shots, who can achieve nothing worth while, are a genuine nuisance, for they bring in no game, make no addition to their own miserable ration, and in consequence of the exercise bring back stomachs fairly shrieking with hunger. . . . The ebbing courage of the men seems to have revived with the return of the friendly sun, for every man begins afresh to hope that this year he will succeed in escaping from the ice and come back to his beloved fatherland. . . .

15 February (temp. max. −39°, min. −48°, med. −43°)

The general health seems to grow worse rather than to improve; increasing bodily weakness caused by undernourishment is showing itself in ailments not before noted by the doctor; instead of the once cheery and active sailors, now one only sees creeping about the shrunken forms of men who have no desire but to sleep. Ah, how it must affect our captain, already weighed down with countless cares and anxieties, when he sees his once-strong, rugged, and hearty crew wasted away and scarcely with the strength to hold themselves upright! The Lord will send him courage to endure and be his one sure Hope.

22 February (temp. max. −42°, min. −52°, med. −48°)

The strongest of the seamen are employed in carrying sand on sledges on to the ice and spreading it in a broad strip from the ship to the mouth of the bay, in the hope that through it the ice may melt earlier in the powerful rays of the sun than if under a white blanket of snow. The intention is, when summer comes, to tow the ship through this canal nearer to the open sea. The men thus employed are to draw a larger daily ration. The ship's armourer is in hospital, and as I have nothing else on hand I have taken over his post and am making small mess-tins for the use of those who in two months will be setting out on a journey. Three dozen have been ordered....

28 February (temp. max. −40°, min. −52°, med. −48°)
As this is the end of the month, our two doctors examined the crew today, and this is the substance of their report delivered to the captain: Not one of the men is fit for heavy work, and their steadily increasing bodily weakness is having a potent effect on their spirits, and will, perhaps in the near future, have bad and alarming consequences. Twenty-one men are now in hospital, and the recovery of some is despaired of; truly a gloomy prospect for us, for in six weeks we must, with those judged unfit to remain longer with the ship, harness ourselves to sledges laden with supplies, and drag them through snow and ice for hundreds of miles. How many of us will in this way see Europe? The answer is: "No one."

But what if we should leave the ship in a body, whither could we go? In this icy region we know of no ship but our own. . . . Mr. Wyniatt, who now visits me frequently, has become much more tranquil, and often has a lucid hour.

3 March 1853 (temp. max. −32°, min. −53°, med. −39°)
This morning after muster the captain addressed the men, disclosing the plan he had drawn up some time before: Because an exact survey had shown that supplies for the whole crew would last only until November, and because it was neither possible nor practical to desert the ship in a body, he would send away only enough to ensure that supplies for those who remained with the ship would last until the following spring, in case the ship again failed to get out of the ice. The officers, Lieutenant Haswell, Dr. Piers, Sainsbury,

and the crazed Wyniatt, with twenty-six sailors whose names were read out, were appointed to go to Port Leopold (500 miles), where in 1848 a hut had been built with food, clothing, and coal in abundance, and where a small steamboat would also be found; from Port Leopold they would endeavour to be picked up by a whaling-ship in Baffin Bay, and so be brought to England. A second party of eight persons, Lieutenant Cresswell, myself as interpreter, and six sailors, would go to the Princess Royal Islands (in Prince of Wales Strait) and there at the depot planted by us in 1850, containing food and a boat, spend three months in a tent; and when the ice breaks up, set out by boat past Wollaston Land, across Dolphin and Union Strait, along the American coast to the Mackenzie River, up to the Hudson's Bay post, Fort Good Hope, and thence with the help of the Indians through the wilds of North America to Montreal and New York. The captain, Dr. Armstrong, Messrs. Paine and Court, with the strongest seamen, would remain with the ship and, in case they again failed to get her out of the ice this summer, would pass yet another winter in her, and in the spring of 1854 would leave her for Port Leopold. The large party under Lieutenant Haswell receives forty-five days' travelling allowance. . . . Our little company, going to New York via the Princess Royal Islands and Fort Good Hope, receives thirteen days' travelling allowance.[1] Also, the captain promised that for a month

[1] The supplies would certainly have proved insufficient to carry the travelling parties to their respective destinations. In 1851 McClintock with a fresh and carefully selected crew had taken eighty days to make a round trip of 760 miles on a route which largely coincided with the course assigned to Haswell and his twenty-six invalids. McClure did not know this, but he was aware that in the same season Lieutenant Cresswell had spent thirty-four days, out and back, on a route corresponding to but rather shorter than the one he was now to cover one way in thirteen days with a party of near cripples. These considerations give an ugly aspect to McClure's subsequent claim that he could have saved the lives of his men without the help of Kellett — a claim that enabled him to secure for the crew of the *Investigator* the entire amount of the 10,000 pounds offered for the discovery of the Passage, to the exclusion of the crews who rescued them.

184

before the date of their departure the travellers would receive a full ship's ration of good food, would be excused all
duty, and would be supplied with candles to make ready
their clothing for the journey. The day of departure is set
for April 15. . . . The men chosen to stay with the ship were
disappointed and downcast at the lot assigned to them,
while many of those appointed to travel have visions of
their corpses lying on the ice, a prey for wolves and foxes.
Yet there are many who, having experienced the wondrous
works of God, in all times rely only on the aid of the Lord,
our true Helper, and show a cheerful spirit. . . .

1 March

. . . Sixteen of the men designated for travel are in hospital,
and among them four men belonging to our little party.
Mr. Wyniatt's mind is so affected that it is impossible to
make him understand that he is to leave the ship and go
on a journey. Bradbury is equally devoid of comprehen-
sion, only he is perfectly docile and must be handled like an
idiot child.

16 March

Today begins the full ration for all who are to leave the
ship on April 15. Two wolves have been shot in these days,
one of 80, the other of 72 pounds. Both the travellers and
the ship's artificers are feverishly engaged in preparing the
things needed for the journeys. I had long known what my
assignment would be, and so during the winter had made
ready what I needed for the journey in the warmth of the
captain's cabin. I am therefore free now and can hunt daily.

27 March

. . . In the evenings I read Easter meditations aloud to the
captain. Those men who are to stay with the ship are busy
writing letters to their friends in England.

31 March (temp. max. 2°, min. −32°, med. −16°)

The weather is very warm in comparison to other years, and this inspires the hope of a really early summer.... General health is the same as last month; yet full rations seem to be giving new courage and strength to the prospective travellers. But scurvy continues to spread in the most alarming way; not one on board is free from it; some are more affected than others. Nine men supposed to travel in fourteen days are still on their backs in the hospital. The ice, measured in five different places, showed a thickness of 6 feet, 11 inches.

April 1853 (temp. max. −6°, min. −16°, med. −11°)

The weather is fine but variable, with strong winds and snow-squalls. In these days our transport has been made ready, the new sledges tested and stowed; all the property we must leave behind we have packed, addressed, and turned over to the ship's master. If ever the ship reaches Europe we shall get it back again. Through a written order of the captain's it has been announced: That all journals, sketches, charts, and other documents, written, drawn up, or prepared in connection with our expedition must, by the 5th of this month, be sealed, marked with the proper address, and delivered to the captain, who will turn them over to the Admiralty whence we may recover them. So my labours of four years must perish here.[1]

[1] At this point ends the part of Miertsching's narrative that was rewritten at a time subsequent to the happenings it records. From here on his journal is a regular day-by-day record.

CHAPTER SEVEN

7 April 1853 (temp. max. −14°, min. −21°, med. −19°)
Yesterday it snowed a little, and today storms and snow-squalls prevented us from hunting. The captain spent the morning preparing for the Admiralty letters and dispatches which we are to carry. About noon the wind ceased completely, and because it was too late to go hunting the idle seamen walked on the ice and on that part of the beach which lay close to the ship. I also walked with the captain on the ice near the ship. We talked of my forthcoming journey through North America and, above all, of the gloomy situation of our *Investigator* and of those who were remaining with her. "Sir," said he, "if next year in Europe you neither see nor hear of me, then you may be sure that Captain McClure, along with his crew, has perished and lies unburied but wrapped in the fur coat which you gave me, enjoying a long and tranquil sleep until awakened on the Day of Resurrection by the Redeemer in Whom is all my hope and trust", etc. As he was speaking these last words he was interrupted by a sailor who approached him and reported that seawards on the heavy ice a black moving point was visible, which however might be a musk-ox crossing the ice from Point Back to the opposite side of the bay.

187

We both saw clearly that it was some living creature, without being able to determine what sort of creature it was. Then a second sailor came running up and cried: "They are men – first a man, and then a sledge with men." The captain looked at me and I at him: neither of us spoke as we went to meet the approaching men. In me a new hope of life had arisen: taking the strangers for Eskimos, I thought that whence these come, thither we can go. For the last twenty-one months we had met no stranger. As we neared these strangers, in dress and nature resembling Eskimos, our hearts beat violently; we were speechless until words spoken in English reached our ears: "I am Lieutenant Pim of the ship *Resolute* in Winter Harbour."[1] These words came like an electric shock, at first stunning us and then instantaneously awaking us as from a dream to the sober assurance that we need no longer doubt the reality of the figure that stood before us. I can do no better than describe this word for word as our sorely-tried captain expressed it in his daily journal:[2] He says: "I will try as best I can to describe the feelings which overwhelmed myself and everyone on board, when this unlooked-for apparition was observed coming over the ice from seawards, some 500 yards away, though any description must fall far short of reality. Picture to yourself a whole crew which had no idea that any ship except their own was to be found in this dreadful region of ice; picture our desolate and hopeless situation, and then in the twinkling of an eye, when the form of a stranger was perceived hurrying towards us with gestures

[1] A curious mistake: the rescue ships were not at Winter Harbour, but some distance to the east on the shore of Melville Island behind an islet named Dealy. The error, which occurs also in McClure's journal, cannot have been Pim's; it is likely that neither Miertsching nor McClure heard him accurately, assumed that the ships were at Parry's old anchorage, and so stated in their journals before they were properly informed.

[2] These are not McClure's actual words, but a re-translation of Miertsching's German version.

of friendship, with his features as black as night from the smoke of the cooking-lamp in his tent. My astonishment, I might say my terror, was beyond belief. How petrified I stood beside my companion, in doubt whether a human being or a spirit from another world had appeared before the eyes. But we were not long in doubt. 'I am Lieutenant Pim of the ship *Herald*,[1] Captain Kellett, in Winter Harbour,' cried the strange figure in a loud voice, and these words proved that he was real English flesh and blood. To rush to him, to seize him by the hand, was the work of a moment – our hearts were too full to speak, while the grimy stranger greeted us and told us who he was and whence he came. And what was it like on the ship when this was noised abroad? At the mention of the stranger the sick, forgetting their pain, sprang from their beds; the healthy forgot their trials and despair, and in less time than it takes to tell it all were out on deck. Tears of joy and gratitude were flowing, and many sighs and exclamations testified to the grateful emotions of the rescued crew. No one who witnessed this scene will ever forget it. All was surprise, joy, animation, and uproar. Our situation was transformed in the twinkling of an eye. But I will say no more; no words are adequate to express in the smallest degree how we felt." While Lieutenant Pim was briefly giving us his most important items of news his crew also came up to the ship with their sledge.[2] Many thankful prayers from joyful hearts were wafted up to the Throne of Grace. This was what we learned from Lieutenant Pim: In the year 1852 five ships were sent from England through Davis Strait under the supreme com-

---

[1]Another example of mental confusion. Kellett *had* been in command of the *Herald* when McClure last met him in Bering Strait, but had since returned from his Pacific cruise and taken command of the *Resolute*.

[2]Pim had left Dealy Island with dog-sledge and a large man-handled sledge in charge of the *Resolute*'s surgeon, Dr. Domville. The latter broke down, and Pim made the crossing of Viscount Melville Sound with the dogs and two men only, Robert Hoyle and Thomas Bidgood.

mand of Sir Edward Belcher.[1] Captain Belcher took direct charge of the ships *Assistance* and *Pioneer*; the *Resolute* and *Intrepid* were placed under the command of Captain Kellett (the very man whose acquaintance we had made in Bering Strait in 1850; subsequently he had returned to England with the ship *Herald*). The fifth ship, the *North Star*, had been anchored off Cape Riley at the entrance to Wellington Channel, where she remained as a depot ship for the other four. At Cape Riley the squadron divided; Captain Belcher sailed with his two ships north up Wellington Channel to seek Franklin in that quarter; and Captain Kellett with the two other ships sailed west to Melville Island where he was compelled to set up his winter quarters at Dealy Island.[2] In the autumn he sent out a number of sledge-parties to search the coasts and plant small provision depots so that in the following spring longer journeys might be made by sledge to the north and west. One of these parties, commanded by Lieutenant Mecham, found the record which our captain had planted on Melville Island, and hurried back to deliver it to Captain Kellett at Dealy Island. The approach of winter, the bitter cold, and the imminent darkness prevented him from sending a sledge to Mercy Bay immediately; next spring on March 10 he sent Lieutenant Pim with sledges and a picked crew to seek the *Investigator*, and after a very cold and trying journey of twenty-eight days he had fulfilled his captain's command – and filled us with joy.

8 April (temp. max. –14°, min. –21°, med. –18°)

Yesterday a death occurred on board – that of the first

---

[1] Captain Austin's former squadron, which had been re-fitted and had returned to the Arctic, with the addition of the *North Star*, under the command of Belcher.

[2] He had tried to get into Winter Harbour, but found it ice-choked.

gunner, Kerr;[1] he had suffered from scurvy, and had grown so weak that for the last two months he had been unable to move a limb. I visited him often, especially as the end drew near, and found him always calmly reconciled to the will of God and to the redemption of Jesus, Whom he acknowledged as his Saviour, trusting alone to His grace to awake to a better life on the day of his passing away. This is the first death since our departure from England.

In consequence of the arrival of Lieutenant Pim our proposed journey has, naturally and to our great delight, been cancelled. The captain is very busy today making ready for a journey: he is to accompany Lieutenant Pim to Dealy Island where he will confer personally with Captain Kellett on the plight of the ship and of ourselves.

9 April (temp. max. −15°, min. −18°, med. −17°)
At 5 a.m. the captain with Lieutenant Pim set off for Dealy Island, leaving orders that Lieutenant Cresswell, Messrs. Piers and Wyniatt, and myself, with twenty-four sailors, should follow him on the 15th for Dealy Island. We were directed to leave *all* our possessions on the ship and to think of nothing but bringing twenty-four men, sick and grievously stricken with scurvy, alive to Dealy Island. The distance from here to Captain Kellett's ships is 40-50 German miles. The journey will be on the ice with no land to bivouac on.

10 April
... In the afternoon the body of the gunner who died two days ago was buried; the coffin, wrapped in black cloth and draped with the English flag, was placed on a sledge and drawn by eight sailors to the open grave on shore; the

[1]There is a discrepancy here: Armstrong and Miertsching agree that three men, Kerr, Ames, and Boyle, died between the 6th and the 13th of April, but differ as to the respective dates, Armstrong assigning that of Kerr to the 13th.

marines in military order preceded the coffin, and the rest of the crew followed it; on the ship the bell was tolled and her ensign lowered to half-mast. The English burial service was read at the graveside, and at the words "earth to earth" the coffin was lowered into the grave. At the conclusion of the service the marines fired three volleys over the grave, which was then closed. The marines marched slowly back to the ship with colours flying.

11 April (temp. max. −3°, min. −15°, med. −10°)
As we must leave all our effects on the ship and may carry only two pairs of socks, in addition to the clothes on our bodies; I have packed up all my belongings: four leather valises, a chest of stones, a chest of Eskimo weapons, a chest of dried plants, and a leather bandbox. It grieves me bitterly to be obliged to leave behind my journals which have cost me so much effort and are worth more to me than everything else.

13 April (temp. max. −1°, min. −11°, med. −6°)
Yesterday the seaman Ames died unexpectedly; he had for a long time been somewhat indisposed and weak physically, but so were many others who were not confined to their beds; so it was most unexpected when we heard of his sudden death. He was buried today. Five men of our travelling party, due to haul sledges two days hence, are still in hospital. We have all made ready for the journey and await only the hour when we are to bid the *Investigator* farewell. Mr. Wyniatt in his diseased condition still cannot properly understand that he is to leave the ship. Ah, it will indeed be a trying journey.

14 April (temp. max. 10°, min. −8°, med. −2°)
There was another sudden death last night: the sailor and hospital attendant, Boyle, was very ill in the night and was

dead before the doctor reached him. Later it was reported that he had poured together the dregs of medicines in various glasses and made himself ill by drinking the mixture. Within nine days three men have died, which has a very disheartening effect on the men who are to remain with the ship. Those, on the contrary, who are tomorrow to leave the ship are good-humoured and are glad, as they say, to be rid of the hunger-ship.

15 April (temp. max. −3°, min. −11°, med. −7°)
Today is the day that we must leave our ship, the ship that has borne us safely through many a storm at sea, and dreadful perils in the ice.... In the morning the weather was unfriendly and stormy, but the sledges were loaded and all things made ready for our departure.... The noon meal, for which an extra ration was issued, was, in view of our impending departure, eaten by all together on the lower deck, after which we parted solemnly from those who were to stay with the ship. At 2 p.m. I had a private gathering and leave-taking with a number of men, and offered up a prayer which seemed to make a deep impression on several, and which, I hope, will not remain unblessed. Even in the last half-hour some of the men remaining behind came to my cabin and bade me farewell with many thanks for the friendship and love I had shown them. A young sailor, once an evil-liver, whom I had later won over, had learned to read and write, and had begun to write poems; this man, previously so coarse, but now, through the grace of God, reformed, gave me as a souvenir sixteen hymns and songs of his own composition, and as I left the cabin where I had spent so many lonely and gloomy, but also so many blessed and happy days, and came on deck, there stood my friend, the poet Nelson,[1] with the comrades who, like him, were

[1]Armstrong, who notices Nelson as a brave and active hunter, credits him with a good elementary education. This is borne out by the technique, if not the content, of his verse.

remaining with the ship, and sang a farewell poem written
by himself:

I

At last, my lads, we're about to part,
Some for our native shore,
And after changing years, perhaps,
We part to meet no more.
But to whatever climes ye roam, And wherever you may be,
Think of Him that sits aloft,
Protecting you and me.

.   .   .   .

4

When you depart, dangers may oft
Beset our chequered way,
And troubles oftentimes arise,
Remember this and say:
I'll put my trust in Him above
Who calms the troubled sea;
And that bright Eye that's still aloft
Will still watch over me.

We harnessed ourselves to the sledges and after respond-
ing to the three loud hurrahs of those who remained behind
set forth with slow and weary paces; Mr. Cresswell, to
whom the command of the detachment had been entrusted,
in the lead, and six men, too weak to bear a hand with the
sledges, following behind. . . . Slowly we marched four hours
on our way, pitched our tent on the sandy cape of Point
Back and there set up our first night quarters.

16 April (temp. max. −4°, min. −25°, med. −17°)
After seven hours' rest – we had very little sleep – we could
no longer endure the cold in the tent; so after eating and
drinking well we resumed our slow advance. Many of our
horses were lame today, although our loads were not heavy,

194

so that, had we all been strong and healthy, we could have stepped forth in cheery mood, yet with so many weak and in pain from scurvy, scarcely keeping up with us by holding on to the sledges, the whole burden fell upon a few healthy men. Often we came upon long stretches of upheaved ice-masses where we had to draw the sledges while crawling on our hands and knees.

23 *April (temp. max. −3°, min. −7°, med. −5°)*
Today we reached Melville Island in bright and friendly weather. For the last four days we have had much fog and snow; we could not see land, sun, moon, or stars; the compass is utterly unreliable in this part of the earth, so that often we were in great perplexity about the direction to take to reach Melville Island; sometimes we steered by the northward flight of the ptarmigan, which cross the twenty-mile[1] strait between Banks Land and Melville Island to pass the short summer on the latter. In my tent are nine men of whom five are so miserable and lame that they can scarcely stand upright and follow the sledges that we draw; it is the same when it comes to setting up the tent: we four must again provide for all. Today at 3 a.m. we set up our tent on the shore-ice; and after wrapping up the lame and putting them in their sleeping-bags, I could not refrain from going on shore, and, exhausted as I was, climbing a low hill. There I stood on Melville Island, and, all starved and wretched as I was, could not suppress the proud thought that here in this polar region I was the only Wend from Germany, and that I had had a share in the North-west Passage, sought for 300 years, and now discovered by us. Returning to the tent, I ate with the best appetite my evening meal consisting of fat pork and biscuit, and drank my quarter gill of rum mixed with snow-water.

[1]German miles, we may assume: Point Back is about eighty statute miles from the nearest part of the Melville Island shore.

30 April (temp. max. 14°, min. 5°, med. 10°)

The weather this last week has been very pleasant. From the beginning of our journey it has been the rule that we sleep twice in the twenty-four hours; that is five hours in the tent, then seven hours of travel, again five hours in the tent and seven hours on the road; so that the twenty-four hour period is filled. We have two very sick men, Anderson and Ross, on the sledges, and several are so lame and wretched that they can barely follow slowly by clinging to the sledges. Our two deranged comrades, Mr. Wyniatt and Bradbury, have caused us a great deal of trouble on this journey. Today we passed Winter Harbour, and saw on land a great herd of musk-oxen. Late in the afternoon we met a sledge-crew from Captain Kellett's ships on their way to Winter Harbour to hunt the musk-ox.

1 May 1853 (temp. max. 17°, min. 2°, med. 9°)

At 7 a.m. we saw through the telescope Dealy Island lying in Bridport Inlet, and, a few hours later, the masts of the ships *Resolute* and *Intrepid*, some fifteen miles away. We were cheered and given fresh strength by the thought that we had come so near to our journey's end. We took a good rest and spent ten hours in our sleeping-bags.

2 May (temp. max. 6°, min. 2°, med. 4°)

After we had had breakfast and, as we hope, the last morning prayer to be pronounced in a tent, we set off in the hope of ending this toilsome journey in one march. By 4 a.m. we were drawing near the ships, they observed us and ran up a flag; and, soon after, Captain Kellett came over the ice with Captain McClure and many officers and men from both ships. They greeted us with the utmost kindness: I was conducted to the captain's cabin, where for the first time in sixteen days I had a decent wash and put on clothes and linen lent me by Captain Kellett. After breakfasting with the two captains, and drinking my first cup of coffee in two and a half years, I went to rest and enjoyed a refreshing sleep until 2 o'clock when I was called for lunch. The ship *Intrepid* – 200 paces from the *Resolute* – has been set up as a hospital for the sick, and twenty-two men of our company placed there immediately. We six sound men remain on the commodore's ship, *Resolute*. All have been provided with the most essential articles of clothing and undergarments.

4 *May (temp. max. 10°, min. −2°, med. 4°)*

Yesterday and today everyone of us has been complaining of severe pain in all our limbs; which probably arises from sleeping on the ice; I have such pains in my right arm and leg that I cannot dress or undress myself. All the officers and men of Captain Kellett's two crews who are strong and fit for heavy work are away, now that it is spring, on journeys in small sledge-parties in different directions to traverse the yet-unknown coasts of Melville Island and to seek, in the faint hope of finding, traces of Franklin's expedition. Yesterday and today our captains have been busy, the one proposing, the other rejecting one plan after another until finally it has been decided that Captain McClure shall return to the *Investigator*, taking with him Dr. Domville, as an unprejudiced party, to join with Dr. Armstrong in examining the crew as to whether, in event of the ice again remaining unbroken this summer, they are willing and able to spend a fourth winter in the ice.[1] Should they find twenty men who are both fit and willing, Captain McClure will remain with them on the ship and send the

[1]McClure was naturally anxious to round off his achievement by rescuing the ship and bringing her through the Passage he had discovered, but Kellett would permit no further demands on her crew except on a voluntary basis. Armstrong acquaints us with the unpleasant fact that in spite of their sufferings McClure kept the men on the ship on short rations until the end of May, when Kellett's order to abandon ship became operative (pp. 569 and 573).

rest of us to Captain Kellett's ships. His party will leave this evening or tonight. My good Captain McClure has promised to send me my journal which he has had in his keeping since April 4, with Dr. Domville when he comes back, or, in event of the ship being abandoned, to bring it himself.

5 May (temp. max. 10°, min. 0°, med. 6°)

I am so lame that I can barely crawl from my cabin to the captain's. . . . Captain Kellett told me this evening that he has decided to send to the depot ship *North Star* at Cape Riley fourteen of the least fit men from both his ships, along with Mr. Cresswell, who is to carry dispatches, and the deranged Wyniatt. Dr. Piers and I are to remain here. Unwell and lame as I am, I would gladly be one of this party. My time is utterly wasted here; and, should the whole crew of the *Investigator* join us, our quarters will become desperately narrow; but the friendly old Kellett[1] is not in the least disposed to gratify my wish, but tells me that this summer he will go down the coast of Baffin's Bay to get at the truth of the stories told by Erasmus York and Adam Beck:[2] for that purpose he required my services as interpreter. With much trouble and in great haste I wrote two short letters to Europe, in case Mr. Cresswell should arrive there before ourselves. With much regret I witnessed the departure of my old ship-mates, Mr. Cresswell and Wyniatt.

22 May

. . . Captain Kellett sent his dog-sledge to fetch me from

[1]"Mein alter freundlicher Kapt. Kellett" — this cordial language suggests that Kellett sweetened his disagreeable order with a little of his native blarney.

[2]Kellett was still unaware that in the previous August Captain Inglefield had disproved the Eskimo rumour that Franklin's crews had been massacred at Wolstenholme Sound far up the West Greenland shore.

the hunting-tent to the ship to re-sole two pairs of boots for him.[1]

5 *June 1853 (temp. max. 35°, min. 24°, med. 28°)*

At 4 a.m. Commander Richards arrived quite unexpectedly from Captain Belcher's ship *Assistance*, which is frozen in Wellington Channel – lat. 77°, long. 97° west. Mr. Richards met Lieutenant Hamilton [of the *Resolute*] on his journey along the coast in lat. 77°, long. 109° west, and learned from him that the ship *Resolute* was in winter quarters at Dealy Island. As the north and west coasts of Melville Island were being explored by sledge-parties from Captain Kellett's ships, Commander Richards, who had planned that survey for himself, found himself anticipated, and began his journey home, making light of a deviation of 150 miles to pay us a visit. He told us many interesting anecdotes of winter life on Sir E. Belcher's ships. Today we saw the first water-fowl. . . .

10 *June (temp. max. 31°, min. 25°, med. 28°)*

Yesterday Commander Richards left with his sledge-crew to return to his ship. Dr. Domville, who had journeyed to the *Investigator* with Captain McClure, came back today with the news that Captain McClure is compelled to abandon his ship, and that he and the crew will arrive here next week with sack and pack: instead of twenty men only three were found willing to stay with the captain on the ship. Our good ship *Investigator* is by now deserted in the Bay of Mercy and will lie on the sandy shore, the haunt of bears, wolves, and foxes. I heard this news with distress, for now are all my natural history collections, plants, etc., lost, as well as all my written records for three years. All

[1]The breezy and informal Kellett must have been on very good terms with Miertsching to make so irregular a request of one who was even a temporary officer on one of H. M. ships. Possibly Miertsching took seriously what was intended as a joke.

my linen and clothing I count as a trifle, for *they* can be replaced by purchase. But there is no help for it and I will rejoice and be thankful to escape to Europe from this region of ice with my bare life.

17 June (temp. max. 38°, min. 31°, med. 35°)

Today at 8 a.m. we caught sight from the upper deck of the crew of the abandoned *Investigator* coming over the ice, some five miles away. The best possible preparations had been made on both ships for their reception. The caravan was moving very slowly: at 12 noon it was still three miles from the ships; to send out help was impossible, for there were none but invalids on the ships; all the strong men were away on journeys. At 1 o'clock I went with the captain to greet the new-comers; but the melancholy spectacle which they presented I will never in my life forget. Two sick men were lashed on to each of the four sledges; others, utterly without strength, were supported by comrades who still preserved a little vigour; others again held on to and leaned on the sledges, and these were drawn by men so unsteady on their feet that every five minutes they would fall and be unable to rise without the help of their comrades, the captain, or one of the officers. The spectacle of this miserable throng brought to my mind the unfortunate Franklin expedition; and had not our gracious and merciful Lord and Saviour intervened, and, by bringing these ships at the right time, cancelled our intended long journey at the last moment, we must all have perished miserably on the frozen sea. . . . At 4 p.m. these poor wanderers reached the ship, where all possible care was given them. Lieutenant Haswell, Dr. Armstrong, and Mr. Court took up their quarters on the *Intrepid*; Messrs. Piers, Paine, and Sainsbury and Captain McClure remain on the *Resolute*. The ship *Investigator*, abandoned in the Bay of Mercy, had been doubly anchored and all openings and ways of entry to the interior of the ship securely closed. All useful provisions and supplies for seventy men for six months, along with all the boats, had been transferred to the land near by. The captain had been unable to bring me my precious journal; though it would have added no more than about two pounds to the load of the sledge; but he would have been obliged to bring also the journals and records of his officers, and this he could not do.[1] Much as I regretted my loss, I consoled myself with the thought that the others were no better off, and one could plainly perceive that the men, broken down by disease, were in condition to do no more than barely save their own lives; and to accomplish that one would give up anything – even the greatest riches on earth. My worthy Captain McClure offered me in the friendliest way the use of his ship's journal, that with it aided by memory I might reconstruct my own; he would endeavour to procure for me writing materials, which are very rare on these ships. I accepted his friendly offer with many thanks. Captain Kellett promised me twelve sheets of paper, Dr. Domville two pens, and Mr. De Bray some ink.

18 June (temp. max. 37°, min. 30°, med. 34°)
Today we were surprised by the arrival of mail by dog-sledge from the ship *North Star*. We learned that the

[1]Miertsching was obviously hurt by the loss of his journal, and with good reason. He was in a different category from the other officers. He had given up several years of a beloved mission to enter the service of a foreign power which could offer him neither honours nor promotion. No officer could dispute his claim to a slight privilege in exchange for such a sacrifice, and McClure was not the man to heed him if he did. The suspicion that the captain was doing his utmost to conceal the cost of his daring voyage in human suffering is strengthened by the circumstance that, when the abandoned ship was visited in the following spring, the officers' journals could nowhere be found. (See entry for June 1854, p. 230.) It appears that Dr. Armstrong *did* salvage his journal, but for this, no doubt, he was indebted to the good offices of his colleague, Dr. Domville, who bore written orders from Kellett and was exempt from McClure's control.

sledge-party which left here at the beginning of May had arrived safely, that the little steamboat *Isabella*, commanded by Captain Inglefield, had arrived[1] and taken Messrs. Cresswell and Wyniatt back to England. . . .

9 July 1853 (temp. max. 38°, min. 32°, med. 34°)
Today we received a visit in our hunting tent from Lieutenant Mecham. This officer, with his sledge-crew of six in the best of health, was on his way back to his ship, the *Resolute*, from a ninety-five-day journey; on his westward route from Melville Island he had discovered two more islands, one small, and one large, the first named Eglinton, the second Prince Patrick Island.[2] He had often seen reindeer and musk-oxen on the coast of Melville Island, but on the two newly-discovered islands, which were low-lying and composed of gravel, there was neither wildlife nor any trace of vegetation to be seen. Petrified wood and much stone pyrites had been found there. On their journey for a period of sixty days they had seen no life – neither insect nor animal.

18 July
. . . Commander McClintock of the ship *Intrepid* came back today with his crew in good health. He had explored the coast of Melville Island to the north and north-west, but, like the others had found no trace of Franklin. He had spent 105 days on his journey, and had traversed 1,200 miles of coast hitherto unexplored,[3] and discovered some more small islands in 78° north latitude. On the way back,

[1]Miertsching must have mistaken the *expectation* for the *fact*: Inglefield can hardly have got his ship in as early as the beginning of June.

[2]Mecham had mapped the southern and McClintock the northern sections of the shores of these islands. An unexplored gap on the west coast of Prince Patrick Island was first visited by Stefansson in 1915.

[3]McClintock had travelled 1,200 geographical or 1,400 statute miles, but naturally the extent of new coast visited was much less.

three days' journey from the ship, he was compelled, owing to wet weather and shortage of provisions, to leave behind tent and all equipment, and with only a little food to travel as light and as fast as possible by the quickest route to the ship. For the last three days his party ate only twice and, having no tent, they hollowed out sleeping places in the snow. . . .

10 *August 1853 (temp. max. 35°, min. 31°, med. 33°)*

The sea water has come up through the broad rents in the ice and overflowed this white, uneven expanse on all sides as far as the eye can reach. All is ready for sailing; we await only the break-up of the ice. Were the ice here at this season of the same thickness as it attains in Germany in the hardest winter, the ebb and flow would soon disperse it; but for this ice, 6, 10, to 15 feet in thickness, a strong ground swell from below, and an even stronger storm from above are required to break it. The captains and crews are growing impatient; and Mr. Nares is sent with six men, and boat and sledge to examine conditions along the coast; but after three days' absence they come back reporting no water, but "all ice". . . .

18 *August (temp. max. 35°, min. 32°, med. 34°)*

The strong wind became a strong gale; the ice began to move; and the ships, with the ice to which they were still fast anchored, were driven out to sea by the high tide. In a few hours the unending level of the sea was smashed to fragments, and the ships no longer had a secure anchorage, but were flung this way and that by the heaving and tumbling ice, and took many hard knocks. The rudder of the *Resolute* and two boats of the *Intrepid* were smashed to pieces. Towards evening the storm died away, and both ships lay tight beset among the ice-masses.

19 August

Driving eastwards with the ice; we are thirty-five miles from Dealy Island. Both ships are so hemmed in by pieces of ice that neither sail nor steam-engine are of use. The rudder is beyond repair – a new one is being hung.

21 August

Both ships still lie helpless, besieged by ice with which they are slowly drifting to the east. We are so far from land that we cannot see it. My fourth birthday in this sea of ice I spent in complete quiet. . . .

22 August (temp. max. 36°, min. 31°, med. 33°)

The strong south-west wind is driving the ice and us with it northwards where the water seems to be somewhat more open; late in the afternoon we came to thinner ice, or rather the ice had more room to yield and open a passage; promptly we exerted ourselves with sail and steam to get out of the ice into more open water near the land, which was coming into sight; but before this could be reached night came down upon us, so progress by sail or steam must be halted.

27 August (temp. max. 34°, min. 25°, med. 30°)

Since yesterday morning we have been out of the ice and tacking slowly to and from the land. To the north, east and, south is one mass of solid ice; on the contrary, to the west is open sea, but our way lies not west but east, and there the ice is packed so densely that not a spoonful of water is to be seen. . . .

29 August (temp. max. 28°, min. 25°, med. 27°)

Last night both ships were again so involved in ice as to lie utterly helpless. This morning came a mighty storm in

204

which the sturdy ships were flung around by the ice like
nut-shells, and threatened more than once with being overwhelmed and sunk by the ice-masses heaving up around
them. By the evident and marvellous help of the Lord both
ships were finally brought from the raging ice to open
water, where they were securely anchored in a small bay
or angle of the fast ice. Here Captain Kellett intends to
remain until a channel fit for a ship opens on the ice eastwards. . . .

*3 September 1853 (lat. 74° 57'; long. 105° 52';
temp. max. 31°, min. 27°, med. 29°)*
In view of the lateness of the season Captain Kellett has
wholly given up the idea of visiting the shore of Baffin Bay:
his one wish is to sail to England by the straightest and
shortest way. Ah, had I been permitted to go with Mr.
Cresswell to the *North Star* I would no longer be in this
ice-waste, so benumbing to the spirit, but might by now be
back in a land the Lord created as a home for man and
beast. I am weary and sick of this idle dreary life at sea.
Byam Martin's Island lies to the east of us and is visible
from the upper deck in clear weather. . . . Our ship, the
Intrepid, daily steams to the rim of the ice to find a way
to the east for both ships, but everywhere is impenetrable
ice and each evening we return to anchor near the *Resolute*.

10 September (temp. max. 20°, min. 16°, med. 18°)
This morning bright but cold weather; in the afternoon
much snow. After breakfast no ice was visible eastwards
from the masthead; Captain Kellett left his own ship at
anchor, came to our ship, and we went with a light wind
under sail and steam to examine the condition of the ice
farther east. After we had sailed east for three hours and
had put twenty-five miles behind us without seeing any
heavy ice, Captain Kellett decided that if this ship could

get through the *Resolute* could do the same. He promptly ordered the signal hoisted for the *Resolute* to follow us; but the order was not acknowledged, so we concluded that the signal was either not seen or not understood. We put about and steamed back with the same signal at the masthead. We had been on the backward course for about an hour when the *Resolute* observed our signal and hoisted an answering flag; in seven minutes we saw her quitting her anchorage under full sail and steering towards us. As soon as the two ships met, the *Intrepid* took the *Resolute* in tow, and we went with full sail and steam away to the east without seeing one piece of heavy ice; every man on board was overjoyed that the idle life at Point Griffiths had ended, and was living in confident hope of an uninterrupted voyage to England. All day there had been a light wind from the north; towards evening it fell calm. We steamed ahead with the *Resolute* in tow until it was completely dark, and then, as we were near the south tip of Byam Martin Island, we hove to without casting anchor for fear of the unmarked shoal which – according to Captain Parry – lay somewhere thereabouts. Seven hundred yards (paces) separated the two ships. The captain's order was: "As soon as the grey of dawn appears both ships proceed with sail or steam."

11 September (temp. max. 15°, min. 7°, med. 11°)
All through the night it was dead calm and very cold. The ship lay as motionless as a house on land. Yesterday in the joyous hope of soon reaching Europe we had tried to forecast the week and even the day of our arrival at London; and some had, in the genuine English style, laid appropriate bets; but to our astonishment when we rose early this morning, as soon as it was day, not only from the upper deck but also from the masthead we saw all our hopes dashed to the ground. As far as the eye could reach not a

drop of water, but one continuous sheet of ice lay before us. One could hardly conceive how great was the fear and the alteration on faces yesterday so bright; and with the continuing calm and severe cold the ice, which had appeared in the night, was growing each minute thicker and more firmly set. The ships could not break through the ice with steam only, unaided by wind – all possible efforts were made to get the ships to Cape Cockburn near by, but all human strength and skill were barely sufficient to move the ships forward ten feet. There is nothing for us but the hope that a gale will soon arise to break up the young ice and open a way out of the new prison.

13 September (temp. max. 18°, min. 8°, med. 13°)
Continuous very cold weather and perfect calm. The new ice is 5 inches thick. Our yearning wish and best hope to reach Europe this year is crushed and extinguished for good and all. Ah! to endure a fourth winter in this life at sea is almost too much. The mood on the ship and the feeling that masters everyone as he looks forward to the immediate future is more easily imagined than described. Ah, Lord, give me patience and trust in Thee as the one Helper and Comforter in time of need.

18 September (temp. max. 12°, min. 9°, med. 11°)
The ice covering the sea with a thickness of 13 inches was shattered today by a strong north-west wind, but there is no thought of a way being thereby opened for the ships. The *Resolute*, which was 2,097 paces from the *Intrepid*, has been driven by the current and the thrust of accumulated masses of ice to within 432 paces, where she is now surrounded by heaped up masses of young ice and seems to be freezing in immovably with a list to one side. In six days the current has driven the whole mass of ice, and us with it, sixty-four miles to the south-east. The two ships

sailed from Dealy Island with nine months' provisions for 175 men;[1] but as it is now accepted as certain that we shall not reach England this year, Captain Kellett has given orders to reduce the daily ration to two-thirds as from to-day; so that the nine months' ration may last for twelve months.

30 September (temp. max. 15°, min. 11°, med. 12°)
Both ships have partly been made ready to serve as winter quarters. The new ice is 2 feet, 3 inches, thick; we are being perpetually driven back and forth with it. We were frozen in in lat. 74° 49′, long. 105° 42′, and afterwards driven, now south, now north, and find ourselves today in lat. 74° 32′, long. 103° 6′, forty-five miles from the nearest land. The weather is very cold and biting; quarters for us "Investigators" on these ships were made ready for the voyage to England only – in the summer months – and now that winter is approaching we already feel the cold; what will it be like in real winter? A number of our invalids are not yet recovered, but are still confined to their beds; in particular, Mr. Sainsbury is very weak. In recent days a number of snowy owls have been shot.

[1]Supposing that he would reach England that autumn Kellett had cached surplus food and clothing at Dealy Island in the faint hope that it might yet be of service to the lost men of Franklin's expedition.

CHAPTER EIGHT

October 1853

... All available unused space on the ships is being fitted
out for winter quarters. All work on the two ships is finished and the crews are utterly without employment; the
time will be shortened by various sports on the ice, especially by a kind of game with a ball that occupies fifty to
sixty men at a time. Also daily visits from one ship to the
other enliven in some degree the weary hours. Many walks
are taken on the smooth ice. The general health is fair on
both ships: five men – Investigators – are lying very ill,
and two of them are, to all appearances, not long for this
world. I often visit them. . . . As for comfortable quarters
on board, they lie beyond our sphere of knowledge: there is
a desperate shortage of space; even the two captains, Kellett and McClure, must live and sleep in one cabin, and
one must lie in bed while the other washes and dresses, and
at breakfast both must depart to the upper deck, while the
steward puts the beds away and sets out breakfast. On the
Intrepid our lot is even worse, for we have neither the
necessary bedding nor warm cabins. Our beds consist of
two woollen blankets (coverlets), one of which each man
brought in his sleeping-bag from the *Investigator*, and the

other issued to us here; more cannot be given us for there is no more to give; and our cabins, framed of canvas instead of plank, are so cold that the temperature never rises above freezing-point.

For the whole month of October: temp. max. 26°, min. −21°, med. 4°.

5 *November 1853*

... Today there were great celebrations on both ships, for the crews were observing Guy Fawkes' Day. (Guy Fawkes was the ringleader of the band of conspirators who, out of religious hatred, would have blown Parliament into the air with gunpowder, but before this frightful deed could be accomplished, it was detected and suppressed. Guy Fawkes was burnt alive in 1605 [sic].) At 7 a.m. there came to our ship from the *Resolute* a band, with horrible music, masked and disguised, drawing a sledge on which, on a chair, sat a stuffed figure representing Guy Fawkes. They sang a few songs which were appropriate to this setting, and presented Captain McClintock with an address in which they requested his permission to pay this visit to his ship. After a frightful display of theatricals and nonsense they returned to their own ship. An hour later the same ceremony was performed by our crew for the benefit of the *Resolute*. The day passed as quietly as usual, but towards evening, when it was quite dark, the display was repeated with uproar by both ships; and then a great fire was kindled on the ice into which both strawmen, partly filled with powder, were thrown in and blown into the air. With loud hurrahs, blazing torches, and darting rockets each crew retired to its own ship, where an extra double grog, the gift of Captain Kellett, awaited them.

Today we saw the sun for the last time this year.

14 *November (temp. max. −20°, min. −15°, med. −19°)*

For several days it has been observed that the ice is now

perfectly motionless; both ships are, according to sights regularly taken for three days, in the same place, and this is lat. 74° 41′ north, long. 101° 22′ west.

The nearest land is Cape Cockburn, thirty-eight miles away, and in bright weather it can be seen from the crow's-nest. After protracted and severe suffering Mr. Sainsbury, lieutenant[1] of the *Investigator*, died today at the age of twenty-six years. Since our departure from England he had been my ship-mate and we had messed together, so that we had become tolerably well acquainted. Dr. Piers and I visited him daily on his sick bed, and, as the end drew near, many nights also. And, when his speech began to fail, we often would read aloud passages from Scripture and other Christian books, which, especially in the last days, seemed to impress him deeply. Yesterday he requested the officers and captains to visit his bed-side, and with hand-clasp and words asked forgiveness for his many shortcomings. His submission to the will of God, and especially his last utterances, give ground to hope that through grace he will find salvation as a poor rescued sinner. Tomorrow, with military honours and the usual ceremonies observed at sea, his body will be sunk below the ice in the deep sea.

> To the sea let these remains
> In hope committed be;
> Until the body, chang'd, obtains
> Blest immortality.

30 *November (temp. max. −12°, min. −37°, med. −21°)*
In the last half of this month we have had continuously stormy and very unfriendly weather; often snow fell thickly all day; the ships were simply buried in snow; and the upper deck, protected from the snow by the housing, was the only place where we could warm ourselves by exercise. In many respects we are better off this winter than in the

[1]He had been promoted *in absentia* during the cruise.

three previous ones, passed in our own ship; the daily ration, although only two-thirds, is sufficient for inactive men. There is no shortage of lighting this dark winter; and these ships have been provided in England with many comforts, necessary for this climate, of which, in our ship, we had no idea; and also the social intercourse that occurs when two ships are together affords diversion and relieves the monotony of the long hours and eternal loneliness which are so oppressive to the spirits. On the other hand with regard to our cabins, bedding, clothing, and many such things essential to human life, we are very poorly provided. We were able to bring nothing from our ship except the clothes we wore, and here they could give us little or nothing, because everything in compliance with the orders of the Admiralty had to be left at Dealy Island. Furthermore, because we expected to be in England in a month or two, we were all prepared for a couple of months only, and now have to taste the bitterness of a polar winter to an extent that we had not yet experienced. The cold nights especially are barely endurable: a man lies rolled up in two woollen blankets in a canvas tent packed inside and out with ice and snow, and tries to warm himself and to sleep in woollen blankets which are frozen and icy from the breath and perspiration of the human body, but he cannot do both; towards morning, tired, stiff and shivering with cold, he falls into a sort of stupor for an hour or two; sleep is wholly out of the question. Were one not permitted to sleep a few hours by day on a bench in the officers' cabin (gun room), he could not endure the lack of rest. But all this deprivation and discomfort will have an end, and may all these experiences work together for the best, and in happier days abide in our memories and fill us with gratitude.

On neither of the two ships can the mood be called pleasant. The unexpected winter in the ice and the deprivation of space and comfort owing to the intrusion of us passengers does not please men who had been accustomed to something better. One can well see here that sympathy, love, and friendship, unless kindled in our hearts by a Christian spirit, cannot endure, and may be likened to blazing straw, quickly kindled and soon extinguished. It is gratifying, especially to our worthy Captain McClure, that the men of the *Investigator*, owing to their good behaviour and peaceful deportment, are doing nothing to provoke unpleasantness. From the very beginning of the month Captain Kellett had planned to present plays and entertainments, to occupy and enliven depressed spirits *through means such as these*. But this project had been postponed owing to the death of Mr. Sainsbury. Dramatic costumes and the like had been brought from England. For fourteen days men have been busy converting the deck of the *Resolute* into a great hall with decorations, stage, and scenery. Those sailors chosen to act go daily on to the ice to learn their parts. Programs – red silk for the captains, blue for the officers, and of paper for the men – have been printed and distributed. This evening at 7 the sound of a trumpet proclaimed the commencement of the play, *The Taming of the Shrew*, followed by the farce, *The Two Bonnycastles*, which lasted until 9.30. All spectators received a pint of beer. November temperatures: max. –3°, min. –42°, med. –20°.

15 December 1853 (temp. max. –37°, min. –42°, med. –40°)

The weather is cold and stormy, but day and night the sky is clear and covered with stars. The general health is not what one could wish. As the hospital is too small, the space next to my cabin has been set up as a second sick-room and equipped with an iron stove; the two patients – a sailor and a married petty officer – are very ill, and, according to appearances, unlikely to outlive the winter. Because the recreations and drama provided by Captain Kellett have not had the success which he desired and hoped to obtain from them, some of the officers are delivering lectures of a sort in simple style, intelligible to uneducated sailors, twice weekly. The men attend gladly and in great numbers, and show much appreciation. Any man may take part in them. These lectures, or, as they are properly named, "time shortenings", are theoretical and practical expositions of astronomy, chemistry, geology or earth-building, mechanics, the system of winds and ocean currents, arctic exploration and travelling, etc. Though very simple and inadequate, they have been well attended and everyone seems to enjoy them. When the men are walking back and forth on the ice their conversation is on learned topics. Without doubt these lectures, if supported by private reading, are much better than theatrical representations.

22 *December (temp. max. −30°, min. −41°, med. −35°)*
Yesterday on the shortest day of the year, at midday, in bright moon and starlight, the finest English print could be read. This evening theatricals of a sort were presented on our ship, the *Intrepid*. First many silhouettes were shown with a magic-lantern, then many wonderful conjuring tricks were performed;[1] after these came a kind of masquerade performed with many songs, burlesque and comic, spoken or sung; and finally a farce, *Box and Cox*, was presented. Every sailor received a glass of grog and a pint of beer; the officers of the ship were entertained by McClintock to supper and punch.

25 *December (temp. max. −40°, min. −43°, med. −41°)*
Today the holy festival of Christmas was celebrated ac-

[1]An anecdote preserved in Markham's *Life of McClintock* reveals that Miertsching enjoyed the conjuring tricks (performed by Mr. Krabbé of the *Intrepid*) more than his own grave narrative would lead one to believe.

cording to the style of the English mariner by eating, drinking, and frolicking. Roast beef and plum pudding are essential to the observance of the day. Seamen's quarters on both ships were very tastefully decorated with flags, pictures, and various mottoes very neatly printed. Because today is Sunday Captain Kellett will observe Christmas tomorrow: Mr. Haswell, Dr. Armstrong, and I, along with Captain McClintock, are invited from this ship to dine with him. The weather is stormy, especially today, and also the snow is driving so thickly that already several have lost their way while passing from ship to ship, and have only been set right by the sound of the ship's bell.

31 December (temp. max. −8°, min. −16°, med. −11°)
Because of the continuous storms and blizzards, all communication between the two ships has often been interrupted, and to overcome this they have set up an electromagnetic telegraph, which works very well. From ship to ship is stretched a wire connected with a galvanic battery and clockwork in both vessels, and with its ends extending through the ice into the sea water. If one wishes to send a message by this "Blitzpost", first of all an alarm is given by the magnetic bell in the works; as soon as this is acknowledged the sending of letters and syllables begins. This contrivance is the cause of endless jokes: often a game of chess is played by means of this "Schnellpost"....

While many of the "Resolutes" are commissioned to study or to learn a new play (its performance is a matter of great doubt) our sailors have been employed in building two rows of pyramids, 12 feet high, from ship to ship, so that we now have an alley of snow pyramids on a straight line, 500 paces long.

The sick on both ships are unhappily no better, and there is little hope as long as this intense cold lasts. The three sick near my cabin, of whom one is weak in the head and the other two beyond the hope of recovery, cause me many disturbed nights by the frightful speeches with which they testify their impatience and, in the daytime, their heathenish opinions – in order to provoke me as a pietist. ... Today yet another year comes to an end. When will the time, the year, the day come, of my deliverance from the sea life which I find so repulsive? Lord, Thou alone knowest this. I must be thankful for the past. December temperatures: max. –8°, min. –44°, med. –30°.

1 January 1854 (temp. max. –43°, min. –46°, med. –44°)

Today, on New Year's Day, there is again much banquetting on both ships. Christmas Day and New Year's Day are the only two festivals in the whole year, except Sunday, which are observed at sea; but unhappily not in an edifying manner, but by eating, drinking, and uproar for which extra rations of food and spirits are issued – a truly English tradition. . . . My three sick neighbours are in a pitiful state; the condition of the poor marine, Hood, is particularly lamentable. This unhappy man has no rest night or day, but groans, curses, and complains unceasingly. I go often to his bedside and try to awaken him to a sense of his pitiful state and of the great danger he is in of being lost eternally, although in his last hours his salvation is possible if he cries for pity and deliverance to the crucified Saviour, Who assuredly will hear his prayers, for He desires not the death of the sinner, but his repentance, that after his death he may dwell with Him in His Heavenly Kingdom with all the souls of the saved; but unhappily, unhappily, all my words seem to be in vain. He absolutely refuses to listen; he has forbidden me to visit him, for he cannot endure religious instruction, and does not believe in it. Daily the doctor reads to him the prayers prescribed by the Liturgy for the dangerously ill, but they leave him unchanged. He does not believe the Word of God; if one speaks to him of his immortal soul, and of the purpose of Man's creation by God, etc., especially when anyone – an old comrade perhaps – speaks of things spiritual, he gives no answer; at best he listens sullenly, and often interrupts the speaker by pronouncing a curse on his own sufferings. Here one may see a fellow-creature in his deepest misery. Lord, take pity on this poor soul which Thou hast purchased with Thine own blood. About 11 p.m. I rose from my bed to visit the sick man, but he was of the same mind as before; I could only invoke the Divine mercy and pity on his behalf. About 2 a.m. he became quite still, neither word nor movement could I hear on the other side of the canvas curtain; I rose, and as I was coming out of my cabin the sentry told me that the sick man had drawn his last breath and lived no more. I went in and found it so; his precious ransomed soul had taken its flight to receive judgement at the throne of the Righteous Judge. Who can fathom the ways and the decrees of the Most High? Oh Lord, be gracious unto *us*.

The four naval surgeons held a post-mortem on the body.

The deceased was a marine, thirty-four years old and thirteen years in the service. Tomorrow the ice will be opened and his body sunk in the sea. When his ship, the *Intrepid*, sailed from England into the frozen seas in 1852 her crew consisted of forty persons, and this is now the fifth death to occur among them.[1] Our ship, the *Investigator*, has been two years longer at sea, namely since January 1850, and up till now only four of her crew have died.

[1]McDougall gives the number of deaths on the *Intrepid* up to this date as four. But Miertsching might have strengthened his point by recalling that the Investigators had been at sea for well over three years, and for much of the period on half rations, before the first death occurred – a record of which Armstrong was not unreasonably proud.

Me for Thy coming, Lord, prepare, grant that I may ready be,
   Whene'er Thou callest, without fear — to meet and welcome
Thee.

18 *January (temp. max. −48°, min. −54°, med. −52°)*

All is going its wonted way in these winter quarters, without disturbance; nothing out of the ordinary occurs except that, often, especially on the *Resolute*, Captain Kellett is compelled to resort to severe rebuke and punishment to keep his unruly crew in order. The health on both ships remains more or less the same; thirty-five names are on the sick list; of these some are dangerously ill, and two men are mentally deranged. The death of the marine on our ship has much affected the other two sick men, especially the petty officer, Wilkie; the prejudice of these men, dead to Christ, because I do not belong to the English High Church, seems largely to have been laid aside; at least my visits to the sick are welcome, and discussion of sacred things is not objectionable to them; and certainly many are most grateful when I read something aloud and give the necessary explanations. It is noteworthy here — it was at first the same on the *Investigator* — that everyone welcomed me and, if opportunity offered, was ready to do me friendly services; but as soon as I began to speak of religious and spiritual matters they drew back because they had the unjust suspicion that in some subtle manner I wished to separate them from the English High Church to which they thought they belonged, and which must be the right church because their queen belonged to it — and to attach them to some sect. But I hope now to overcome these prejudices.

31 *January (temp. max. −52°, min. −55°, med. −53°)*

For the last half of this month the weather has been bright and calm, but bitterly cold; and we feel it, especially in our threadbare clothing; we are wearing the same clothing consisting of one suit only, since April 1853, wearing it daily and often by night as well, and it is now beginning to wear, to grow thin, and to give little protection against the extreme cold. . . .

2 February 1854 (temp. max. −36°, min. −44°, med. 40°)

Last night another of my neighbours died, the ice-quartermaster, Wilkie, aged thirty-six years; he leaves a wife and three children in England. In complete resignation to the will of our Lord in Whose grace and merits alone he trusted, and remembering our Saviour's death and sufferings, he bore the pains of sickness with the greatest patience; I often heard him imploring his Saviour for a speedy release. I have often had very edifying conversation with him. When his ship-mates visited him he would often admonish them with tears to reform their careless lives, and show them that the Bible was the only rule by which to lead a life pleasing to God. For the last two days he could neither speak nor hear; often his uplifted arms and gaze fixed on high showed that he was praying. Shortly before his death he bade us farewell.

We Investigators were notified today by Captain Kellett that we were to make ready to journey from here to the *North Star* at Cape Riley at the end of March or the beginning of April, in order to sail from there to England in the coming summer, as from Cape Riley on, the water will be open.

This was cheering news to all of us, for we are heartily sick of living on these two ships, and although we have a journey of fifty German miles on foot over the ice before us, we will rejoice on the day of our departure.

28 February

. . . Of my sick neighbours two are dead, and the third has

been taken back to the regular hospital; unhappily they have carried off not only the sick man, but also the stove which used to make my cabin so magnificently warm. Once again I am to be frozen solid. When my servant brings my water in the morning I must be quick, for in a few minutes it is frozen in the wash-basin; the most disagreeable consequence of which is that I must dry myself with a towel which is frozen stiff whereby I often scraped my skin. . . .

15 March 1854 (temp. max. −36°, min. −45°, med. −41°)
Today Messrs. Mecham and Krabbé [master of the *Intrepid*] were ordered by the captain to get ready for travel – each with his own crew to make a journey and search the coasts to the west for traces of the *Enterprise*. Mr. Mecham with six men and a sledge is to visit Prince of Wales Strait; and Mr. Krabbé with six men and a sledge will go to our ship, the *Investigator*, in the Bay of Mercy. . . .

. . . .

3 April 1854
Today the two sledge-parties under Messrs. Mecham and Krabbé took their departure. They will travel in company as far as Dealy Island, where they will draw supplies from the depot for the rest of the journey, and from there to Point Providence,[1] whence Krabbé will continue westwards and Mecham will turn south. Krabbé has orders to bring back the journals of the officers which were left on the *Investigator*. . . .

10 April
. . . Our Investigators are full of life and good spirits at the prospect of soon quitting these ships; they live to get away,

[1]One of the two capes that mark the northern outlet of Prince of Wales Strait, Point Peel and Point Russell, must be intended here.

to hold together among themselves, to do their duty well and promptly without grumbling, to give no opening for unpleasantness; and when the others devote the evening hours of leisure to their wild enjoyments, our "pietists", as they are sneeringly called even by some of the officers, gather on our ship, where we have already had many agreeable and blessed private gatherings. Today in the afternoon our "postal" sledge under Mr. Hamilton arrived from Cape Riley bringing letters and strict orders from Sir Edward Belcher to Captain Kellett:[1] To leave the ships *Resolute* and *Intrepid* in the ice, and take his entire crews over the ice to the *North Star.* . . . Towards evening two sledges were made ready for the journey of Messrs. Haswell and Paine with twenty men to the *North Star.*

12 April

The day before yesterday two sledge-parties left, and again yesterday another two set out for the *North Star* with twenty-two men under the orders of Dr. Armstrong and Pim. Today Captains Kellett, McClure, McClintock, and Richards held a secret session at which it was resolved to send a petition to Sir Edward Belcher and request him to revoke his order for the desertion of these two ships, *Resolute* and *Intrepid*, and to permit Captain Kellett with fifty men to remain another summer in order to bring these ships to England. Captain McClintock left us today with the dog-sledge to deliver this petition in person to the commodore, Sir Edward. Captain Richards left at the same time to rejoin his ship *Resolute*[2] in Wellington Channel.

14 April

Today the rest of us Investigators took our leave from

[1]Actually the orders were not "strict", but so ambiguous that Kellett insisted on a clearer mandate before he would comply.
[2]The *Assistance* — an obvious slip of the pen.

here bound for the *North Star*. We have three sledges under Captain McClure, Dr. Piers, and me. We took our leave of these ships without regret, for every step brings us nearer to Europe, and it is as good as certain that if we reach the *North Star* the ice at last will no longer be an impassable obstacle on the way to England. We are beginning our 200-mile journey on foot with pleasure, and hope to be at Cape Riley in twenty days. This is the second time that we find ourselves without a ship. When we were compelled to desert our good ship *Investigator* and leave all our belongings behind, each took with him only what he wore on his person; now we have been in these clothes and linen for an entire year on these ships, and they are well worn; we could leave nothing behind on these ships, for we brought nothing to them and received little or nothing there. It has been good for us all that in love and friendship we could conduct ourselves differently from the crews of these ships; the "pietistic Investigators" have often been mocked and have suffered much unfriendly handling which, with ordinary seamen, would have caused much unpleasantness, and demanded retaliation and reprisal; but in this as in other matters our sailors show themselves grateful for the love and friendship they have enjoyed, and apologize when any unintentional fault has been committed. Also, I cannot enough thank the Lord Who rules in the hearts of men for the thoughtfulness, love, and friendship shown me by the captain, officers, and men. Before we left the ships, Captain Kellett assembled us all on deck and thanked us publicly for the regular discipline and exceptionally good conduct which to the very last had characterized the men of the *Investigator*; he handed to our worthy Captain McClure a letter to the Admiralty in which he gave the crew of the *Investigator* a character so good that one would rarely find other ships worthy of it.

25 April

Today we pitched our tents hard by Cape Hotham, the western angle of the entrace to Wellington Channel. From here on, it should be another forty miles to Cape Riley where the *North Star* is frozen in; the ice should be quite smooth and free from snow. The journey from the *Resolute* to this point has not been as difficult as we at first expected it to be. For the most part the ice has been smooth and level; only in a few places have the upheaved masses been forty-five feet high. Terribly exhausting is the snow on the level ice: at every step the foot sinks six to eight inches in snow with the texture of dry sand. Our days are so arranged that we step out briskly for five hours and then spend seven in the tents, so that in twenty-four hours we sleep twice and march twice. Night is no hindrance to this because it is already beginning to be very bright: it is dark for only about two hours at midnight, and those hours are passed in the tent. If the weather is very cold and windy we spend an hour more in the tent and a shorter time on the march. The sledge-loads which we are required to draw are not heavy, the men are cheery and good-humoured; also the daily ration is more than one needs, and so the days pass full of cheer and vigour, ever forward over the frozen sea, and every stride brings us nearer to our appointed end. Also, there is no lack of those incidents, interesting though not always enjoyable, that one may justly call adventures, and which when they are over are a great source of conversation and do much to banish monotony. It happened, for instance, in Mr. Ommaney's[1] tent that after evening prayer, when all had got into their sleeping-bags for a

---

[1] The occurrence of this name is a mystery: a Captain Ommaney had been second-in-command of the previous Austin expedition, but no officer of that name is listed on the *Investigator* or on any of the five ships under the supreme command of Sir Edward Belcher. Furthermore, Miertsching has expressly stated that the tent commanders were McClure, Piers, and himself.

night's rest without remembering to secure the tent-door, that a polar bear poked his head into the tent. The officer, who alone observed this, snatched up his gun which stood in the corner of the tent, but as he was taking his aim it went off – probably by an unintentional pressure of the man's finger – and instead of going through the bear the bullet went through the tent and cut the ropes; the tent collapsed overwhelming its inmates and, along with them, the bear. It was a piece of good fortune that three tents stood together; the men in the other two, aroused by the shot and the uproar, sprang up and shot the bear down. The entire tragedy was over in less time than I require to relate it. Only a few days before, it had happened that our cook had been negligent in fastening the tent-door, which was opened by the perpetual stirring of the wind; we heard the tread of feet outside, but, supposing that it was some-one from the next tent, lay with our heads buried in our sleeping-bags until the sound of a peculiar snort brought our faces out of our bags, and we perceived above us, inside the tent, the head and long neck of a polar bear snorting and breathing heavily. Here was a situation where good advice would have been worth much: we lay in a narrow tent packed together like herrings, in bags too, and scarcely capable of moving; a sailor had the happy idea of drawing his large knife, and reaching out from his bag with one arm, he cut an opening in the side of the tent; and in a few seconds we all crawled out of the tent with our bags, snatched up our guns, loaded with ball, from the sledge, and with one volley laid our unwelcome guest dead at our feet. These disagreeable and unwelcome occurrences are interesting, especially when they have a happy ending; they furnish a topic of conversation and inspire many genu-ine sailors' jests to enliven the weary travellers. . . . It often happens that the beard of a sleeper freezes to his woollen sleeping-bag because in the bitter cold his breath congeals into ice and, because he cannot set out on the march with a sleeping-bag hanging from his chin, he must submit to a process of liberation devised for freeing one's beard when such an accident befalls a traveller. The process is this: the man's tent-mates sit close around him with their short to-bacco pipes well ignited and by this means finally succeed in separating the man from his bed. This is a genuine vapour cure, for the smoke of from six to eight pipes under his nose brings him to the verge of suffocation. When this first cure has been accomplished he must take his boots, which he has used as a pillow, and try to thaw them sufficiently to be drawn onto his feet. While this is going on, the cook is busy outside the tent melting ice or snow in a kettle with a spirit lamp; when this has been done, powdered cocoa and brown sugar are added–and the cocoa is ready. The tin cups – which since the beginning of the journey have not been washed or cleaned of the frozen dregs of successive meals – are brought from the sledges; frost or snow adhering to them is removed with a glove and the due portion of cocoa is poured in. If a man brings this tin cup to his lips before the hot cocoa has warmed it he leaves skin hanging from the cup, as happens in Germany with ice or cold metal – and so those little incidents are produced which seem to occur so often in daily life, but which one cannot fully appreciate unless he has experienced and shared in them. The proverb, "A jest breaks no bones", is as applicable to polar life as to life elsewhere. We had a day's rest at Cape Hotham – that is, instead of five hours in our tents we remained for ten because of the wind and drifting snow. We had set out again on the road and had marched for barely an hour when we met Captain McClintock with his dog-sledge. He had been conferring with Sir Edward Belcher, and was now on his way back to Captain Kellett. He bore a positive order from Commodore Belcher to Captain Kellett to abandon his ice-bound ships *Reso-*

lute and *Intrepid* as soon as possible, and with the entire crews to start without delay on the journey to the ship *North Star*. The chronometers and other valuable instruments are to be brought along, but everything else is to be left behind.

26 April

On our last journey by night we arrived at the tip of Cape Hotham, close to the mainland, and visited the depot planted there by the *North Star*, and stocked with provisions for the use of Franklin or Collinson. We found there a number of broken chests and kegs and as we were short of fuel we loaded a good supply on our sledges. As the ice was smooth thereabouts and there was no need for the officers to lend a hand with the sledges, I went some distance ahead and as I was thus walking alone I saw on the ice some distance away an extraordinary dark point; with my gun at the ready I drew as near to it as I could, fired and heard the bullet strike – but the supposed wild animal remained as motionless as before. I went up to it and found that it was a tin chest and that my bullet had gone clean through it; on opening it we found fourteen pounds of coffee, which caused great rejoicing among the sledge crews. We had just before obtained a sufficiency of fuel, so at every halt a regular cauldron of coffee was prepared and every man drank as much as he pleased. This afternoon we met six sledge-crews laden with provisions from the *North Star* and on their way to Cape Hotham to add to the depot that is being left there for Franklin or Collinson.[1]

28 April

Now we are back on a ship and it is to be hoped that it is

[1]They had no idea of Collinson's whereabouts – he had been unreported for two and a half years. He had been as far east as Cambridge Bay, but at this time was far away, frozen in on the north shore of Alaska.

the last we shall board before reaching England. This morning we reached the *North Star* in excellent trim, and we found the comrades who had preceded us in excellent health. Captain Pullen and his officers gave us the friendliest reception. The people who came with us must busy themselves in preparing a dwelling-place for us on the lower deck of this frigate; until this is done our abode will be in tents on the ice near the ship. This ship, the *North Star*, is a twenty-six-gun frigate; Captain Pullen and his six officers seem to be the finest of fellows. The bay in which this depot ship has now lain for two years is named Erebus and Terror Bay; the headland that encloses it from the east is Cape Riley, a perpendicular cliff 740 feet high; the west side of the bay is formed by Beechey Island, which is a volcanic pile irregularly thrown together and formed of sandstone and limestone, a grey clinker-like mass; its height is 900 feet above sea-level.

4 *May 1854*

Today my cabin was ready; we have only four carpenters and these have to prepare twelve cabins with accessories and sixteen tables with benches for the seamen on the lower deck; as I was weary of sleeping in a tent on the ice, I borrowed some tools and in three days built a cabin and fitted it with bed and wash-stand, and will occupy it tonight. Tomorrow I will make myself a wooden table. As yet I have done little sight-seeing in these parts, and what I have seen does not please me. The lofty, ragged masses of rock of which the whole landscape consists have a repellent aspect. Although the entire desert land from Bering Strait to this point can fairly be described as a barren wilderness of rock, sand, snow, and ice, yet in places vegetation, though poor and stunted, does occur; nor is there a complete lack of charm and beauty in the shape of plain and mountain. But this is no longer the case when one begins to pass east through Barrow Strait – here is the genuine Chaos. The 100th degree of longitude seems to be a dividing line: west of it as far as Bering Strait the land is flatter with many small patches of grass and moss; but to the east the aspect of the land is repulsive: lofty but shapeless heaps of stone or rock which seem in part to be formed of petrified shell-fish and sea-weed. No grass, moss, or vegetation is to be found here, and very little wild-life, and that only towards the end and the beginning of the year. It is utterly impossible for larger animals to clamber over these masses of rock. The tiny Beechey Island, which is about an hour's walk in circumference, lies about three hundred paces from the spot where the *North Star* is frozen in. I have twice strolled over to it; one finds there many traces of Franklin's expedition; it appears that here he spent his first winter. Tenting-grounds, fragments of cable, wood shavings, iron hoops, glass, earthenware, and the like are found in a number of places. In addition there are three graves, each marked by a black-painted oaken slab on which the following epitaphs are carved:

I

Sacred to the memory of W. Braine, R. M., H. M. S. *Erebus*, died April 3rd, 1846, aged 32 years. "Choose ye this day whom you will serve."

II

Sacred to the memory of Ino. Hartwell, A. B., H. M. S. *Erebus*, aged 23 years. "Thus saith the Lord of Hosts, Consider your ways."

III

Sacred to the memory of Ino. Torrington, who departed this life Jan. 1st, A. D. 1846, on board Her Majesty's ship *Terror*, aged 20.

The year and the dates show when Franklin was here with his ships; these are absolutely the only traces that have yet been found of that unfortunate expedition. No other written record has been found here.

228

28 May

Today Captain Kellett with his crews from the *Resolute* and the *Intrepid* reached the *North Star* in good condition; their sledges were loaded down with nautical instruments and personal belongings. Until now we had passed the time fairly comfortably and agreeably on this ship, but now we are packed quite close together because four crews are jammed on to one ship; we must endure by the exercise of much patience what it is to be hoped will last for only a few months; for the relations between the men already here and the new arrivals are not of the best. . . . Sir Edward Belcher's ships, the *Assistance* and the *Pioneer*, are frozen in on the east side of Wellington Channel, fifty-four miles from Beechey Island. Every week sledges arrive from there loaded with nautical instruments. Again yesterday came the sledges from Sir Edward with more chests of instruments; one of these, marked "nautical instruments", was broken while being hoisted aboard; it had to be opened and the "instruments" which it contained were found to be three dozen bottles of *Franzbrandwein* and a few fox-pelts. It seems that Sir Edward is contemplating the abandonment of his two ships also in the ice, and is taking care to transfer his personal belongings to the *North Star*. . . .

June 1854

The carpenters are feverishly engaged in building a wooden house on Beechey Island, which will provide a comfortable home for sixty men and will be stocked with food and other necessities in case Franklin or Collinson should wander in this direction. . . . On the 10th Messrs. Mecham and Krabbé returned in fine fettle from their long journey. Mr. Mecham had reached the Princess Royal Islands and had found our depot in good condition. Near this provision depot we had built a pile of stones (cairn) and left a record in a metal box; in this box Mr. Mecham found a full report of the doings of Captain Collinson. The *Enterprise*, which had left Honolulu four days ahead of us by way of Petropavlovsk, arrived [at Bering Strait] fourteen days after us and learned from Captain Moore that we had sailed ahead into the ice. After repeated but fruitless efforts to follow us Captain Collinson found himself compelled to sail back to China (Hong Kong) and there to winter. In 1851 he was able to follow in our course, but before he reached the Mackenzie a lieutenant and a sailor of his crew were murdered by the Eskimos. At Cape Bathurst he learned from the natives in what direction we had sailed in the previous year. At Nelson's Head and again at the Princess Royal Islands he found our records, but on account of the ice could press no further to the north, and wintered in Walker Bay near Prince Albert Land where he was visited on his ship by the Eskimos of those parts, but owing to lack of an interpreter could not speak with them. Whither the *Enterprise* intended to go in the summer of 1853 – whether she will try to come our way or sail back to Bering Strait – could not be ascertained from the record she had left. Mr. Mecham has travelled a thousand miles on his sixty-eight-day journey on foot. Mr. Krabbé with his sledge-party found our old ship, the *Investigator*, in the Bay of Mercy much as we had left her in April 1853; according to appearances the ice again remained unbroken last summer. He stayed there for a week and put ashore the good provisions which he found aboard, and other articles. The orders of Captain Kellett – that he should bring back our journals which Captain McClure had left behind – he did not fulfil, *because he could not find any*!?[1] No traces of Franklin were found, nor had Captain Collinson come to the Bay of Mercy. . . . One of our sailors (Morgan), who had been sick continuously since 1852, and extremely ill for the last eight months, was

[1]This extraordinary incident can only be assigned to the neglect, accidental or deliberate, of McClure, for Krabbé must have made sure where the records were to be found before leaving the *Resolute*.

early this month called by God as a poor pardoned sinner to a better life. His body was laid near the graves of Franklin's three men on Beechey Island. He leaves a widow and four little children in England. . . .

July 1854

In the first days of this month Sir Edward Belcher sent his two lieutenants, May and Cheyne, here to the *North Star* because he can no longer endure them. They are no longer officers of the expedition, and will be regarded as passengers. At the same time came Mr. Sherard Osborn, commander of the tender *Pioneer*, also as a passenger. He had fallen into disfavour and for two months had been held under arrest by Sir Edward.[1] The regular sledge trips between here and Sir Edward were discontinued at the middle of the month. Snow, melted by the sun, had so covered the surface of the ice with water that the sledge floated, while its crew were wading knee-deep in water; also the clefts that appeared in the ice after the last spring tide make sledge journeys no longer possible. Sir Edward has sent an order to Captain Pullen to equip the house on Beechey Island as a comfortable residence; for in the course of the month he himself intends to take up his abode there. On the 20th we had the pleasure of seeing this interesting man, Captain Sir Edward Belcher, C. B., Commander of the Arctic Squadron, coming with three sledges and two boats, and taking immediate possession of the house. It was formally opened for use and named North-

[1]When the expedition reached home the Admiralty would not permit this feud to continue, and refused Osborn's application for a court-martial, while in effect exonerating him by immediate promotion.

Both Kellett and Belcher were in the awkward position of having less knowledge of the Arctic than some of the officers under their command: Kellett had managed by tact and good sense; the capable but arrogant Belcher had not. The latter got himself a bad press by making enemies of two distinguished arctic historians, Sherard Osborn and Clements Markham, but a recent, more balanced estimate of him by Noel Wright (*Quest for Franklin*, pp. 209-10) does little to redeem his character.

umberland House, by Sir Edward. He sent the men who had come with him back to his ships, keeping only six to be his bodyguard or watch and to live in the house with him. A cairn has been built on the summit of Beechey Island; it is twenty-three feet high and a series of steps leads up to it. Also, Sir Edward has had a monument erected to the memory of those who have died in the polar regions since 1850: their number is thirty-two. Towards the end of the month the ship will be ready to sail.

August 1854

With joyous hope we saw in the first days of this month the frozen sea cracking and opening rents which daily grew wider. In order to get the ship as early as possible to the open sea where the ice occurs only in fragments, we were obliged to cut a canal 900 paces long and 20 broad through ice 15 to 25 feet thick, and this was accomplished with all available help employed, partly by sawing, partly by blasting. It was a hard and wearing task occupying three weeks, but it was finished on the 20th and the ship was immediately towed through the canal into open water and anchored on the margin of the land-ice. From the top of a 900-foot mountain near by it was seen that the frozen surface was broken into fragments; only in Wellington Channel does any fast ice remain.... The summer is almost over, and new ice is forming, especially by night and on sunless days, in all places where the water is not kept in motion by wind, tide, or swell. The weather is good for the most part, the nights are cold. The sea-fowl are flying back to the south. We had hoped that a vessel would come from England to carry us "shipless" ones home, but our hope and wish has not yet been fulfilled; and our old frigate, the *North Star*, which has fought on the shores of China and Borneo, and has suffered many a shock on polar journeys, must carry us all home.

26 August

Early today at 8 o'clock came the last boat from Belcher's ships, and at 9 the anchors were hoisted, three cheers given, sails hoisted, and with a light west wind we set forth for the beloved homeland for which we had so long yearned; here on one ship are the crews of six: the total number is 278 men. Pleasing emotions stirred everyone of us as we sailed forth, and as far as the eye could reach a great open sea presented a strange sight, for never since August 1850 had we seen so much water. Our worthy Captain McClure, with whom I stood on the ship's poop, could not restrain his tears; gratitude overwhelmed him at being thus set free after years of imprisonment in the ice. We gazed long, yearningly, and happily; but even more pleasure was to be ours on this happy day. We were barely in the open sea and just rounding the tip of Cape Riley when the cry resounded from the look-out in the crow's-nest: "Sail ho! Two sail right ahead". And so it was: two vessels, a sailing-ship and a steamer, were coming towards us from the east with flags flying. We greeted them with great unspeakable joy. It was Captain Inglefield with the ships *Phoenix* and *Talbot*, coming from England. They accompanied us back to the anchorage: the mail-bags were opened, and now, after remaining so long with no word from my beloved homeland, letters and papers from England and Germany were handed to me.... With joyful heart I could praise and glorify Him Who had preserved us from so many dangers, and had granted to me even to this hour to enjoy His precious grace; praise and thanksgiving to His name for His everlasting compassion.

27 August

After the supplies brought by the ship *Talbot* for Franklin had been landed on Beechey Island and added to the depot, the crews of Captain Kellett's ships were transferred to the

Phoenix and those of Sir Edward Belcher to the *Talbot*. Captain McClure remains with us on the *North Star*. . . . At about 1 p.m. all was ready for sailing, and soon the signal was hoisted, and we sailed away hoping that we would not again cast anchor before arriving in England. . . .

29 August (lat. 73° 50'; long. 81° 4')
We sail cheerily on day and night, meeting nothing in Barrow Strait except a little floating ice. This morning we were off Port Dundas in Maxwell Bay. . . . We sailed slantwise across Lancaster Sound to Navy Board Inlet. . . .

30 August (lat. 73° 6'; long. 75° 30')
. . . We lay at anchor here for two days, and encountered a frightful gale which raged with such fury that one of the two chain cables which had been let go snapped, and sixty fathoms of it were lost along with our best and strongest anchor. Only by the wondrous power of God and with the help of the steamer was our ship saved from being driven on shore. . . .

10 September 1854 (lat. 68° 52'; long. 53° 50')
We have sped over Baffin Bay unhindered by ice, saw on the 5th the land named Svarte Hoeke, and today coasted by Disco Island on the coast of Greenland where we cast anchor at Godhaven, a Danish trading settlement. The two ships *Phoenix* and *Talbot*, which parted company from us on the 6th, are very fast sailors, and had waited for us for three days. We had no sooner cast anchor than a boat brought an order from Sir Edward Belcher to our Captain McClure requiring him to transfer to the steamer in order to make an early arrival in England with the other captains. Our captain was sorry to part from his people, whose joys and sorrows he had shared for so many years, but he had no choice but to obey. . . .

234

11 September (lat. 67° 22'; long. 54° 26')

. . . And now the tiny flotilla set a course in company for the desired homeland.

13 September (lat. 63° 15'; long. 54° 54')

. . . We intended to put in to Holsteinburg . . . but were prevented by the strong land wind, so we sailed away southwards and towards evening passed out of the Arctic Circle. Since the 27th of July 1850, when we crossed that line in Bering Strait, we have been in the Arctic Circle. I hope that never again shall I cross that line.

14 September (lat. 63° 15'; long. 50° 53')

Late this afternoon we arrived off the entrance to Baal's River, where our mission-station, New Herrnhut, is established. Sir Edward Belcher seemed to be much interested in this, and wished to study one of our mission-stations in this cold zone. He has seen our establishments in the West Indies, Surinam, and Cape Colony, and was well acquainted with other missions in the South Sea Islands, the East Indies, and Borneo, but he neither wholly approves nor fully understands the purpose of these missions, because they are inspired by true Christian principles, which he will not understand, because the pure Word of God is a Rock of Offence to his shallow Christianity. A strong contrary wind and the ebb-tide hindered the ships from entering the bay, and, as standing off and on outside meant the loss of much time, Sir Edward abandoned his purpose and gave the order: That now each ship should sail independently for England. . . .

24 September (lat. 52° 4'; long. 21° 50')

We passed Cape Farewell on the 20th without seeing it. For several days we have had heavy seas and strong contrary winds; in addition, it is growing intolerably warm;

also, the rolling of the ship, to which we have long been unaccustomed, is causing many severe headaches. . . . To-day we saw our first ships: two American and one English.

1 October 1854

Since the 25th of September we have had for the most part weak contrary winds and at times calm, but there has been a heavy swell which causes a most unpleasant movement to the ship. The weather is intolerably warm: everyone is complaining of headaches and weakness in the limbs; neither on deck nor below does one find relief. There is no thought at all of serious occupation, for one has neither the patience nor the urge for reading or writing. Every day we see ships sailing by in all directions. Today, towards evening, a fresh breeze arose from the north-west. We sighted land: probably the southernmost tip of Ireland.

4 October

. . . In the afternoon a Frenchman spoken to: she has come from San Domingo; no news. The Lizard lighthouse passed in the evening. . . . The ship is making 10 knots.

5 October

. . . We are sailing along the beautiful English coast at 9 to 11 knots. In the evening saw the lighthouse of Beachy Head and the lights of the town of Hastings. I cut off my beard of four years' growth.

6 October

Pleasant weather, light wind; innumerable sailboats and ships near by. At 8 a.m. we were at anchor off Ramsgate. Captain Pullen hired a steam-tug for forty-five pounds sterling to tow us to Woolwich. I knew that the Labrador ship *Harmony* was usually on the way back from the coast of Labrador to England in September and October, and so

236

from the day when we first saw a ship at sea after passing Cape Farewell I carefully observed every ship which we met in the hope of seeing our little brig; but I always looked in vain. Even Captain Pullen and the officers, who had shown interest and wished to see the mission-ship themselves, gave up, and each one bet me a bottle of wine that I could not pick the brig out of the countless ships. Today after luncheon I came on deck and as usual was beginning to examine the many ships near by when I caught sight of a trim brig with two white stripes and seven dummy ports boldly delineated sailing by; I looked through the telescope and found – it was the *Harmony*! The captain and the officers confirmed this; for with the telescope they made out the name *Harmony* on the forward part of the ship, and on the stern could see the painted forms of the polar bear and the reindeer. Among the few seamen on her deck we saw three passengers standing – two men clad in sealskin and a woman in European dress; I could not identify them at that distance. I mounted to the poop and waved my hat, which greeting was observed by the two brothers on the *Harmony* and acknowledged. Our tug was towing us at the rate of 8 knots, so the *Harmony*, sailing with a light breeze, was left far behind. In the evening we cast anchor at Gravesend, because of a sand-bank that could not safely be passed at night. We had fresh meat and vegetables brought aboard from the city, and fairly revelled in these for us unaccustomed delicacies, and, undisturbed by the uproar of this strange new world, lay down to sleep.

7 October

Early this morning we learned that Captain Inglefield with his steamboat, the *Phoenix*, had landed Captains Belcher, Kellett, and McClure in Ireland, and himself already lay at anchor in the Woolwich dockyards. As yet there is no word of the *Talbot*. As soon as it was day and the ebb tide allowed us to proceed, we went up the Thames towed by the tug. It will be long before I forget that day, favoured as it was by the grandest weather; the banks of the river were adorned with green trees and beautiful houses, and in the green meadows were no savage musk-ox or reindeer – but real, tame, useful animals were grazing, and men were going about, busy with their various tasks; railway trains thundered by, and, in a word, we saw, full of life and activity, the fruitful, cultivated world to which we had become strangers. We stood and gazed like delighted children. Oh, the feelings of rapture which overpowered everyone of us are beyond all description! From the 4th of July 1850 to this very day we have seen neither tree nor bush; the scanty vegetation of the ice- and snow-covered polar lands has often filled us with a passionate yearning for our beloved homeland; ah, and *today*, in a moment, has given us all that we had so long pined for. It is almost too much for us seafarers, long inured to loneliness and deserts. We forgot all about eating and drinking; and before we deemed it possible someone called out: "This is Woolwich." At 10 a.m. we cast anchor in the outer harbour of Woolwich. They had been advised of our coming the day before yesterday by the telegraph. To get me to London as quickly as possible Captain Pullen took me ashore in his own boat, and pointed out the way through the dockyard to the railway station; but I had barely passed the admiral's residence when I was called back and sent with Captain Pullen to the ship. We are not to dock here, but at the naval base of Sheerness. Most disappointing I found it, but had no course but to obey. The little steam warship *Monkey* took our ship in tow and tugged us back once more down the Thames. The beauty of river-bank and landscape were the same as when we were sailing up, but I could no longer enjoy the glorious beauties of nature which surrounded us, because the plan I had resolved upon of being in London that afternoon was wholly upset, and because, though not an officer of the navy, I was still denied, after the arrival of the ship, the liberty of going to the city and becoming free. But, as it was throughout the journey, so it was at the end – the sweet has always an admixture of bitterness. At 8 p.m. when it was already very dark we cast anchor at Sheerness between two great warships, the *Waterloo* and the *Royal Albert*.

8 October

An Admiralty bulletin had been published in the newspapers announcing that our ship had arrived in England and was lying at Sheerness. So the wives of officers and men had assembled on the dock with their children to welcome back husbands and fathers from their long, long journey. Unhappily there were some truly piteous scenes; more than one mother with children, who had come in joyous expectation of welcoming the father whom they had never seen, received from the captain the heart-breaking intelligence that the father had *not* come back, but had found rest in an icy tomb. Ah, happy the man who has never had to witness such scenes! With the deepest sympathy men saw the heart-broken and sorrowing widows and orphans leaving the ship. At 9 a.m. came orders from the Admiralty that we Investigators – those of us who had been passengers on the ship *North Star* – were immediately to be transferred to the warship *Waterloo*, which lay at anchor beside us, and there await further orders.[1] Here a letter from the Admiralty, addressed to the crew of the *Investigator*, was delivered to and read aloud by the Commodore himself; in this the Admiralty, with the warmest praise of the crew as well as the officers for their good conduct and zealous service in the ice-fields for a continuous period of five years, thanked

[1] They could not be paid off until a court-martial had inquired into the loss of their ship.

them with the warmest acknowledgements. This was now the fifth ship to which we had been posted, and no one could blame me for yearning to be quit of my idle life at sea and to be reunited with members of the Brotherhood in London; I wrote a letter to the Admiralty in which as one who was not an enlisted member of the navy I requested leave of absence and permission to go to London. After an hour or two I received an answer and four days' leave. Never was anyone so happy as I. In a few minutes I was in a boat, landed on the dock, went to the town in my worn and patched sailor's garb, entered a large shop, and emerged therefrom after half an hour freshly equipped as a "gentleman", boarded a steamboat and sailed in company with Captain Pullen to Strood, and went from there by railway to London, where a cab delivered me at 6 p.m. at the house of our worthy Brother W. Mallalieu; there I received the best and kindest reception from Sister H. Mallalieu, and from Sister Warhoes and Brother Kern, newly arrived from Labrador, who had come for tea; soon Brother Mallalieu also came home and invited me to his house with the warmest brotherly love. To me it was a regular feast of joyful reunions. . . .

When I had in some measure adjusted myself to this life that was so new to me, I called on my worthy Captain McClure and on Captain Kellett, who lived in London, and when, in answer to my application, I had received a written discharge from my ship, I went on Thursday the 12th to Sheerness to bid farewell to my ship-mates who were berthed on the ship *Waterloo*. I spent there a few very pleasant hours; and when it was time to go they all accompanied me to the steamboat on which I was returning to London. The parting from my ship-mates was distressing for them as it was for me, and several seamen, their features hardened by storm and foul weather, were not ashamed to shed tears. . . . Through the Lord's grace alone are we here again in England; five men out of 76 [66] have by God's will ended their lives in the frozen seas. . . . Several have lost some part of their limbs by frost, so that they can no longer follow their accustomed trade; others, after years of suffering, hope to recover their health in their homeland. . . .

The purpose of our expedition – to find Franklin and his unlucky crews – has been, as far as we are concerned, without success. . . . The famous arctic traveller, Dr. Rae, who has recently returned to England in a Hudson's Bay ship from a journey made this year, has brought from a tribe of heathen Eskimos near Repulse Bay a number of small articles which are beyond doubt partly Franklin's property, partly that of his officers. According to the story told by these Eskimos a party of Europeans was seen in 1850 near King William Land travelling with sledges and boats, and in distress for want of food; according to this story many corpses are lying, naturally unburied, on some cape. How far these Eskimos reports are true will, one hopes, be revealed by the expedition which will be sent from England next spring (1855).[1] Our other ship, actually our flagship, the *Enterprise*, Captain Collinson, to whom the command of our expedition had been entrusted, we never saw after April 1850. From the dispatches[2] which Captain Collinson sent to England from Bering Strait by way of Panama, which have just now reached the Admiralty, it appears that the *Enterprise* also has totally failed in her mission. After a year in China and three years in the frozen seas she

[1] In 1855 the Chief Factor James Anderson was sent down the Great Fish (Back's) River to the arctic shore, but his canoes were unfit for the crossing to King William Island, and he did little but confirm the report of Rae. With her own funds, aided by public subscription, Lady Franklin sent McClintock in the *Fox* (1857-9) and he obtained definite information as to the cause and actual scene of the disaster.

[2] Part of Miertsching's entry for 8 October must have been inserted during a later revision; Collinson's Alaska dispatch did not reach England until December 1854.

is now returning through Bering Strait and is sailing by way of China, the East Indies, and Africa to England where her arrival is expected in April or May. Our *Investigator* had the task of bringing Franklin's fate to light; in this she failed; but another task, the object of centuries of endeavour, a task in which many expeditions besides Franklin's had been sacrificed, was fully achieved, so that we now know of not one but two Northwest Passages, which, however, are without significance and useless for navigation as long as the climate in those parts is so severe and the sea covered with ice 50 to 60 feet thick. Although our ship was left in the ice as a lasting memorial for future times, so remains the fame of her crew, the first and only men to pass through the waters encircling America, and by that to show to the world that America is an island. . . .

When I look back on that period, now ended, of my life at sea, I must prostrate myself in the dust and with the deepest penitence cry: "Lord, I am not worthy of all the grace and goodness which Thou hast shown me." With the deepest gratitude I can acknowledge to my Lord and Saviour that I have come back with health as good as when I left England five years ago, and with all my limbs sound. For the whole period the Lord granted me good health. Although the first year was a difficult and disagreeable one for me, owing to personal relationships, yet outwardly my lot was very good: from the beginning I enjoyed the friendship, love, and attentive care of the men and also the officers, and especially of Captain McClure, of whom I shall always preserve the most grateful recollections; and this good fortune I enjoyed not only on our own ship but in my relations with that noble fellow, Captain Kellett, and his crew; and also from Sir Edward Belcher and Captain Inglefield I enjoyed the most courteous proofs of affection and regard. . . .

I much regretted that I had so little opportunity to communicate with the Eskimos living in heathen darkness, the natives of the north-west coast of America; and for a long time could not console myself; but in this also the understanding cannot fathom the will and the ways of God. The coast from Bering Strait to the Coppermine River, and also Wollaston Land, are inhabited by Eskimos who are utter heathens. A glorious harvest for missionaries!...

10 October

... Today in company with Brother Mallalieu, I visited Captain McClure – Salisbury Street 13, Strand – and Captain Kellett, and also the Admiralty, where I met a number of old ship-mates. I presented to the Admiralty my application for discharge and they promised to attend to this ....

12 October

As I had now received my discharge from the ship I went to Sheerness to take leave of my old ship-mates.[1] I received a cordial welcome on the *North Star*, was invited to luncheon, took my departure in the afternoon, and in company with Mr. Court went by steamer from Sheerness to Strood, and thence by rail through Chatham to London. In Sheerness and Chatham I saw many Russian prisoners of war.

27 October

In the morning I called on Captains McClure and Kellett, who took me to the Admiralty and introduced me to H. Barrow [John Barrow, Jr.?] who promised me for my service on board ship this year 161 pounds; and told me that I could draw my pay at Somerset House. There I met a number of our sailors, and also Sir Edward Belcher, Captain Pullen, Haswell, Hamilton, and Shellebear....

---

[1]Evidently the same leave-taking – enlarged upon in the expanded entry for 8 October.

28 October

Today I went with Brother Mallalieu to Somerset House where I was given a cheque of 733 pounds, which I cashed at Whitehall. . . .

30 October

. . . I received today the second written request from the Admiralty to join another polar expedition, its purpose being to search for those relics of the Franklin expedition described to Dr. Rae. Though these offers were most advantageous to me I have answered them with an emphatic "no". Lady Franklin is trying to persuade me to join by the promise of money, but my resolution is fixed: I make no more such polar journeys.

10 November 1854 [the day preceding his departure for the Continent]

. . . Captain McClure visited me at Mallalieu's.

EPILOGUE

In May 1855, seven months after the return of the "Investigators", the indestructible Collinson brought the *Enterprise* and her crew home by way of Bering Strait and the Cape of Good Hope. Their cruise had lasted five years and four months.

As McClure had no doubt anticipated, a handsome monetary reward was proposed for the discoverers of the Passage, and a parliamentary committee was set up to examine his claim and to determine in what proportion, if any, Collinson, McClure's commander, and Kellett, his rescuer, should share in the bounty. The former gave up what little claim he had by curtly testifying that McClure had not violated the letter of his orders by his escapade at Cape Lisburne. Kellett was in a far stronger position: all that was original in the *Investigator*'s achievement was due to him: without his aid she would merely have duplicated the last Franklin voyage with a triumphant discovery followed by an overwhelming disaster. He did not grasp the point of McClure's diplomatic jockeying at Dealy Island, and it must have been with no small chagrin that he heard the latter blandly inform the committee that the help of the *Resolute* had not been essential to his preservation: he could have either extricated the ship or brought her men to the Port Leopold depot without assistance. He was able to make this monstrous assertion with no evident inconsistency because he had never admitted failure and had contrived that the ship should be abandoned by Kellett's order, not by his. His officers' journals had, by accident or design, been suppressed, and the medical testimony, which also might have been embarrassing, was only partially presented. The Crimean War was on, and Armstrong was at sea with the Baltic squadron; Dr. Domville was permitted by what seems to have been a pro-McClure committee to be cautious and non-committal in his evidence as to the condition of the *Investigator*'s crew when the order to abandon ship was given. The committee therefore awarded the entire ten thousand pounds to the officers and men of the *Investigator*, dismissing their rescuers with a brief commendation, which, under the circumstances, was the most galling of insults. The loyal Kellett was hurt, not for his own sake, but because of the slur on his crew. He would gladly, he said, contribute fifty pounds to a fund for their benefit. The politicians who made up the committee probably had more than an inkling that they were doing an injustice, but were not displeased that the nature of the testimony permitted them to make a finding that if inequitable, added dignity to a national exploit and was highly popular. McClure had what Collinson and Kellett lacked, the "colour" that wins public favour.

Miertsching's portrayal of this celebrated seaman clarifies the impression that the careful reader gets from Osborn's glowing but somewhat evasive panegyric and from the guarded hostility of Armstrong. He was aloof, unstable at times, with a driving ambition, coupled with more selfishness and less scruple than quite befitted his rank and profession. Yet he was not a wholly unpleasing character nor unworthy of the honours he obtained. His remoteness was due more to insecurity than to lack of feeling. Miertsching, the only person on board with whom he felt that he could converse freely, he treated with a uniform kindness, which the young German, though fully alive to his faults,

246

repaid with the sincerest affection. In an emergency he could overcome his diffidence and appeal to the men with force and emotion. If the lack of confidence between himself and his officers was a fault, it serves to emphasize the resolution with which he maintained discipline for a long period of hardship and privation; he welded Miertsching's "shameless sinners" into such an orderly, self-respecting unit that Kellett gave him a written testimonial certifying the good conduct of the "Investigators" while attached to his command. He had much luck in his historic voyage, but the use he made of it marks him as a brave and skilful navigator.

CALENDAR OF THE FRANKLIN SEARCH (1848-59)

1848. The search began for Sir John Franklin's *Erebus* and *Terror*, which had been in the Arctic, and unreported, for three years.

1848-9. Sir James Ross took two ships into Lancaster Sound and found Barrow Strait blocked by ice. In company with Lieutenant McClintock, Ross searched part of the east shore of Peel Sound.

1848-9. Based on Great Bear Lake, Franklin's former companion, Dr. (Sir John) Richardson, and Dr. John Rae searched part of the continental shore between the Mackenzie and Coppermine rivers by boat.

1850-1. On foot and by boat Rae searched the south shore of Victoria Island (Prince Albert Land to McClure), and the west side of Victoria Strait between Victoria Island and King William Island.

1850-1. The four ships of Captain Horatio Austin and a number of private vessels entered Lancaster Sound. Austin's ships were frozen in at Griffiths Island in Barrow Strait (close to the modern station of Resolute Bay). In the spring of 1851 extensive sledge-journeys were made on the island shores on both sides of Barrow Strait. Lieutenant Sherard Osborn on the south-western shore of Prince of Wales Island was not far from the track of Wyniatt of the *Investigator*. McClintock made the long journey to Winter Harbour and there deposited the record found a year later by McClure.

Captain Kennedy and Lieutenant Bellot of the French navy in the *Prince Albert* entered Regent's Inlet and discovered Bellot Strait.

1850-4. The voyage of the *Investigator*.

1850-5. Collinson failed to enter the Arctic in 1850, succeeded in 1851, and wintered in Prince of Wales Strait (Walker Bay). In 1852 he took his *Enterprise* through the intricate shallows of Dolphin and Union Strait, a piece of navigation much admired by Amundsen, and wintered at Cambridge Bay. In the spring of 1853 he searched the west side of Victoria Strait — had he crossed to the east side he might have solved the Franklin mystery. On the way home he spent the winter of 1853-54 on the north shore of Alaska, and he reached England in May 1855.

It was Collinson's misfortune that, having unintentionally followed routes earlier traversed by McClure or Rae, he did not make a large contribution to original discovery.

1852-4. Austin's four ships, with the addition of the depot ship *North Star*, were sent back under Belcher and Kellett.

Belcher, Richards, Osborn, and May made search on the north shores of Devon, Bathurst, and Melville islands. Belcher discovered North Cornwall Island.

Kellett rescued the crew of the *Investigator*. Mecham and McClintock discovered and mapped Eglinton and Prince Patrick islands.

Belcher was much criticized for the desertion of his ships and barely escaped censure by court martial.

1853-4. Rae made a journey from Repulse Bay to Boothia and there was told by the Eskimos that a number of Europeans had died on the west shore of King William Island and in the estuary of Back's River four (actually it was six) years before.

1855. Chief Factor James Anderson of the Hudson's Bay Company descended by canoe from Great Slave Lake to the estuary of Back's River, but did little except confirm the report of Rae.

1857-9. In command of Lady Franklin's *Fox*, McClintock entered Prince Regent Inlet and berthed his ship at the east end of Bellot Strait. By sledge-journeys to the estuary of Back's River and around King William Island he and his officers gathered much information from the Eskimos and found one written record. Franklin's ships, they ascertained, had been beset by ice on the northwestern shore of King William Island and their crews had perished of scurvy and starvation while trekking towards the mouth of Back's River. Twenty years later Lieutenant Schwatka of the United States Army learned that the strongest had barely reached the continental shore and had perished at Starvation Cove, a little to the west of the estuary.

McClintock proved that Franklin's men had found the last link of a Northwest Passage before the final catastrophe, anticipating by two, or possibly three, years the claim of the *Investigator*.

REFERENCES

Shortly after the *Investigator*'s cruise Sherard Osborn published *The Discovery of the Northwest Passage*, a lively, uncritical account, based on McClure's personal record (London: Longman, Brown, Green, Longmans, & Roberts, 1857, 2nd ed.). Having been himself an active participant in the Franklin search Osborn has some fine descriptive passages. He praises Miertsching as a good shipmate and a great contributor to morale.

Dr. Alexander Armstrong's *Personal Narrative of the Discovery of the Northwest Passage* (London: Hurst and Blackett, 1857) is a lengthy volume, full of interesting material. G. F. McDougall, *Eventful Voyage of H. M. Discovery Ship Resolute* (London: Longmans, 1857), Sir Clements Markham's *Life of Admiral Sir Leopold McClintock* (London: J. Murray, 1909), and Parliamentary Papers are most helpful.

Two modern publications that deal at some length with the voyage of the *Investigator* are L. H. Neatby, *In Quest of the Northwest Passage* (Toronto: Longmans Canada, 1958), and Noel Wright, *Quest for Franklin* (London: Wm. Heinemann, 1959).

R. J. Cyriax, in *Sir John Franklin's Last Arctic Voyage* (London: Methuen & Co., 1939), provides a richly documented survey of the voyage itself and all rescue expeditions, and Wm. Gibson, F.R.G.S., who knew the King William Island area well, in *The Beaver*, June 1937 ("Sir John Franklin's Last Voyage"), furnishes an excellent commentary on all that has been learned of the fate of Franklin's crews since the voyage of McClintock.

INDEX

Aleutian Islands, 34ff.

Altin, Mr., Honolulu merchant, 27, 29

Anderson, seaman, 15, 159

Armstrong, Dr. Alexander, Surgeon, published "Narrative" of cruise critical of McClure, xi, xii; estimate of, xvii-xviii; *Investigator*, 7; relations with Miertsching, 65n.; humiliated by officers, 103; open quarrel with Captain McClure, 158; competence, 217n.

Attua, Eskimo chief, 45-6

Austin, Captain Horatio, R.N., commander of 1850-1 Franklin rescue expedition, 90, 163, 248

Back's River, 248

Baffin Bay, 234

Ballast Beach, 134-41

Banks (Baring) Island, sighted by Parry, viii, 89; designated "lofty, mountainous land", 67; name "Baring's" assigned, 104 and n.; almost circumnavigated, 131-49 *passim*

Barrow Strait, viii, 234; this name applied by Miertsching to its extension, Melville Sound, 89

Beechey Island, *North Star* berthed near, 227; Franklin's 1845-6 winter quarters, 228

Belcher, Captain Sir Edward, R.N., commander of 1852-4 rescue expedition, 190, 221, 225, 231ff.; Miertsching's questionable anecdote about, 229; court-martial acquits, 249

Bellot, Lieutenant J.-R., French naval officer volunteer for Franklin search, 248

Bering Strait, 36

Bradbury, seaman, 170, 196

Bridport Inlet (Melville Island), 196

Byam Martin Island, 205

Cape Bathurst, 58ff.

Cape Cockburn, 211

Cape Crozier, 144

Cape Hotham, 223, 225-6

Cape Lambton, 121, 132-3

Cape Lisburne, 39

Cape Parry, 66

Cape Riley, 190, 223, 227

Cape Virgin, 17

Cape Walker, 105 and n., 110

Collinson, Captain Richard, R.N., of *Enterprise*, x; receives Miertsching, 5-6; permits him to remain on *Investigator*, 18; work in Arctic, 151, 230, 241 and n., 248; 247

Colville River, 43

Court, Stephen, sailing-master, *Investigator*, xvii and *passim*

Cresswell, Lieutenant Samuel G., R.N., second officer of *Investigator*, xvii, 7; sledge journeys along Banks Island shores, 107, 111-12, 121; conducts party from Mercy Bay to Dealy Island, 194-6; leaves for England, 198

Damon, the Reverend, 29, 33-4

Dealy Island, Captain Kellett's 1853-4 winter quarters, 189n., 190-1, 208

Dease, P. W., *see* Simpson, T.

De Bray, enseigne de vaisseau, French Navy, volunteer on Kellett expedition, 201

Disco Island, 234

Dolphin and Union Strait, 66, 117, 248

Domville, Dr., surgeon, H.M.S. *Resolute*, 189n.; assists in medical examination of *Investigator*'s crew, 197, 199; his testimony, 246

Eglinton Island, 202

Enterprise, ship of Collinson, *q.v.*

Erebus and *Terror*, lost ships of Sir John Franklin, viii

Erebus and Terror Bay, 227